The King's Best Highway

The Lost History of
the
BOSTON POST ROAD,
the Route
That Made America

ERIC JAFFE

SCRIBNER

New York   London   Toronto   Sydney

SCRIBNER
A Division of Simon & Schuster, Inc.
1230 Avenue of the Americas
New York, NY 10020

First Scribner hardcover edition June 2010

SCRIBNER and design are registered trademarks of The Gale Group, Inc.,
used under license by Simon & Schuster, Inc.,
the publisher of this work.

For information about special discounts for bulk purchases,
please contact Simon & Schuster Special Sales at 1-866-506-1949 or
business@simonandschuster.com.

The Simon & Schuster Speakers Bureau can bring authors to your
live event. For more information or to book an event contact the
Simon & Schuster Speakers Bureau at 1-866-248-3049 or
visit our website at www.simonspeakers.com.

Book design by Ellen R. Sasahara

Map on pp. x–xi copyright © 2010 by John del Gaizo

Manufactured in the United States of America

3   5   7   9   10   8   6   4

Library of Congress Cataloging-in-Publication Data

Jaffe, Eric.

The King's best highway : the lost history of the Boston Post Road,
the route that made America / Eric Jaffe.
—1st Scribner hardcover ed.
p.   cm.
1. Boston Post Roads—History. 2. Post roads—Massachusetts—Boston
Region—History. 3. Post roads—New York Region—History. 4. Boston (Mass.)—
Relations—New York (State)—New York. 5. New York (N.Y.)—Relations—
Massachusetts—Boston. 6. Roads—United States—History. 7. Transportation—
Social aspects—United States—History. 8. Transportation and state—United
States—History. 9. Social change—United States—History. I. Title.
HE356.B6J34 2010
388.10974—dc22   2009051453

ISBN 978-1-4165-8614-2
ISBN 978-1-4391-7610-8 (ebook)

For my parents

Contents

Author's Note

THE GENERAL COURSE of the "King's best highway" requires a moment of introduction. The original highway used by English settlers was not quite a single way at all—rather, it was a collection of Indian paths that, over time, colonists would commandeer, consolidate with minor adjustments, and christen as one in the name of the king. When the dust settled, this system of trails twisted and turned from Boston toward New York, but each precise twist and turn is far less important to grasp than the basic outline: A northern, or inland, branch led west from Boston to Springfield, then down along the Connecticut River through Hartford to New Haven. A southern, or coastal, branch led south from Boston to Providence, then along the shore of Long Island Sound, also to New Haven. From there both branches unified en route to New York. (A less vital middle branch from Boston to Hartford fell outside the scope of this narrative.)

In short, seen from above, the highway as a whole resembles a lasso tossed from Manhattan toward the Bay, its knot landing at New Haven, wrangling southern New England.

The name of the road—rather, the lack of a consistent one—requires another moment to introduce. Over the course of its existence the "King's best highway" has avoided a single, editorially pleasing designation. In colonial times it was often called the "high road" or, simply, "highway." The name "post road" stuck through Revolutionary and stagecoach days. When rail travel largely replaced common roads the route was covered by numerous segments—most notably the New Haven railroad, along the coastal branch, and the Boston & Albany railroad, inland. The interstate era labeled the coastal highway U.S. Route 1 and the inland branch U.S.

Route 20 (with some exceptions), though many local regions simultane-ously granted their sections nostalgic names such as Boston Post Road and Kings Highway.

This overview covers only the meager basics. An exhaustive name list, from Bowery Lane in Manhattan to Main Street in Hartford and Providence to Washington Street in Boston, would require a book of its own. For this reason I've generally called the highway whatever name people living along it used at the time—abandoning this approach only when clarity seemed to demand.

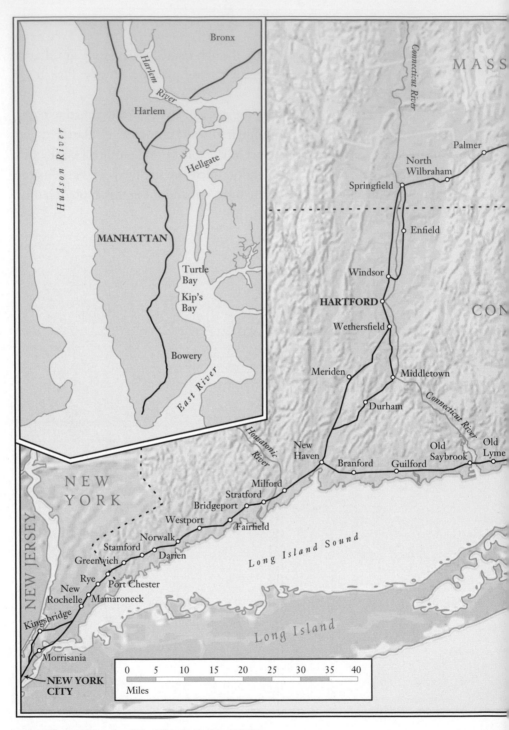

Adapted from Stephen Jenkins, "The Old Boston Post Road," 1913

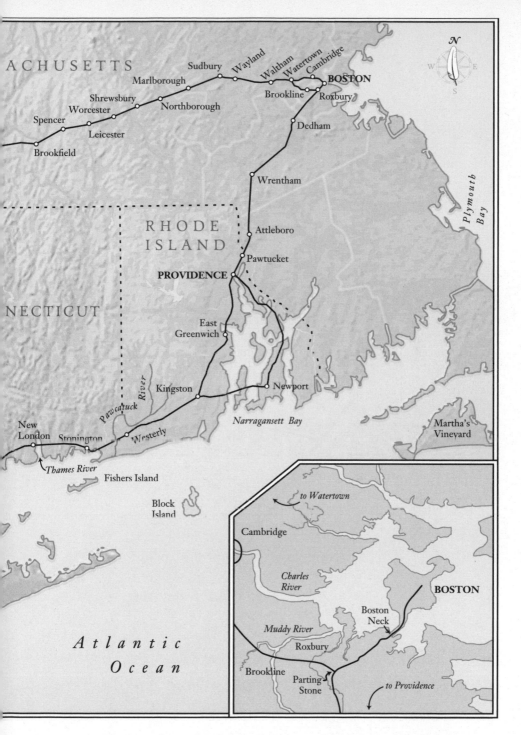

The Boston Post Road around the time of the American Revolution.
(Place names are modern.)

Part I

From Indian Path to Post Road

Each first Monday of the month he sets out from New York, and is to return within the month from Boston to us again.

— Francis Lovelace, governor of New York, to John Winthrop Jr., governor of Connecticut, December 27, 1672

Chapter 1

The "Ordinary Way"

IN SPRINGTIME OF 1631 the town of Boston resembled a swollen head clinging to the body of America by a long, thin neck. Freckling this head were three large hills that had inspired the town's original name, Trimountain, and the inhabitants, numbering roughly one hundred fifty, lived in the shadows of these mounds—in low wooden houses, with private gardens. This peculiar birthmark aside, Boston had several features prized by the colonial settler: a potable stream, an abundance of pastures, a favorable and defensible port. Very few trees encumbered the head, bald as a newborn, and when the people needed wood they journeyed from head to neck to body on a lonely, winding road—the single vein connecting the town with mainland New England.

The stream is gone now, and private gardens are hard to come by, but vestiges of this early seventeenth-century Boston do survive today. The middle mound, slightly dulled, is Beacon Hill. The main pasture, neatly contained, is Boston Common. The neck, purposely fattened, is Back Bay. And the solitary road, for decades Boston's only true highway, lives on as Washington Street.* Back in 1631 John Winthrop, the gover-

---

*At times there have been numerous Washington Streets in the Boston area. Only two sections—one leading west from Brookline Village toward Watertown, the other south from downtown Boston toward Roxbury—can be considered modern derivatives of the original highway.

3

nor of the Massachusetts Bay Colony, lived in a house just a few modern blocks east of the foot of this highway, which ended at present-day State Street. He had a great hall, a parlor with a hearth, a service wing—plenty of space to entertain his many guests, including a rather unexpected one who dropped by in early April.

He was an Indian, this visitor, who went by the name of Wahginnacut. By the time he reached Winthrop's home, Wahginnacut had traveled five days by land from the Connecticut River valley—covering roughly one hundred sixty miles—with a request he was "very desirous" to see fulfilled. Along the way he had enlisted English-speaking Natives John Sagamore, a frequent ambassador in the Bay, and Jack Straw, who years before had served Sir Walter Raleigh. As they dined in the governor's home, Wahginnacut informed Winthrop of the Connecticut River valley's exceptionally fertile countryside. He offered an annual payment of eighty beaver skins—a high form of currency at the time, the other being wampum, which was Indian money made by stringing beads on hemp or meat tendons—if only Winthrop would send two men back with him to examine the fruitful region themselves.

Winthrop refused, and his instincts proved sharp; he later found that Wahginnacut's true intention was to gain English protection from the bellicose Pequot tribe. But the idea of westward expansion had been planted in some of Massachusetts Bay's most migratory minds, and it quickly grew ripe, like so much corn in Connecticut River valley soil.

The first to act on this impulse was a contentious man named John Oldham, whose strong temper was matched only by his spirit of enterprise. Originally a Plymouth settler, Oldham had been banished by that colony for insurrection. When he returned without permission an entire guard "was ordered to give him a thump on ye brich" with the butt ends of their muskets. He was eventually accepted into Massachusetts Bay society despite an independent mind-set unusual for his time and place, and saw in the highway toward Connecticut the prospect of land and wealth—a pathway to freedom that his move to the New World had not quite secured.

In the fall of 1633 Oldham and three other Bay men ventured out along the highway and into the river valley to trade with the Indians. After leaving the Boston neck the route wriggled through Roxbury and up through present-day Brookline toward the Charles River. There travelers crossed to modern Cambridge—after 1635, they rode a ferry—where the path continued west through Watertown, then out toward neighboring Connecticut. All Bay settlers knew the course, but Oldham would have been particularly familiar with it; he took it regularly between Boston and Watertown, where he kept a small clapboard home, which had recently burned down when he started a fire inside before having built a chimney.

Oldham's party returned from this maiden expedition with beaver skins, superior hemp, graphite they mistook for lead—and an introductory glimpse of the pioneer route connecting Boston to interior New England. Fitting that a person of Oldham's volatile temperament would be the first to scout the highway. While the broad lens of history shows the Native road as the foundation for travel in northeast America, in early colonial times it was regarded entirely as wilderness, and so reserved for the wild at heart.

When passing through settled towns, the road west from the bay served as a de facto main street. Outside these pockets of civilization the highway joined a well-worn Native path that used the natural terrain to its advantage. Each November the Indians engaged in a primitive act of paving termed "bush-burning" by the Dutch. They set fire to bramble, seedlings, and fallen twigs, lest this underbrush "overgrow the Country, making it unpassable," in the words of a contemporary traveler, William Wood. The process doubled as a hunting technique: game, attracted to the fresh growth, flocked to such paths, tamping it down even more over time.

Native trails skirted rivers and lakes to provide travelers with fishing access and refreshment. (Of New England's waterways, "there can be no better water in the world," wrote Wood. "I not preferre it before good Beere . . . but any man will choose it before bad Beere.") When the path did cross water, it typically forded the shallowest parts. Often the road led through Indian villages—during their first foray Oldham and his companions bunked in wigwams, which fellow colonist Daniel Gookin called "as warm as the best English houses."

Not that the route could be considered tame. Merely surviving in colonial times was a chancy affair, but in Oldham's day, and for decades beyond, those who ventured far out along the road tempted hazard and mayhem. The great path often slipped into narrow stretches no wider than a foot and a half—wilderness corridors filled, come night, with "terrifying darkness." Some of the river crossings, though not impassable, were dangerous. One imagines a general index of perils, from slippery rocks to unfamiliar insects to raw winds—to say nothing of quieter burdens like hauling food and drying wet clothes. Even staying sane proved difficult: in 1634 two Bay men lost their way on a Native trail for six days before they were found, "almost senseless for want of rest."

Although colonists commonly marked trees along the trail, most of the route required Indian guides. Heavy snows would have camouflaged the course; rains and spring thaws would have muddied it beyond all hope for speed. When high tide hit the neck of the bay, the highway dipped below the water level, causing the head of Boston to dangle, disembodied, in the sea. John Winthrop never went traveling without a match, a compass, and a remedy for snakebite. Even as late as 1635, well after Oldham's first trip west, Winthrop found it so remarkable that a lone traveler had gone "by land to Connecticut, and returned safe," that he noted the accomplishment in his journal.

Oldham's exploration came at a critical time in colonial development. The urge to flee westward strained the Bay government and the Puritans leading it, who had come overseas to knit the tight community they had been denied in England. For a while Massachusetts refused to authorize official moves toward Connecticut. At the same time, life on the tiny head of Boston had grown claustrophobic. Cambridge residents lacked proper pasture space for their livestock. Even the population of Watertown, then firmly in the hinterland at eight miles west, neared saturation. If New Englanders failed to claim the Connecticut River valley, the Dutch sure would—they already held a riverside fort in modern Hartford, called the House of Hope.

Soon the scouting trips into Connecticut became routine, and eventually they inspired others to follow. By summer of 1634 Oldham and several others from Watertown had built log cabins along the Connecticut River, at modern Wethersfield. In July of that year six men from Cambridge scooted just upriver from Oldham's crew and, ignoring protests from the Dutch, surveyed present-day Hartford. The following fall, John Winthrop Jr., son of the Bay governor, returned to Boston, having successfully sold English investors on the promise of the Connecticut River valley—to the hefty tune of £2,000. (Winthrop Jr. had also gone back to pacify the discontented throne, which had come to view American colonists as idlers "whose only end is to live as much as they can without the reach of authority.")

The land grant secured by the younger Winthrop, known as the Warwick patent, unleashed on the Bay a general settlement fever. Civilized New England soon scattered west along the path blazed by Oldham. A week after Winthrop Jr.'s arrival, a group of sixty men, women, and children traveled along the highway and planted themselves in the Connecticut River towns that would become Windsor and Wethersfield. The following May, the Reverend Thomas Hooker of Cambridge led most of his congregation toward Hartford on the same route, their livestock bouncing behind them all the way. By summer of 1636 the fur trader William Pynchon had settled Springfield, Massachusetts. A southern branch of the colonial highway began to emerge around the time when Roger Williams, banished by the Bay Colony for religious dissidence, moved to present-day Providence, in early 1636. That March the younger Winthrop traveled south this way himself, to settle at the mouth of the Connecticut River. In honor of the investors he had attracted back in England—Viscount Saye and Sele, and Baron Brooke—Winthrop Jr. called this town Saybrook, a name it keeps in part today, as Old Saybrook.

John Oldham lived to see this initial burst of settlement along the highway he had tamed, but not much longer. In July 1636, Oldham, who had sufficiently recovered his once-tarnished reputation to become a confidant of the mighty Winthrop family, was involved in a diplomatic conference held at Fort Saybrook between New England colonists and the increasingly bothersome Pequot tribe. There the Indians were issued an ultimatum that Oldham had delivered to Wintrhop Jr. on behalf of the Bay Colony: in short, the Natives were told to surrender or to fight. A few days later Oldham's merchant ship was discovered on Block Island, off the southern coast of Rhode Island. His body was found stowed beneath the ship's seine, naked, with a hatchet planted in the skull.

The gruesome death of John Oldham touched off a period of violence between the colonists and Natives known as the Pequot War.* For a while, most of the effort that had gone into colonial settlement was concentrated on the fight. But Oldham had shown the way down a road that now rested firmly above the fluctuating tides of discovery—a road that, a century later, steered post riders and stagecoaches; a road that, two centuries later, guided the railroad tracks that carried the Industrial Revolution; a road that, three centuries later, inspired the need for, and the location of, interstate expressways. That is getting ahead. But even by the middle of 1637, Oldham's course was so familiar that the elder John Winthrop, writing in his journal, referred to this route—heretofore approached with caution or fright, when it was approached at all— as the "ordinary way."

THAT JOHN OLDHAM passed the torch of highway knowledge to John Winthrop Jr., one of the last to see him alive, can only be considered a historic coincidence. But Winthrop seems to have accepted this legacy—it was he who would later be charged with uniting the distinct paths of the "ordinary way" into the cohesive "King's best highway"— and the story of how he achieved enough fluency to earn this charge really begins on November 11, 1645. That day he commenced a tour of the highway unprecedented for its time—a time when the vast bulk of long-distance travel was confined to the seas. Even official Massachusetts Bay surveyors Nathaniel Woodward and Solomon Saffery had failed to travel as much of the route as Winthrop would. It was the type of mad journey attempted by firebrands like Oldham, or natural-born

---

*Although Oldham's murder is widely considered the direct impetus for the Pequot War, there is a bit of mystery surrounding his death, which came at the hands of a Narragansett Indian, not a Pequot. One theory holds the killing as possible retribution for the smallpox outbreak that infected Natives after Oldham's initial journey on the highway, back in 1633.

nomads like Winthrop—a man who, all told, lived in at least six New England towns, founding three—and who, beginning in youth, rarely felt at home except when on the move.

If the well-rounded man is hard to categorize, then John Winthrop Jr. formed the perfect circle. He was scientist, alchemist, diplomat, financier, entrepreneur, and devoted husband, all in one. He was physician to some seven hundred patients. He was governor of Connecticut longer than anyone in the colony's—and subsequently the state's—history. His sighting of the fifth moon of Jupiter two centuries before its official discovery is doubted today, but the telescope he used later became Harvard's first scientific apparatus and contributed to Newton's great work *Principia Mathematica*. His father is a far more famous settler, yet it was the son who first proposed leaving England for the New World (the elder John was originally "loath" to the idea). His shoes—quite literally for his time, at size eleven—were large to fill.

Some of the restlessness that came to define him might trace back to his conception. On May 9, 1605, the elder John Winthrop and his new wife, Mary Forth, attended a feast thrown in their honor at Groton Manor. The young couple likely had more on their minds than banquet fare, because nearly nine months later to the day, on February 12, 1606, Mary gave birth to her first child, who was given the name of his father. The younger John Winthrop shifted through his youth. He left for Trinity College in Dublin around age sixteen, but abandoned his studies after a year. He puttered about London for a while as a lawman, then felt instead an "inclination to the Sea."

Twice he felt so inclined. The first such urge landed him aboard the *Repulse,* a warship sent to relieve French Huguenots on Île de Ré. Around the time English players were performing *Hamlet* on the Continent, John Winthrop the father, sounding like a Puritan Polonius, advised his wayward son to "seeke the Lorde in the first place," to "keepe diligent watche over your selfe," and to "be not rashe upon ostentation of valor, to adventure your selfe to unnecessarye dangers." Winthrop glimpsed battle but failed to satisfy his unrest, so he set out again in the summer of 1628. This second trip, with its cruise ship itinerary and frequent requests home for funds, is proud ancestor of the modern teenage spring break. But a series of trials near its conclusion, including a monthlong quarantine in Lazaretto, seems to have finally soothed Winthrop's agitated spirit.

He returned home to find that his father had joined the Massachusetts Bay Company and would soon embark for New England. The son decided to follow, declaring his intention in a tone far more resolute than restless: "I have seene so much of this vanity of the world that I esteeme noe more of the diversities of Countries then as so many Innes, whereof the travailer, that hath lodged in the best, or in the worst, findeth noe difference when he commeth to his Journies end." Seen enough, perhaps, to contribute to the dominant facial feature of his middle years: large hooded eyes engaged in a perpetual battle between retiring and pressing on—the eyes of a veteran traveler.

Even the most veteran of voyagers would have found the twenty-six-day trip in late fall of 1645 a rough affair. Traveling on foot—he loaded his horse, instead of riding it—Winthrop faced driving rains, heavy snowfall, and temperatures "below the freezing point." He defended against "violent winds" with walls built of pine boughs, and filled a net with grass for a blanket—nevertheless claiming to sleep "quite comfortably." He lost his way at times, nearly got snared in a trap set for Indians, fell up to his waist in one stream, and cut down a tree to make a bridge across another. It was an altogether grueling journey, hardened traveler or not, and Winthrop returned so exhausted that this typically scientific thinker was reduced to a basic spiritual flourish when penning the final entry of his travel diary: *"Deo gratias."* Thank God.

The original purpose of Winthrop's trip was to "lay out a convenient place for iron works" in a region of coastal Connecticut some twenty miles east of Saybrook—a place that would come to be called, rather boldly, New London. (Winthrop had also hoped to tour a graphite mine in Sturbridge, Connecticut, which he had purchased about a year earlier—quite possibly the same mine encountered by John Oldham during his river valley exploration in 1633—but he missed the turnoff leading to it.) In the process Winthrop acquired a rare, intimate look at the tiny societies developing along the course of the road, as well as the role the highway played in shaping these raw worlds.

Toward the end of his first day Winthrop reached the town of Sudbury, Massachusetts.* Sudbury was an example of how the "ordinary way" naturally pulled communities inland. When towns swelled toward overpopulation—or, often, dissension—local leaders traveled the route and surveyed a spot ripe for new settlement. Years earlier, when Watertown had neared capacity, the colonist Peter Noyes rode along the trail until he reached an area seven miles west, where the plains were webbed with fresh springs, the meadows were ripe for pasture, and the woodlands were filled with game. Its location along the highway would provide access to Boston's market and its harbor—in short, Noyes was convinced that life could carry on away from the coast without fear of total isolation. Noyes reported back favorably, and in 1638 Sudbury was born. Similar acts of fission carried Dedham from Boston, Milford and Stamford from New Haven, and, eventually, Marlborough from Sudbury.

Soon after picking a site for a town, settlers typically chose a site for their meetinghouse. In colonial New England, meetinghouses served as places of worship and general fellowship. As each community's civic core, they were naturally given central placement, often directly on the old highway, or just off it. Private homes surrounded this core—by law, at first. In 1635 Massachusetts Bay ruled that no resident could build a home more than half a mile from a town's meetinghouse. Boston's first Meeting House was located just off the foot of modern Washington Street; the second was built directly along it. Often, as with Washington Street, private homes simply flanked the highway as it led toward these centers of congregation.

In time the highway made new settlements not only possible but desirable. When requesting permission from the government to form a new town in the late 1660s, a group of Massachusetts colonists spoke of a site twelve miles west of Marlborough, "in the roade way to Springfeild." This "roade way" was the "ordinary way," and the colonists argued it was a good place for a town because settlement there would "unite and strengthen the inland plantation, and in all probability will be

---

*There is a modern Sudbury, Massachusetts, but the Sudbury of Winthrop's day is presently Wayland.

advantageous for travelers." The product of this request appeared a few years later, when settlement began in the town of Worcester.

During his journey of 1645, Winthrop reached Springfield over the so-called Bay Path, named for leading travelers toward Boston. His trip also took him along parts of the Connecticut Path, widely considered Oldham's route, and the Pequot Path, running through Providence. Altogether these Native paths formed the blueprint for what became the official colonial highway between Boston and New York. In Springfield he slept in the home of William Pynchon, perhaps the most successful fur trader in New England. From there he continued south along the Connecticut River to Windsor, where for three pence per person and twelve per horse he crossed on the ferry, tended by John Bissell.

In Hartford Winthrop spent the night at a tavern kept by Thomas Ford. Connecticut leaders had asked Ford to set up shop a year earlier, noticing an increase of visitors suffering "want of entertainment." At the time taverns served multiple functions, and if not the equal of the town meetinghouse, they were a close second in importance. They were inns for travelers, complete with stables for horses, as well as the only places in town permitted to sell wine or liquor. As taverns were typically among a town's finer buildings, colonial courts often convened there— oblivious, it appears, to the irony of passing temperance laws in a house of refreshment. ("Whoever drinks himself drunk," remarked a Dutch colonist upon visiting Hartford a few years before Winthrop, "they tie to a post and whip him, as they do thieves in Holland.")

Since 1639, the Boston tavern kept by Richard Fairbanks had served an additional purpose—doubling as a post office for overseas letters. The Fairbanks tavern–mail room was situated, quite conveniently, right at the foot of Washington Street, at the Boston end of the old highway. Back in May of 1638 the colonies had asked King Charles I to authorize a postal system, describing it as "so useful and absolutely necessary," only to be refused. That Boston established one at its own cost reflected a growing need for improved communication. This demand, in turn, demanded better roads, and laws on highway maintenance began to litter the colonial records. In 1643 Connecticut adopted a law giving two highway surveyors per town the right to call on every fit man to mend highways once a year—particularly roads connecting "Towne and Towne." Those who refused incurred a five-shilling fine. Massachusetts had similar laws on the books after the late 1630s. The job was taken quite seriously; in Sudbury, from the very start of settlement, Highway Surveyor was listed as a major town position, alongside Constable and Tax Gatherer.

Before he reached what would become New London, Winthrop passed through his old town of Saybrook—badly run down since its founder departed shortly after the start of the Pequot War. Nature granted some revenge against its absconded proprietor; the weather forced Winthrop to wait six days to cross the mouth of the Connecticut by ferry, and when he finally did, waves bombarded his boat. Once across, Winthrop toured New London for a place to plant his ironworks—and, hindsight suggests, to plant his family. Evidently satisfied, he entered the last leg of his trip, on the highway along the coast of Long Island Sound.

This final stretch brought Winthrop to Rhode Island's major trading house, Cocumscussoc, then owned in part by Roger Williams, stationed on the southern branch of the highway, in modern Wickford. Trade headquarters remained locked beside harbors in colonial days—the process of loading and unloading merchant ships required it—but in time buyers and sellers from far along the route flocked toward these emerging commercial centers. By 1645 Boston's market had operated for more than a decade: Every Thursday, Bay Colony merchants dragged their livestock, produce, and other wares to the intersection of modern Washington and State streets. Connecticut had recently started a weekly market in Hartford, where people from near and far could trade commodities, cattle, "or any merchandise whatsoever."

In Providence Winthrop stayed with Benedict Arnold, great-grandfather of the infamous Revolutionary War traitor of the same name, and a few days later he reached Boston and home. He had traveled the highway because it was the primary thoroughfare between settlements, but to describe it as merely a route connecting Point A to Point B, even as early as 1645, was already to reduce much of its significance. Taken as a whole, the road represented a conduit of cultural progress.

A meetinghouse would appear, then a tavern, then a marketplace—and soon the route had conferred upon its New World residents a sense of permanency, safety, and hope. Whether Winthrop picked up the awesome entirety of this significance is unknown but irrelevant; the experience alone engraved his mind with a clearer picture of inland travel and settlement than anyone else in New England had at the time—a familiarity with life along the highway that would come in handy down the road, so to speak, when tapped in the service of the throne.

Chapter 2

Of Fidelity and Fate

BY THE SPRING of 1649, John Winthrop Jr. and his whole family—wife, Elizabeth, and, by then, eight children—had settled in New London. They perched themselves in a stone house at the top of a rock ledge. A wide river, the present-day Thames, fed into the Sound toward a checkmark-shaped landmass called Fisher's Island, where Winthrop's goats munched away their days, bleating goatish wisdom in the blue Long Island breeze. One day in late March a solitary Indian on horseback entered this scene. Nahawton, a "Trustie & swift" Indian messenger, had hurried along the highway from the Bay bearing a letter for Winthrop. His presence was requested in Boston. His father had died.

For years after the death of the elder John Winthrop, several colonies made a push to secure the junior Winthrop's favor. Connecticut made him a "freeman," a title of advanced social status and a prerequisite for holding office, and in 1651 elected him a magistrate—reelecting him the next two years though he failed to attend a single session of the colony's General Court. Peter Stuyvesant, governor of the Dutch colony of New Netherland, invited Winthrop and "any others that shall come along with yow" to live near him in the capital, New Amsterdam, on present-day Manhattan. New Haven, then an independent colony every bit the equal of Massachusetts Bay, Connecticut, or Rhode Island, briefly won his favor. But in late May of 1657 fate intervened in the form of a rider coming down the highway with a message that Winthrop had been chosen governor of Connecticut—less than a week before New Haven's own elections.

This bold move by Connecticut would shortly prove brilliant. Back in England, King Charles II regained the throne in spring of 1660. Puritan rebels—including Winthrop's father-in-law, Hugh Peter—were shown to the gallows. A cousin sought Winthrop's advice on migrating some families to New England, "if times press them." The crown cast a newly skeptical glare at its colonies; only a royal patent could ease the anxious times, and only Massachusetts Bay held an unquestioned one.

So, as the other colonies raced to prove their authenticity, a dependable foreign envoy was at a premium, and John Winthrop Jr. was one of the most dependable around. When England briefly considered a position of General Governor over New England, Winthrop was among the final three nominees; "which however that Designe ripened not, yet Your Name keepes up an high esteeme," Roger Williams wrote him in March of 1660. That May, the same month Charles returned to England from exile, Connecticut made another move both bold and brilliant— lifting its ban on consecutive terms so Winthrop could remain its governor indefinitely.

The restoration of Charles II set the highway astir. Colonial commissioners scattered toward important meetings. Letters burst with news, taverns buzzed with fear. Many Indian messengers, formerly considered "Trustie," grew unreliable. Some refused to deliver a letter if they suspected it concerned them; Roger Williams was known to promise new pants to Native messengers, provided they brought back a response. Neither could shipmasters be trusted with sensitive mail. For a small bribe they let anyone read a letter before delivering it to an official. The practice grew to be so routine that New Amsterdam passed several laws against it.

Out of necessity, the colonists formulated an impromptu version of the postal system they had been denied by the first King Charles back in 1638. A letter sent by Winthrop from Hartford to Boston in December of 1659 noted "this weeks passage" by a messenger willing to "adventure through the wilderness"—a clear hint that thought had been given to an organized pipeline between New England's two great capitals. Correspondence was often entrusted to servants, fellow townsmen, even reputable travelers passing through. A good example occurred in October of 1660, when John Davenport, the preacher who had founded New Haven, overheard in a tavern that someone was heading for the Bay. Davenport asked the Boston-bound man to take a letter to Winthrop—the presumption being that the man would pass Winthrop's home in Hartford along the "ordinary way."

The need for regular communication by land now exceeded the danger of highway travel. In warmer times word from New Amsterdam typically reached New England by boat into Milford, Connecticut, where Alexander Bryan, postal dispatcher of sorts, forwarded it along the route to New Haven and beyond. In winter, when the harbors froze, it was not out of the question to send a letter from New London to New Amsterdam by land; that was often, in Winthrop's words, the "spediest oportunity possible of passage." Life itself kept a quicker pace: in the early 1660s Boston enacted a speed limit so that galloping horses would avoid running over children, "who are ordinarily abroad in the streetes, & not of age or discretion suddainly to escape such danger." Through it all, the highway dutifully conducted the urgency of the time.

In the summer of 1661, the Connecticut court asked Winthrop to return to London to request a royal charter. (The Warwick patent he had secured years earlier, always suspect at best, would no longer stand.) Winthrop left Hartford with an official, obsequious petition, and £500. Instead of setting sail from Boston, however, he wrote to his friend Peter Stuyvesant and secured passage across the Atlantic on a Dutch vessel embarking from New Amsterdam—a very curious move, one with "no small motive," as Winthrop put it, because it meant he would have to return to London via Holland. He made one more curious move, departing for New Amsterdam by boat from Saybrook rather than from Milford, as was typical at the time.

He arrived with a bang. Twenty-seven pounds of gunpowder, to be exact, greeted his boat at Manhattan's southern shore. Fort Amster-

dam towered above the base of the island. Out front, near the Bowling Green, the marketplace hummed. Farmers, Indians, and merchants
from around the world convened here to exchange goods of all kinds.
Winthrop soaked in the scene. He gazed up at the fort, perhaps making
mental comparisons with one he had drawn for his father decades earlier. Its sides stretched one hundred yards; sixteen guns were mounted
on its walls; six more were mounted on each of four bastions. The
orange, white, and blue of the Dutch West India Company flag waved
overhead.

Eventually Winthrop and Stuyvesant moved north on modern
Broadway—then often called Heere Straat, or High Street—passing
houses built with glazed yellow bricks and roofs checkered in red and
black tile. They saw the burying ground and the company garden, and
passed the jail where, two months earlier, deputy guard Hans Vos had
been too weak to stop prisoner Richard Bullock from escaping, or too
drunk to care. They entered the feeble gate of the wall at modern Wall
Street and crossed the stream that connected the Collect Pond with
the East River. They were on the *Heere-weg* now, Dutch for "highway";
today it's called Bowery, this road, because it meandered through the
farms—the *Bouwerie*—divided among the Dutch settlers. The biggest
bowery, spanning some three hundred acres, belonged to Stuyvesant,
and when they reached his manor, in the vicinity of present St. Mark's
Church, they pulled to a stop.

Stuyvesant had secured a place for Winthrop aboard a ship with an
English-speaking captain. Five days later, after nearly one hundred fifty
pounds of gunpowder expended in salute, Winthrop sailed for the Continent in the *Trouw*—Dutch for "fidelity."

At this point, the reason for some of Winthrop's curious moves
became more clear. Not long after the *Trouw* reached the Atlantic, William Leete, the governor of New Haven, feverishly raced along the
Sound, clutching a charter petition he hoped Winthrop would present
to King Charles on his colony's behalf. As the most vocal antiroyalist
settlement, New Haven had no diplomat as qualified as Winthrop to
represent its charter claim in London. The town feared being swallowed
by Connecticut and losing authority over its uniquely strict lifestyle; it

saw Winthrop, a former resident, as its only hope of remaining independent. Leete had expected to intercept Winthrop on his way to New Amsterdam; after all, Winthrop would have passed through New Haven en route to Milford. Eventually Leete rode along the coastal highway in a blind and furious search, but when he reached Saybrook he was informed that Winthrop had left from there a week earlier, "and so I was wholly disapointed."

Seen from today, the move seems slippery, but at the time it made a good bit of sense. New Haven had recently drawn the ire of the restored monarch by harboring two fugitives—judges who had helped hang Charles I. Sympathizing with the town would have been politically foolish. And Leete was not alone in chasing after Winthrop; the Plymouth colony also sought his help. After discovering that Winthrop had left unannounced, Plymouth's governor wrote a scathing note to "the son of such a father as was our very honored friend, and of a public spirit, whose careful and painful endeavor was not confined within the limits of his jurisdiction." Taking up too many causes would no doubt hurt them all. If fidelity were to play a role in Winthrop's mission, it would have to be toward Connecticut, and Connecticut alone.

Back in London, Winthrop stayed in a house beside St. Stephen's Church, where a young John Davenport had once preached. He spent much time with the Royal Society, and may have played an important role in the throne's official acceptance of the group.* Finally he met with the king. His old friend Lord Saye and Sele, it seems, helped Winthrop secure a royal entrée by writing a letter of introduction to Edward Montagu, who served as lord chamberlain to Charles II. Once inside, perhaps the astronomer in Winthrop found some common ground with a king known to enjoy his telescope. However he worked his charm, Winthrop left no small impression on the court. The patent he secured for Connecticut stretched infinitely southwest of Massachusetts from the Narragansett Bay, consuming New Haven—and also New Amsterdam—in the process.

Both territories were furious upon his return. Soon enough, how-

---

*Winthrop was the first North American admitted to the Royal Society.

ever, neither grievance would matter. Preferring any authority to that of the king, New Haven reluctantly acquiesced to a union with Connecticut, forever relinquishing its hope of independence. Then, in midsummer of 1664, four royal commissioners arrived in New England with the intention of "reducing" New Amsterdam—acquiring it, this meant, as property of James, Duke of York. Winthrop joined these commissioners in western Long Island, at the base of their approach. He dashed off a letter to his friend Stuyvesant, ensuring the fair treatment of the Dutch and agreeing to "avoid the effusion of blood," if only the residents of Manhattan would give themselves over to England's throne.

With that, the reason behind Winthrop's other curious moves from earlier became clear as well. The commissioners had consulted a map of Fort Amsterdam, often called the Duke's Plan, drawn with startling precision and dated about a month after Winthrop left Manhattan back in 1661. If Stuyvesant felt betrayed, he had reason. Winthrop may have provided the details used to draw the Duke's Plan; years later, a description accompanying the map was found among the papers of the Royal Society. Winthrop's cousin, George Downing, helped orchestrate the takeover, and the two certainly kept in contact during Winthrop's charter visit.

Stuyvesant, enraged, tore up the note. But New Amsterdam's officials wanted no part of battle; besides, as reports would later confirm, their fort had run irresponsibly low on gunpowder. Amid cries for "the letter!," Dutch leaders gathered fragments of Winthrop's note and made a copy. They set a meeting of capitulation, and on August 27, 1664, Winthrop once again traveled to Stuyvesant's bowery—this time joined by eleven other riders. When these delegates emerged they had reached the agreement that turned New Amsterdam into New York, Fort Amsterdam into Fort James, and the dust churned up on the *Heere-weg,* settling softly in their wake into the Highway of the King.

ON JANUARY 22, 1673, Mathias Nicolls finished reading the postmaster's Oath of Fidelity—"You doe sweare by the Everliving God, that you will truly and faithfully discharge the Trust reposed in you as a Post-Master"—prepared by Francis Lovelace, the governor of New York. With that America's first regular mail carrier began his journey up the Highway from the southern tip of Manhattan toward Boston, under explicit instructions to stop first at the Hartford home of John Winthrop Jr., "from whom you shall receive the best Direction how to forme the best Post-Road."

After leaving Fort James, this rider veered northeast at what is now Park Row, formerly called the High Road to Boston. When he reached Bowery Lane he continued north. Just off the road, near the present corner of Thirteenth Street and Third Avenue, stood a pear tree Peter Stuyvesant had transplanted from Holland years earlier. The tree would survive this cold season and many more—it served as a reminder of the city's Dutch roots until 1867—but Stuyvesant was no longer around to tend it. He had died in early 1672, about a year before the first post ride, permitted by the English to live out his days on his beloved farm beside the Highway.

The rider looped toward modern Madison Square Park, where the Highway diverged from the road to Bloomingdale—the precursor to Broadway as it exists today—then ran northeast along the curvy Indian trail once known as the Wickquasgeck Path. By the early 1640s Wick-quasgeck Natives "passed daily" along this road to trade on Manhattan, according to Dutch settler David de Vries. At about Third Avenue and Forty-fifth Street, near modern Turtle Bay, the rider had traveled some four miles. Continuing along the Highway he approached the town of Harlem, established by the Dutch toward the northern end of the island.

If this section of the Highway had improved since its time as the old Wickquasgeck trade route, Francis Lovelace was largely to thank. A few years earlier he had ordered two men to enlarge the route into a "good Waggon path betwixt this Citty & the Towne of harlem," with the idea that a better road would stimulate communication and trade. At present-day Fifth Avenue, near Eighty-ninth Street, the Highway crept into what's now Central Park. It continued up the heights of Harlem along modern St. Nicholas Avenue toward Spuyten Duyvil, the Dutch name given to the creek that separated Manhattan from the mainland. There the affable ferry keeper, Johannes Verveelen, one of Harlem's original five patentees, came into view. Because the post rider was a colony official, Verveelen would have waived the typical fare—seven pence for horse and man—and shuttled them across the creek and into the present-day Bronx.

The rider continued east toward Pelham and Mamaroneck, New York, where he likely met, respectively, with Thomas Pell and John Richbell. Pell and Richbell maintained an ongoing boundary feud, but together in 1671 they had put aside their differences to improve "a new road to New England" through their towns. The rider continued along the shores of Long Island Sound through Stamford, Norwalk, and Milford, Connecticut, and on into New Haven, called Rodenberghs by the Dutch for the two large red hills straddling its center. He rode north along the Connecticut River toward Hartford, then made his way to the home of John Winthrop Jr., just as Governor Lovelace had instructed.

Though the English colonies had sought an official postal system since 1638, only under Lovelace did the scheme find its energetic ambassador. He had announced its creation on December 10, 1672, and by the time the first rider left, six weeks later, the basic plan had been drafted.

Once a month this postman—an "active, stout, and indefatigable" fellow, according to Lovelace—would journey from New York to Boston and back with the mail. He would mark the letters "post-paid" and drop them into separate bags classified by destination. But the post rider's role went far beyond slinging a few notes into a portmanteau—it stopped just short of making him general conductor of northeast America. The rider would survey the best place to leave letters in each town, and notify the inhabitants of his approximate return. He would mark trees to direct travelers who might take the route on their own, and scout strategic locations for inns and taverns. When someone wished to travel with the rider, he would assist them civilly, "that I may heare noe Complaint of you," ordered Lovelace. If necessary he even would apprehend fugitive soldiers and servants, by which Lovelace might have been referring to Isaac Ratt, his one-handed cook who had run away the previous June.

The system was designed to enhance trade and to provide, in

Lovelace's words, "a more speedy Intelligence and Dispatch of Affayres." The affairs of 1673 centered on the lingering threat of attack from the Dutch. In the years following the seizure of New Amsterdam by the Duke of York, tensions between England and Holland had remained high. The possibility of assault was a primary reason Lovelace wanted his system in place so urgently. Initially the post rider was supposed to leave on January 1, 1673, but Lovelace held him back so that he could forward to Winthrop the latest news of the Dutch approach: forty Dutch men-of-war had been spotted near the West Indies. "If so," Lovelace wrote, "it will be high time for us to begin to buckle on our armor, and to put ourselves into such a posture of defence as is most suitable to our several conditions."

For Lovelace, this "posture of defence" took the form of a finely carved postal road from New York to Boston. Along this route swift messengers would carry the words that moved New England's leaders and roused New England's armies. Lovelace believed in this avenue of intelligence—this "handsomer resistance," as he later called it—with a passion that, at times, clouded his judgment. For Francis Lovelace was not a natural wartime governor. His bloodline* ran poetic and so did his letters; once, writing to England, he described life in America as harshly remote, "as if wee had as well crost Lethe, as the Athlantiq ocean, so that the effects are commonly past with you, before the causes arrive." Missing English refinement, he established in New York a culture club that met twice weekly in the evening, drank brandy punch from silver tankards, and simply chatted. In many ways he was a man of the mind, and seemed to feel the best defense was an informed one.

Above all, Lovelace felt that John Winthrop Jr. was the man to see the plan through. In two lengthy letters to Winthrop, delivered by this first rider, Lovelace described the colonial postal system in detail. Winthrop was to direct the rider toward Boston and, more generally, to improve the route between Manhattan and the Bay. "I desire of you to favor the undertaking by your best skill and countenance," Lovelace

* Richard Lovelace, the notable seventeenth-century English poet, was his brother.

wrote—the skill of a man whose overland journeys had given him intimate knowledge of interior New England, and the countenance of one whose lifetime of public service made him known across this same land. "It would be much advantageous to our design," Lovelace continued, "if in the interval you discourse with some of the most able woodmen to make out the best and most facile way for a post, which in process of time would be the King's best highway."

The John Winthrop Jr. who met the first post rider in 1673, however, was a weary man with a worried mind. Still shaken by the death of his wife, Elizabeth, months earlier, Winthrop was then, and would long remain, enfeebled by the throes of bereavement. For months after Elizabeth's death this otherwise restless figure hardly stirred. More than a year later, in a letter about the "irreparable losse of my deare wife," he blamed himself for aggravating Elizabeth's illness; she had been nursing the governor, himself sick at the time, and Winthrop felt quite sure this loyal care had put a strain too great to bear on her own failing health.

Winthrop did muster the strength to receive America's first post rider—he marked the letters from Lovelace received on February 6— and although one can only guess at the course this man rode toward the Bay, his finish line was clear.* When the rider neared the end of his journey he passed through the small gate in Roxbury, on the neck of the Bay, and entered the head of Boston town. It was a far different Boston from

---

*The first post rider's precise path from Hartford to Boston is not described in Lovelace's instructions, but the mystery deserves a moment of academic consideration. The safe and traditional assumption is that Winthrop guided the rider along the Indian paths he had followed during his trip in 1645. But one must consider that these paths traversed Indian villages, while the purpose of Lovelace's postal system was to inform New England's top leaders. As a result, it would have made sense for Winthrop to steer the rider on a route that more closely resembled the modern Boston Post Road to Boston through Springfield, Brookfield, and Worcester. Winthrop could have guided the rider first toward Springfield's John Pynchon, son of William, who had been among those present at Stuyvesant's bowery during the English takeover—surely worthy of this new colonial loop of information. Pynchon could have pointed the rider toward Brookfield, a town he had helped establish by 1665. As the most isolated settlement between Boston and Hartford—it stands out as such on a contemporary map from 1677 under the name Sqaboag—Brookfield would have needed a regular avenue of correspondence more than most. There the rider could have stopped at the tavern run by Pynchon's business associate, John Ayres, located on the original highway. Last, a "new" Bay Path formed in 1673 to connect Brookfield and Worcester, perhaps as a consequence of the first post rider's mission.

the one Wahginnacut had entered some forty years earlier—now a mini-metropolis of several thousand, furnished with "handsomely contrived" shops and cobblestone streets, according to one contemporary traveler. The home stretch was on a segment of present-day Washington Street, newly widened in 1671. It took him past the town gallows toward the intersection of modern Milk Street, site of the elder John Winthrop's second Boston home, later site of the Bay's second meetinghouse, the Old South. Across the street stood a wooden home later rented by Josiah Franklin, whose wife would give birth there, in 1706, to a son named Benjamin.

Finally the rider reached the intersection of modern State and Washington streets, filled with the sounds and smells of a market square. Here stood the Town House, Boston's two-story center of commerce, government, literature, and life, and likely where the first leg of the post rider's round-trip came to a halt. The Bay governor, John Leverett, seems to have greeted him on February 11,* because on this day Leverett wrote a "very affectionate & consolatory letter" to John Winthrop Jr., upon hearing about the death of Elizabeth.

A FEW MONTHS LATER, wishing to discuss his postal system at further length, Francis Lovelace followed the route of his first post rider into Hartford, arriving on a midsummer evening in 1673. Escorts led the governor north through an ox pasture to the bank of a purling stream that curled east across the town and disappeared into the Connecticut River, beyond a meadow. Moving west along the banks of the stream they reached the corner of the town's main street—so aptly placed that, more than three centuries later, it remains Main Street—and stopped at the home of John Winthrop Jr. Lovelace retired that night weary from his journey; the governor had chosen, quite significantly in those seafar-

---

*To the author's knowledge, no one has previously affixed the date of the post rider's entrance into Boston. Some writers have marked this entrance two weeks from the rider's departure. Such a statement discounts Winthrop's reception of letters on February 6 and appears to be inferred from Lovelace's request that the entire trip take one month. An arrival on the eleventh fits not only with Leverett's letter, but also with the length of time it had taken Wahginnacut to reach Boston from Connecticut back in 1631—five days.

ing times, to come "all the way by land." And if he spared a moment for reflection before falling asleep on Friday, the twenty-fifth of July, Francis Lovelace likely felt the next few days would change communication in colonial America.

To Lovelace, son of a knight of Kent and onetime governor of Carmarthen Castle in Wales, the Connecticut capital must have seemed painfully modest. Hartford held at most a few hundred souls. They lived in one- or two-story houses built of clapboard siding, patched with sandstone quarried from the stream. The better roofs were shingled; the poorer, thatched with grass and clay. The main street running through the town, like the Highway leading into it, was little more than a dirt path. Rain turned it quickly into mire.

A stone and log causeway—colonial sidewalk of sorts—guided dry feet to a cleared patch of land that served as an open market and yard for the Meeting House. On Sundays the town gathered here for service, and those who listened poorly to the Reverend Joseph Haynes perhaps grew familiar with the opposite end of the yard, where the whipping post and pillory stood before the jail. Most other days the townspeople flooded back onto the main street and into the central tavern and inn. There Jeremy Adams served cider and rum, regaling patrons with the "passionate distempered speeches, loud language, and unmannerly carriage" that had once earned him public censure from the colony's General Court, which held its sessions in his establishment nevertheless.

The stars had seemed aligned against the meeting. It had been delayed at least twice since the post rider's first run, in January, and at the last moment nearly fell apart entirely. It was initially set for July 19; when the day came, Winthrop sent three men to Milford, Connecticut, on the coast of Long Island Sound, to receive Lovelace and his party. But just as the governor had prepared to leave New York, Captain John Manning, who was set to accompany him, plunged sixteen feet off a wall of Fort James. The accident left Manning "bruised and hurt much, and taken to his bed," jeopardizing the Hartford trip Lovelace had pestered Winthrop several times to secure.

About a week later Lovelace set off for Connecticut anyway. If leaving New York in Manning's bumbling hands was risky, he may have felt waiting any longer nearly as dangerous. The Dutch threat had intensified—their men-of-war had been spotted near Virginia as recently as March—and Lovelace remained convinced that an efficient system of correspondence was crucial to colonial defense. His conference with Winthrop was later described as an "urgent occasion."

Precisely what the two governors discussed about the "King's best highway" is unknown; if minutes were taken, they didn't survive. Presumably they smoothed out the details in the model Lovelace had already proposed in his letters. It's even reasonable to assume they took things easy: the John Winthrop Jr. of late July 1673 described himself as "something ill lately." He had grown dismayed with public service—Connecticut had chosen him governor yet again, in May, despite his objection—and remained in a state of powerful grief. If Lovelace offered any further sympathies about the death of Elizabeth, they surely echoed those he had already sent: "I heartily condole with you the loss of your excellent lady; but we must all stoop to Fate."

Whatever they discussed, Lovelace no doubt left quite pleased. Certainly this visit had gone better than the last time he left Manning in charge of the fort to discuss his postal scheme. That was back in March. A winded rider had called him back from Pelham, a town in present-day Westchester County, with word of a Dutch advance on Fort James. Lovelace dashed home but found no true danger, dismissing the scare as just another one of "Manning's alarms." Though Lovelace raised funds to solidify parts of the fort, he had done nothing with the money by the time he left for Hartford in summer.

Francis Lovelace left the Connecticut capital on July 29, setting off toward New Haven in morning. Raindrops tapped on Hartford's white-oak leaves and shingled roofs. As always, rain softened the road, so that a clatter of hooves would have stamped a muddy track atop the new wooden bridge that crossed the little stream that rolled toward the Connecticut River. Captain Daniel Clarke and his troop escorted Lovelace back through the ox pasture and south along the Highway, past Wethersfield. From there Robert Treat, a high-ranking resident of New Haven, led them into town. They arrived by dusk.

Perhaps once again Lovelace held a thought before shutting his eyes, or maybe he just fell asleep, his mind now cleared of its obsession. No longer conjuring visions of a solitary rider carrying his dream through the darkness—like the one who had left Boston that same day with word of a recent Dutch attack in Virginia, or like that other one, approaching New Haven from the west. . . .

He awoke to the news and hurried along the Highway toward Fort James, long after his arrival would have mattered. At John Richbell's, in Mamaroneck, the second rider told him of Manning's surrender to the Dutch fleet, and he hastened off a note to Winthrop. By Friday night the news had reached Hartford, and Winthrop read the letter's two requests: that he forward the news to Boston, and that he and Lovelace meet again soon, "if not heare yet hereafter, which is much better."

Winthrop sent the rider on his way toward Boston that very evening, and sent another along the southern route, toward New London and Providence. He stood alone, planted at the crossroads of New England, the restless youth now stooping to his Fate—directing men this way and that, toward their journey's end.

Chapter 3

Benjamin Franklin, Postman

FOLLOWING FRANCIS LOVELACE'S fateful meeting in 1673, the postal system, in measure with America, ebbed and surged along the Highway—the Post Road, rather, for that's what it had become. Shortly after the Dutch reclaimed Manhattan, the new governor, Anthony Colve, outlawed correspondence with New England. Colve sentenced English post rider John Sharpe to "the inner and nethermost Dungeon" for four days, and banished him for ten years. When the Treaty of Westminster restored New York to Britain in 1674, Governor Thomas Dongan tried to set up post offices along the entire Eastern Seaboard. His efforts, if nominally endorsed, rallied little assistance: "You are pleased to say I may set up a Post-House," Dongan wrote to one member of the British Parliament, "but send mee noe power to doe it."

Dongan's successor, Edmund Andros, fared slightly better. He arranged for post rider John Perry to carry letters between Boston and New York once a month in winter, and once every three weeks in summer. But in the early 1690s, with New York under the tumultuous reign of Jacob Leisler, Perry was caught on a post ride and tossed in jail for at least a week, "without baile."

Little matter that the postal system failed to flow smoothly during this period—had it been clockwork, few would have been around to tell the time. A brutal fight with the Indians, known as King Philip's War, ravaged numerous towns along the Post Road beginning in the summer of 1675. Along the upper branch, the Massachusetts towns of Worcester, Marlborough, Brookfield,* Springfield, and Sudbury neared total destruction. Along the coastal branch, the Rhode Island towns of Providence and Wickford were deserted, and all but one house in Warwick had been burned to the ground. New York did all it could to keep the battle outside its borders. Boston grew so tense that the drunken, accidental discharge of a gun thirty miles away sent the town into a panic. In the end the colonists paraded King Philip's head on a pole, but fighting in his name produced a higher death rate than would the Civil War—by double.

For many Post Road towns the recovery process took upward of a decade. Little by little, houses were rebuilt, post riders released, tavern cups refilled. By the close of the seventeenth century, stability had been largely restored. A contemporary map drawn by Philip Lea and dated 1690 traces the highway's two major branches and labels towns along the way. (See pp. 32–33. Brookfield appears as Squabaug.) Lea's map includes a middle road, splitting the northern and coastal courses, but it's drawn with clear erasures and passes through few towns—suggesting by comparison the more established routes.

Right about this time, in 1693, England granted royal minter Thomas Neale a patent to run the American post office. Despite efforts by the colonies to aid the system, it continued to sputter—in part, no doubt, because Neale never set foot in America. Few letters were actually required to travel by post; mail between merchants and private notes between friends did not have to use the system at all, and most government correspondence was exempt from postal fees. Ferrymen were supposed to carry post riders across waterways immediately for free. But

---

*Brookfield played host to one of the war's most devastating encounters, known as Wheeler's Surprise. Captain Thomas Wheeler and a band of men were forced to retreat into the highway tavern kept in Brookfield by John Ayres. Every inhabitant of the town— about seventy in all—squeezed into the makeshift garrison, which the Natives would have burned down had fortuitous rains not intervened. A dozen years passed until Brookfield was reoccupied, and five more until it built another tavern.

with a poor understanding of the system, or showing blatant disregard for it, they often charged post riders crossing rates or kept them waiting until a full boatload of paying passengers had accrued.

Then there was the matter of price. Sending a letter from Boston to New York cost nine pence, the same as sending one to Europe. The charge merely reflected the difficulty of highway travel—forty years after Lovelace's original design, the post rider still needed two weeks to reach Boston from Manhattan—but it resulted in a service too expensive for general acceptance. This expense, in turn, created a critical problem of funding. At the time, recipients, not senders, paid for postage. As a result, the cost of any mail that went delivered but unclaimed came out of the postmaster's pocket. Neale's American deputies often struggled to stay afloat; the postmaster of New England, Duncan Campbell—a firm believer in a system "of so great a benefit to this country"—frequently petitioned for reimbursement. Still, by the time his son, John, assumed the position in the early 1700s, the office lost a considerable £275 a year.

As for the post rider himself, his role had changed very little by the turn of the eighteenth century, but at the same time quite a lot. He still hastened messages along the highway into Connecticut, but now he mainly took the branch along the coast. He still made his delivery to Governor John Winthrop, but now that man was Fitz-John, son of the late John Jr., who lived in New London instead of Hartford. He still carried the day's most important news, but now it was neatly compiled by John Campbell into a handwritten "Journal of Public Occurrences" that would soon become the country's first newspaper.

One late September day in 1703 the post rider left Campbell's office on modern Washington Street and hurried across the skinny neck of Boston. The Post Road's southbound route led riders out of the Bay toward Dedham, Massachusetts, along present-day Centre Street, en route to Rhode Island. Just south of East Greenwich, near the modern intersection of Forge Road and U.S. Route 1, the road crossed a stream known as Elizabeth Spring—so named because Elizabeth Winthrop had liked to stop there for a drink whenever she and John made their way south on the highway from Boston. The road continued west past sparsely populated coastal towns toward the Pawcatuck River

Detail, Philip Lea, "A New Map of New England . . ." (1690), Lionel Pincus and
Princess Firyal Map Division, New York Public Library, Astor, Lenox and Tilden Foundations

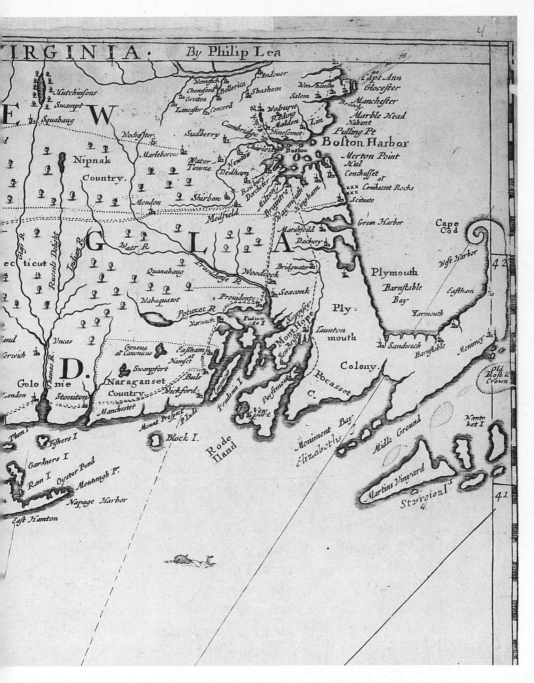

Philip Lea's map of New England, dated c. 1690,
shows the Post Road's two main branches, inland (top) and coastal,
during early colonial times.

that marked the boundary of Connecticut, then on through Stoning-
ton across an uneven countryside, eventually reaching the ferry at the
Thames River—where high winds placed entrance to the governor's
New London home at the mercy of the gods.

A Boston woman named Sarah Knight rode this route with a post
messenger the following fall, and surviving details from her diary provide a rare, vivid glimpse of the Post Road at the time. If making the
trip by foot had been exhausting for John Winthrop Jr., it was no easier
on horseback for the postman and his fellow traveler. The obstacles of
nature still riddled the untamed wilderness. Rocks and swamps encumbered the passage, as did thick fog and steep hills. Pesky travelers in need
of a guide slowed the journey—Knight often struggled to keep pace
with her postal escort. Weary horses stemmed numerous river crossings
when they could. Otherwise young boys led rider and horse across high
waters in canoes that seemed ready to capsize at a single wave's whim.

A day's ride began long before sunrise. Sometimes the journey was
so taxing, the burden of rider and mailbag and haste so oppressive, that
horses keeled over en route. Branches and bushes closely flanked the
narrow path, scraping at the locked sacks packed with letters for Providence, New Haven, New York, and a few towns in between. Occasionally the western rider encountered the eastern post, and they exchanged
letters heading in the opposite direction. When night fell before he
reached the next stage the rider had no choice but to hustle on, deep into
the woods and blind into the darkness. The occasional sliver of starlight
toyed with the tired mind; in the words of Sarah Knight, "each lifeless
Trunk, with its shatter'd Limbs, appear'd an Armed Enymie."

Along the southern route of the highway one might stay at Wood-
cock's tavern in North Attleboro, or the Billings inn near Sharon, with
its inquisitive hostess. There was also clean, comfortable Haven's tavern, in North Kingstown, or the lodge some twenty-five miles west, run
by the irascible Mr. Devil and his homely twin daughters. Beds were
often short or shared, and bedrooms were partitioned from noisy par-
lors by thin boards. On the other side patrons downed dram after dram
of rum—"tyed by the Lipps to a pewter engine," Knight noted. Nearly
everyone inside was a man; consequently, Madam Knight caused quite

a stir upon her arrival. On the strength of this tonic, Knight recalled, the men held smoky, all-night debates on matters as provincial as the meaning of *Narragansett,* and as profound as how to fit a triangle into a square.

Eventually the post rider announced his arrival into New London with a blare of his horn, and quite likely a sigh of relief. When he arrived on that particular day, in late September of 1703, he delivered the latest "Journal of Public Occurrences" to Governor Fitz Winthrop. Amid the written news, and whatever other breathless tidings the rider passed along, John Campbell had slipped Winthrop a personal note: "I must represent to your honor & Assembly the state of the post office," the postmaster begged, "in order to have some encouragement for the support of it . . . else of necessity it must drop."

JOHN CAMPBELL NEVER quite found the "encouragement" he sought from Fitz-John Winthrop in the fall of 1703.* He did occasionally rally some monetary support from the Bay government, but rarely as much as he required, and every pound was hard-fought. The post office found new patronage in 1707, when the government of Queen Anne purchased the system from Thomas Neale's successor. Parliament soon passed the Post Office Act of 1710, but the core of Neale's faulty system remained largely intact. Generally speaking, the act did little to improve either the efficiency of the post or the fortunes of the postmaster.

Nevertheless, John Campbell didn't carry out his threat to "drop" the poorly funded post office. Instead, he seems to have found in the "Journal of Public Occurrences" a reason to endure the fiscal hardships of his postmaster position. If the role didn't bring Campbell a rightful living, then controlling the information that spread across northeast America along the Post Road at least earned him a considerable prestige.

By April of 1704 Campbell's weekly updates to Fitz Winthrop had

---

*Though not the postal patron his father was, Fitz Winthrop did influence the system simply through his choice of residence. In the Post Office Act of 1710, Winthrop's home of New London, and no longer Hartford, was considered the post's "Chief Town in Connecticut," a distinction that temporarily elevated the coastal branch of the Post Road into the highway's primary route.

grown too immense for his scrawling hand to contain. He arranged for the "Journal of Public Occurrences" to be printed at Bartholomew Green's shop near the Boston end of the Post Road. Green laid each word by hand, letter after painstaking letter, then moved the entire frame to his wooden press and spread ink atop the font with leather balls. A large screw helped him lower the plate against a blank foolscap sheet. Colonial newspapers contained very few pictures; those that did appear often depicted a post rider blaring his horn. After Green finished a few hundred sheets—pressing one side at a time—he brought them down the Post Road to the corner of modern Washington and Water streets, where Campbell waited in the post office.

The result was the first regular newspaper in America, and it continued unrivaled for fifteen years. Campbell called it the *Boston News-Letter*.

From that time on, colonial postmasters considered it their right—some, like Campbell, their duty—to publish a newspaper. The dual role made sense. The postmaster's official salary was low, so publishing books, legal forms, bills of sale, or newspapers supplemented the income. News also gravitated to the post office. Houses had no addresses, let alone mailboxes, so anyone wishing to send or receive a letter walked to Campbell's place and made the exchange in person. On days the post went out or arrived in, he stayed there from seven in the morning till seven at night, and if he received the mail past dark, Campbell opened his door and set out a lantern.

A person might read his letter immediately and discuss its contents with Campbell before heading home, or dash off a response right away rather than miss the next mail or make another trip. Merchants awaited the mail so eagerly that one man applied to start a tavern near the Boston office, so that people could bide their time until the letters arrived and were sorted. Between this daily gossip and his own subscriptions to London newspapers, the postmaster became local and foreign correspondent, metro and world editor, head of advertising and lead page designer—in short, a one-man media machine.

Updates cycled back to postmasters naturally. Campbell filtered the latest events into the *Boston News-Letter*, and the post rider carried it from town to town. The rider dropped off the paper along with the mail in local taverns—only a few towns had separate post offices, and even these were not major buildings—where subscribers debated the incoming stories and shared information from their own letters. News bubbled inside pewter mugs, swelled inside opinionated mouths, found shelter inside the post rider's ears. Eventually it gathered again at Campbell's, where he culled the chatter and began the process anew.

As post riders made their laps along the Post Road, certain taverns became preferred stopping points. Eventually these reached landmark status; early travel guides measured distance not from one town's meetinghouse to another but from tavern to tavern. Before long these destinations had become familiar itineraries. New York's first almanac—prepared in 1697 because the author had "little else to do"—lists an inn for each town along the coastal route of the Post Road to Boston and the mileage between them. A 1730 almanac dots the taverns on the inland route from Boston to Springfield and tabulates the trip at an efficient ninety-four miles—just four more than it takes on Interstate 90 nearly three centuries later.

In 1719 the postmaster who replaced Campbell started the *Boston Gazette*, the country's second newspaper, and the decades that followed brought many more. The competition filled columns—it was a regular occurrence, in those precopyright times, to reprint entire articles from other publications. Anyone with the resources could begin a newspaper, but for a while postmasters held an advantage over private news printers because the post office allowed them to distribute their paper for free. Many bribed post riders not to carry the papers of their competitors. The *Boston Gazette* remained in the hands of five straight postmasters until 1734, when the next postmaster started the *Boston Weekly Post-Boy*. This trend continued until midway through the eighteenth century. By then newspapers relied on the post for their livelihoods—so much so that printers in New York and Boston raised an uproar when the post office considered closing the inland route through Hartford, in December of 1767. By February the news publishers had won out, and the post office reopened this branch, at a loss. News went as the post went, and the post went as the Post Road allowed.

The physical road expanded to keep pace with an increasingly communicative society. Bridges spanned Rhode Island's major rivers. Boston built a stone drainage system along the highway across the neck. New York cleared the "Ruinous, and almost impassible" Post Road, widened it to fit coaches, and replaced the Spuyten Duyvil ferry with a drawbridge, calling the new structure Kings Bridge, a name still attached to the area today. Wagon lines shuttled passengers and goods between Hartford and New Haven, and Providence and Boston. Small, interior Connecticut towns pestered the government with requests for highways "branching out of the now post road," to ease their own transportation needs; residents of Norwich went so far as to raise this money themselves, lest the town lose touch with the Post Road's loop of information.

Decades after the debut of the *Boston News-Letter*, when patriotic editorials replaced straight news, urban politics began to shape provincial mind-sets. New York's events informed New Haven's thoughts; New Haven's thoughts, New London's conversation. Big-town ink dignified small-town rumor. Come 1774, toward the eve of revolution, John Adams stopped in a tavern in the small Post Road town of Shrewsbury, some forty miles west of Boston. There Adams heard five local yeomen—"common people," he called them, "of very narrow views"—nonetheless arguing city affairs. If Parliament could take away John Hancock's wharf, one reasoned, what would stop it from taking away your barn? The Post Road now carried knowledge inland from the metropolis, connecting towns with the thread of common culture, and before long, of common cause.

These elements of exchange took decades to coalesce following John Campbell's postal plea to Fitz Winthrop in the autumn of 1703. Had this infrastructure of rebellion been in place earlier, America's frustration with England might have progressed more quickly. Shortly after Parliament announced the Post Office Act of 1710, colonists took objection to parts of the law: Revenue from the American mail would go toward defraying the cost of Queen Anne's War, fought against the French, and once a certain profit had been reached, proceeds could be used at Parliament's discretion, instead of automatically feeding back into the colonial postal system. In fact when details of the act reached

America, in 1718, "a great Clamour was raised against it," reported Alexander Spotswood, then lieutenant governor of Virginia—for many people considered "ye Rates of Postage" not a public service, but a tax.

As it happened, the American post office failed to produce a profit for half a century following the postal act of 1710, reducing the "great Clamour" to mere noise. The sound is mentioned here as an overture to the fury that followed: four events triggered by four newspapers in four Post Road towns that, blurred by their momentum, reached one conclusion. It was during this period that the Post Road evolved into a conduit of revolution; that the post office itself became seen not just as a tax but as the prelude to all taxes; that what the Crown regarded as mere delivery became grounds for a mad dash toward deliverance.

Before any of this could happen, though, someone had to give the post office what Thomas Neale, Fitz Winthrop, and Queen Anne herself had not: the proper encouragement.

IF THERE REMAINS an underexplored aspect of Ben Franklin's life—an admittedly large *if*—it is his role in shaping modern mail service. Franklin was born in 1706 in a small Boston house where the Post Road met Milk Street, and was baptized across the road at the Old South Church. From a young age he wrote essays under the name Silence Dogood for the *New England Courant,* a seditious paper run by James Franklin, his brother. But Benjamin's grand introduction to publishing came when he was just seventeen. James had been told to submit each issue of the *Courant* to the government before publication. Pretending to have "intirely dropt the Undertaking," he put out the paper in Benjamin's name to evade this primitive prior restraint.

In 1737 Alexander Spotswood, by that time America's deputy postmaster, named Franklin the postmaster of Philadelphia. Ironically the man Franklin displaced was William Bradford, who, as New York's only printer in 1723, had too little work to support an apprentice, and so recommended that young Franklin head south. Bradford, as postmaster, had blocked delivery of Franklin's *Pennsylvania Gazette.* It was this postal power that led Franklin to seek the position—not so much for revenge as for the ability to mail the *Gazette,* and his *Poor Richard's Almanac,* free of charge. When Franklin learned of the failing health of then–deputy postmaster general Elliot Benger in 1751, he lobbied hard for the post office's highest position in America. Two years later he was named joint deputy, with William Hunter of Virginia.

Franklin's first order of business was fairly unprecedented, and its impact entirely sweeping. In June of 1753 Franklin set out on a personal inspection of the country's most important post roads and offices. The tour actually began some six weeks before he had secured the deputy position; it resumed in fall of 1754—about the time his "New Experiments and Observations on Electricity, Part III" was printed in London—and would not end until the following March. Whereas his predecessors had managed the system from afar, Franklin would examine the post with a scientist's scrutiny, stage by stage, and address the problems that had lingered, nearly unchanged, since Thomas Neale's regime. Hunter eventually joined the survey trip but "relaps'd into his last Summer Fever" along the way and spent months recovering in Boston. The bulk of the effort, it seems, belonged to Franklin.

Much of his attention focused on the Post Road between New York and Boston. This stretch was by far the most traveled in the country; only the road from Philadelphia to Manhattan approached its activity. Yet postal decay had befallen the route. Back in 1714 the rider had alternated between Boston and New York; once a month he made the full trip along the northern branch to Hartford, switching next time to the coastal course through Providence. At the time of Franklin's inspection, however, every ride followed the coast. When Hartford wanted mail the townsmen hired "a poor little Man" named Brooker to ride down to the shore. Even the coastal branch was far from ideal. After leaving New York, Franklin encountered no post offices, or postmasters, until he reached New London—one hundred twenty-five miles east.

Franklin wasted little time implementing a change. He passed through New Haven in late June of 1753, and soon took steps toward creating a post office there. By fall he had ordered supplies from London—"20 lb Quotations; 2 good Composing Sticks; A compleat good new Press," among others. He rented space for a shop near Yale, and

James Parker, his partner in New York, agreed to run the location. By spring of 1755 Franklin's office in New Haven was producing the *Connecticut Gazette,* the colony's first newspaper. Parker had become the town's postmaster. Poor little Brooker had been hired full-time to carry the mail between the coast and Hartford. The office lost money at first, but it filled a major gap in New England's information loop. "You may ask why we did it?" Parker later wrote to Franklin. "Tho' had we not hired that Rider not a Letter from any Post-Office would have gone to or come from Hartford and Middletown."

Franklin then devised a thorough set of postal guidelines. They were as exhaustive as those proposed by Lovelace a century earlier, but excepting a frivolous rule that forced riders to blow their horns every five miles, they were far more practical. To help postmasters keep better books, Franklin provided them with precise accounting tables. Dates and destinations were recorded, paid, unpaid, and "post free" letters were tallied; senders were even alphabetized by surname. If a letter sat in the post office for a month unclaimed, the recipient's name would be published in the newspaper. If it sat for two months, it was sent to Philadelphia—the birth of the "dead letter office." Home delivery even became an option, with the rider rewarded an extra halfpenny per letter for his troubles.

Lazy riders need not apply: "You are not," Franklin demanded, "out of Friendship or Compliment to any Person whatsoever, to delay his Majesty's Post one Quarter of an Hour." Those arriving late would be interrogated about the cause of their delay. Illegitimate mail carriers, if spotted, were to be reported immediately. Letters were placed in separate bundles by town, to help tabulate cost. Perhaps to lighten the loads, Franklin dissuaded riders from carrying nonpaper valuables—"Money, Rings, Jewels" and the like.

If they wished, senders could pay for their letters in advance. Otherwise, no letter passed for free without the deputy's blessing, marked "Free. B. Franklin." The high rates set by Queen Anne could not be changed, but if merchants could recoup their postal costs through quicker transactions they might patronize the official post instead of hiring private riders—a considerable problem at the time. Efficiency sustained, figured Franklin, would in time offset prohibitive postage.

One of Franklin's more drastic changes hit closer to his heart—and his purse. By 1759 John Campbell's solitary newsletter had multiplied into ten regular newspapers along the Post Road.* With the added weight the post riders wanted additional money. Printers, meanwhile, had great trouble collecting fees from their far-flung subscribers. Some simply failed to pay the rider; others had the nerve to "die, become Bankrupt, or remove out of the Country" unannounced.

Franklin corralled the chaos with two simple steps. He added a shipping charge to each subscription. The extra money appeased the riders, even after postmasters kept a twenty percent commission "for your Care and Trouble." He also gave postmasters the power to refuse delivery to delinquent subscribers. This made collection easier for printers. Both rider and printer benefited from the elimination of excess print runs. Those hurt most by the reform were postmaster-printers like Franklin, who lost the advantage of sending their own newspaper for free while their competitors had to pay postage. But it was worth the cost, he told his fellow postmasters, "not to discourage the Spreading of News-papers, which are on many Occasions useful to Government, and advantageous to Commerce, and to the Publick."

Franklin's civic duties called him to England in 1757. Upon his return, five years later, Franklin launched another postal survey, this time with his new co-deputy, John Foxcroft.** Touch-ups, those earmarks of accomplishment, were all that remained. Franklin devised an odometer that measured distance between routes and laid milestones that both guided riders and helped them calculate rates. He hung rate tables in every office: one such chart, dated 1763, listed five offices between New York and New London on the Post Road's coastal branch, where none had existed during Franklin's first journey a decade earlier. He slashed the speed of exchange between New York and Boston: "By making the Mails travel by Night as well as by Day," he wrote, "Letters may be

---

* *Evening Post, Gazette, News-Letter, Post-Boy* (Boston); *Gazette or Weekly Post Boy, Mercury, Weyman's Gazette* (New York); *Connecticut Gazette* (New Haven); *New London Summary* (Conn.); *Newport Mercury* (R.I.). At that time Newport was on a regular branch of the Post Road.

** In Franklin's absence James Parker essentially ran the American post office alone. William Hunter, still very ill, had gone to England; he died in 1761.

sent and answers received in four Days, which before took a fortnight."

Taken altogether, Franklin's designs essentially drew the modern postal blueprint. They made communication in America strikingly efficient. Finally, come 1761, they even made it profitable. It had taken eight years, but the colonial post office finally earned money for the English government: a modest £494. Over the next three years the American office sent the mother country roughly £2,000 more.

What happened next, no doubt, is pure coincidence: the throne took a renewed interest in the colonial post. War upon war had made England an international power, but its national debt matched those global proportions, surging to nearly £130 million. So in 1764 King George III ordered the colonies to set up ferries, erect offices—whatever it took so "the Posts may meet with no delays or interruptions." The franking privilege, that perk of the postmaster's job, had been abused "to the Detriment of the Publick Revenue," and was banned. Soon the crown decreed that anyone caught embezzling mail funds, or robbing the post "upon the King's Highway . . . shall suffer Death as a Felon." Parliament even revamped Queen Anne's postal laws, cutting rates by thirty percent, because Franklin believed greater usage would follow. His word had become true postal gospel.

But something else whispered "upon the King's Highway" at the same time—something that would build off postal success and earn even larger revenue, but provide the colonies with far less of a service. In the summer of 1764 that something prompted Thomas Whately, England's colonial policy maker, to inquire of one New England leader "how many newspapers are circulated in ye Province." His reason for asking, wrote Whately, was that Parliament was considering a new tax, and he needed to ascertain which documents "ought to be stampt."

By early 1765 the Stamp Act had become inevitable. Franklin traveled to England to try to prevent it, in vain. "The Stamp Act, notwithstanding all the Opposition that could be given it by the American Interest, will pass," he wrote in February. "I think it will affect the Printers more than anybody."

What he failed to see was how the printers, more than anybody, would affect the Stamp Act.

Chapter 4

❧❧❧

Inflammatory Papers and
Tavern Politicians

L ET READERS BE reminded that what the Stamp Act meant by stamps is not what is meant by them today. Tiny profiles of John Winthrop or Peter Stuyvesant were not placed in the upper-right-hand corner of envelopes. Envelopes themselves were a century away; colonial letters were folded and sealed with wax. Nothing whatsoever was licked. Besides, postage fees were still typically paid by recipients. A stamp at that time, rather, referred to a royal imprint emblazoned on certain types of paper. The Stamp Act slapped a surcharge on such paper and required it be used for newspapers, almanacs, legal documents, merchant bills, even playing cards—just about any printer's entire inventory.

What might seem a boost to printer revenue, however, was actually a bane. The cost of publishing a newspaper would rise when it was printed on stamped paper, while the number of subscribers, already reluctant to pay old rates, might fall. A print shop's sundry other goods faced boycott by angry colonists. The problems Franklin predicted for printers would also become postmaster problems, because these men were often one and the same. Stirred together, these factors served a dangerous cocktail to the men controlling communication along the Post Road.

Such was the cultural backdrop facing one of the most important print shops of the Stamp Act era, the one started by Ben Franklin in New Haven. By July of 1765 the town's publisher-postmaster lineage had passed from James Parker to John Holt to Thomas Green to Benjamin Mecom, Franklin's nephew. Mecom revived Connecticut's first newspaper at a crucial moment. It was at his *Connecticut Gazette* print shop located in the New Haven post office—not at the meetinghouse or during sessions of the legislature—that the strongest political jabs of this volatile era were exchanged. The quote Mecom festooned across the front page of his first issue set the tone that would characterize New England in the months to come:

There is a Tide, in the Affairs of Men,
Which, taken at the Flood, leads on to FREEDOM.*

New Haven had evolved a great deal since the departure of its founder, John Davenport. By 1765 it had a customhouse and traded regularly with the West Indies. Its brand-new courthouse was but two years old, and its founding church had split into three, each with a view more progressive than the last. Fifteen hundred people now lived in New Haven proper, and several thousand more filled its fringes; East Haven had expanded so much that it wished to form its own government. After no small fight the town had wrestled Yale College from several suitors, chiefly Saybrook. The matriculating population, weaving through the campus on modern College Street, infused the stodgy town with a youthful, rebellious spirit.

The face of New Haven's discord was that of its royal liaison, Jared Ingersoll. When Connecticut sent Ingersoll overseas to challenge the Stamp Act it had chosen a man torn, like his town, between love for the new country and loyalty to the old. On the one hand, Ingersoll felt the Stamp Tax out of line. As a colonial representative in England, along with Ben Franklin, Ingersoll exhorted George Grenville, the

---

*Mecom apparently adapted this quote from *Julius Caesar* (act 4, scene 3). In Shakespeare's version, Brutus uses the word *fortune* instead of *freedom*.

Stamp Act's architect, against its passage. He even appears responsible for the tax not being higher. "I must tell you then, that I think the Parliament have over-shot their Mark," Ingersoll wrote to Thomas Whately, a Grenville cohort. "'Tis difficult to say how many Ways could be invented to avoid the Payment of a Tax laid upon a Country without the Consent of the Legislature of that Country."

On the other hand, Ingersoll heard Parliament's arguments with an open ear. The crown spent a hefty £300,000 a year just to maintain military presence in northern America in the aftermath of the French and Indian War. People living in Britain paid a stamp tax, and it made the kingdom about that much money each year. The notion of colonial representation in Parliament also had flaws. The Americans would never achieve a majority; besides, it might cost the colonies more to support representatives living abroad than the Stamp Tax itself would cost.

In the summer of 1765 Ingersoll returned to New Haven with mixed feelings—"I don't love to say convinced but, confoundedly begad & beswompt as we say in Connecticut." Regardless of his conflicted sentiments the act had passed, so Ingersoll agreed to serve as Connecticut's stamp distributor—each colony had one—when the new paper went into official use on the first of November.

Late summer neared fall, and the Stamp Act became colonial America's foremost topic of discussion. As the leaves lining Elm Street collected on New Haven's center green, the mounting tensions collected at the post office, and Mecom raked the best of them into the pages of his *Connecticut Gazette*. Columnists emerged, writing under names like Philologus and Philopolites, splitting the town into factions. Colonial speech, so typically coy, grew empowered by pseudonymity.

The loudest voice was that of a Yale professor writing under the name of Cato. Before the close of summer Cato was calling Americans "brethren" and Englishmen "foreigners." He vilified Ingersoll for accepting the paid position of stamp distributor, challenging his allegiance to the land he called home. Ingersoll, under the name Civis, parried each thrust, and the debate raged on for weeks. The tax had passed, wrote Civis, so someone had to collect it. "If every American had bravely refused to become instrumental in enslaving his country," responded

Cato, "it would have given all sensible and Free Britons an exalted Idea of our Patriotism." Civis thought the American idea of patriotism had emerged clear enough: it was leading to "Nothing less than a Trial of Strength with the Mother Country."

Mecom, for his part, aired both viewpoints, admirably printing fewer advertisements than most papers at the time to leave more space for the fiery discourse. Franklin's postal reforms had helped newspapers reach nearly every town in New England, and the debate spread well beyond New Haven. November grew near, and with each passing bundle of mail the pressure against stamp officials rose along the Post Road. One by one the royal agents caved. Andrew Oliver resigned after a thirty-six-hour standoff with the town of Boston. "The News Papers," he wrote to Ingersoll on August 26, "will sufficiently inform you of the Abuse I have met with." The republication of some Cato letters in the *New York Gazette* led to the resignation of the New York stamp man, James McEvers. "I have Been Threaten'd with Mr. Olivers Fate," McEvers told Ingersoll, "if not Worse." By September the contagion had spread to Rhode Island; its stampmaster hopped aboard a ship out of town, fearing for his life.

Ingersoll held out longest. He assured the Connecticut people, through the *Gazette,* that he would not force stamped paper upon anyone, and explained that the position of stamp officer had been thrust upon him. His only wish was "not to be judged unheard, & by no other proofs than the most base & wicked insinuations in Newspapers."

But the newspapers indeed had published Ingersoll's fate. By mid-September a large patriot coalition was plotting to overthrow him. This band, some ten thousand strong, had split into three groups, taken a week's worth of provisions, and assembled along various parts of the Post Road. They stationed guards at key points along the highway. On September 19, so went the plan, they would rendezvous in Branford, eight miles east of New Haven on the Post Road. The following day they would ambush Ingersoll in his hometown.

These patriots went by the name of Sons of Liberty—a name that Ingersoll seems to have unwittingly popularized in America. While in England, Ingersoll had heard a rousing speech by Colonel Isaac Barre denouncing the Stamp Act. Speaking to the British House of Commons, Barre roared that Americans had originally fled English tyranny "to a then uncultivated and unhospitable Country," and that ruling them with too strong a hand will only cause "the Blood of those Sons of Liberty, to recoil within them." Ingersoll relayed the speech home in a letter to the governor of Connecticut, and soon his words reappeared in the *New London Gazette*. Newspapers between New York and Boston quickly picked up the story. Pretty soon the name Sons of Liberty became synonymous with rebellion throughout America.

By September 17, Ingersoll knew he was a hunted man. At a town meeting held that day, residents of New Haven called for him "to resign his Stamp-Office immediately," but he refused. The following day he left New Haven, along with the governor of Connecticut, Thomas Fitch, and rode north toward Hartford along the Post Road. Ingersoll wanted to hear from the colony's officials before deciding on a course of action—though he may simply have sought protection in the state capital. About eighteen miles into the trip, two riders appeared from the wilderness. They wielded long white staves that, to Ingersoll, looked freshly carved.

Ingersoll knew immediately who the men were, and he allowed one to detain him for the night at a nearby inn. He also agreed to meet the Sons of Liberty in Hartford—he wanted to avoid a showdown in New Haven that might damage his property or endanger his family. The rider led the way to Bishop's tavern, a stone inn just off the Post Road, in Meriden. From there letters were dispatched, telling the patriot factions to convene in Hartford. Governor Fitch cautioned one of the Sons to consider the full weight of his actions. The man replied sternly that he "lookt upon this as the Cause of the People, and that they did not intend to take Directions about it from any Body."

The next morning Ingersoll and his escorts set out north on the Post Road for Hartford. A few miles outside Wethersfield they encountered five more riders; half a mile farther they found thirty more; and not much beyond that, Ingersoll faced the paralyzing sight of five hundred riders, each brandishing a freshly carved white staff. The mob guided Ingersoll to Wethersfield's village center. They rode two abreast on modern Broad Street, stopped under an elm tree, and, forming a circle, pushed Ingersoll toward the center. It was here—not in Hartford, where he might get protection from the Connecticut officials—that the Sons of Liberty intended to force Ingersoll's resignation. "What if I won't resign?" he asked. A lone voice answered: "Your fate."

A short while later Ingersoll accepted this fate. He mounted a chair in the center of the circle, removed his hat, and read a statement of resignation prepared by the Sons of Liberty. After he finished he tossed his hat into the air and gave three cheers for "liberty and property." The crowd cheered and shook his hand—a few Sons even led him to a nearby tavern to dine.

Afterward the whole group marched to Hartford, where the capitulation was repeated in front of the General Assembly. And if there remained a single person in the state who had not heard of the proceedings, he or she soon read about them in the *Connecticut Gazette,* which published Ingersoll's detailed account a week later. "We having now got rid of all the Stamp Officers," Ingersoll wrote to a friend in New York, "I suppose we have nothing left for us to do but just to get rid of the Stamp Act itself."

ONE MORNING later that fall John Holt arrived at his office on Broad Street, in downtown Manhattan, to find a sinister note awaiting him. The former postmaster of New Haven now published the *New York Gazette,* and on this particular day he was no doubt quite busy. By Thursday he would have to decide whether to print his weekly paper as usual, though it would mean defying the Stamp Act that had gone into effect since the previous issue. But if after reading the note Holt took a moment to reflect on its contents, or to breathe deeply, or even to set a chair in front of the door to his print shop entrance, no one would have blamed him:

Mr Holt, As you have hitherto prov'd yourself a Friend to Liberty, by publishing such Compositions as had a Tendency to promote the Cause, we are encouraged to hope you will not be deterred from continuing your useful Paper, by groundless Fear of the detestable Stamp Act. However, should you at this critical Time, shut up the Press, and basely desert us, depend upon it, your House, Person and Effects, will be in imminent Danger.

The collapse of stamp officials along the Post Road gave the northeast colonies—which for so long had operated in relative isolation—a heightened sense of solidarity. "It is evident that a secret correspondence has been carried on throughout all the Colonies," New York's Lieutenant Governor, Cadwallader Colden, informed English officials a few days after Ingersoll's confrontation, "and that it has been conserted to deter by violence the Distributors of Stamps from executing their Office."

But the stamp officers themselves were mere agents; their ousting, however liberating, did nothing to halt time's steady march toward November first, when the Stamp Act would officially go into effect. One of the greatest fears among patriots of 1765, as John Holt quickly learned, was that when this day arrived the newspapers would stop publishing—that the Post Road's unifying voice would be silenced while there remained so much to say.

The *New York Gazette,* like many newspapers at this time, filled four pages with advertisements, letters, serial essays, and reprinted articles. The top of the first column usually listed the latest prices of wheat, flour, rum, and other goods, and the estimated times of high and low tide. The rest of the contents appeared rather haphazardly; it was not uncommon for a diatribe on human rights to be juxtaposed to an ad calling for the return of a runaway slave. Overseas news—sometimes snatched from rival publications, sometimes nipped from personal letters—lagged two to four months behind. Font size varied greatly, even among headlines or within single columns. Occasionally a tiny icon would be printed, like the finger that pointed readers to an ad placed by Jacob Abrahams: "As soon as Raisins come to hand, the Publick shall know."

Between spring and fall of 1765 the tone of the *New York Gazette* grew steadily more agitated. In March, big news had been the death of a 1,947-pound ox in Morrisania. But soon after, the latest whispers on the Stamp Act began to appear—and with them emerged the publisher's voice. When Holt printed a list of items that would bear stamps in early April, he added that they "must make the Ears of every American (who conceived himself to be a Freeman, according to the British Constitution) to tingle, and fill him with Astonishment." When he printed a rumor that part of the stamp tax would go toward improving the post roads, in late May, he provided a bracketed warning: "Who can murmur at slavery when it is to answer such valuable and necessary purposes?—till it is grown familiar—!" He published volatile essays by writers assuming names like Publicola, An American, and, simply, Freeman, through the summer.

Every week "inflammatory Papers . . . distributed along the Post Roads by the Post Riders" continued to alarm Governor Colden. Two days after Ingersoll's removal, a special paper called the *Constitutional Courant* hit the streets of New York. The name of its publisher was fabricated, as was its place of publication "at the Sign of *the Bribe refused*"—but the true author was one of Holt's assistants, William Goddard. The words "JOIN or DIE" appeared in the banner above a picture of a snake, chopped into pieces to represent each of the colonies. The cartoon mimicked one printed years earlier in Ben Franklin's *Pennsylvania Gazette*.

The *Courant* was instantly popular and widely reprinted throughout the colonies. After its appearance Colden convened an emergency meeting at Fort George, at the Manhattan end of the Post Road. He wanted to somehow stop the newspapers, but New York's attorney general thought that any legal action would come at the cost of personal safety. "Considering the present temper of the people," Colden concluded, "this is not a proper time to prosecute the Printers and Publishers of the seditious Papers."

If Colden had any power left over New York, the seditious papers soon stripped him of it. In late October the *Gazette* learned that stamped paper had been secretly shipped to Manhattan's harbor from England—"so privately, that not a Passenger in the Ship knew of their being on board." The leak flung New York patriots into action. On October 31, the eve of the Stamp Act's enforcement, the *Gazette* ran an ad in the first column of its first page. It announced a meeting that afternoon, at 4 p.m., at the City Arms, a tavern kept by George Burns on the Post

Road: "Gentlemen who have their Country's Good and their Poster-ity's Interest at Heart, are desired to attend."

The notice was nothing short of a blatant call for rebellion. While Cadwallader Colden was taking the Stamp Act oath in Fort George, two hundred New York patriots gathered three-tenths of a mile up the road to determine the city's true course of action. The group, mostly merchants, met in the long room of Burns's tavern, on the west side of Broadway between modern Thames and Cedar streets. They decided to boycott English goods until the Stamp Act was repealed and appointed five men to scatter along the Post Road and share this decision with the rest of the colonies. By the end of November the *Boston Gazette* called for its patriot population to follow suit.

When the meeting ended, the participants marched down the Post Road to Fort George, lingered ominously for a moment, and dispersed. The following day the fort received a notice: Either Colden would swear, under oath, never to enforce the Stamp Act, or "we can certainly assure you of your fate." Had the meeting at City Arms accomplished little else, it would have held some historic significance. What came next, however, was a major escalation of American insurrection. The confrontation that had merely threatened Jared Ingersoll turned violent.

That night, around seven, several hundred people gathered at the Common—the name for the fields adjoining modern Park Row, where the Post Road branched toward the Bowery. There, hanging from a movable gallows, head in a noose, was a likeness of Colden. The gover-nor was holding a piece of stamped paper as the devil whispered into his ear. Six hundred candles, clutched by the mob, cast the effigy in a haunt-ing glow, and soon the swarm marched down the Post Road toward the fort. When they were not allowed inside, the mob stormed the coach house and removed Colden's carriage. They transferred the effigy from the gallows to the coach and wheeled it through the streets. At Bowling Green they tore down the palisades and used them to build a fire that "reduced the Coach, Gallows, Man, Devil, and all to ashes." The next day a terrified Colden decided to do nothing with the stamped paper until Henry Moore, the new governor being sent from England to han-dle the crisis, arrived.

Once again the newspapers had delivered the fate of a colonial leader—this time no mere stamp officer but a royal governor. The next issue of the *New York Gazette* included an account of the attack. It was Holt's first paper since November 1. He had decided, after all, to publish despite the Stamp Act. But the man John Adams later called "the liberty printer" did alter one part of his newspaper in response to the royal law. Its banner now read: "*LIBERTY* and *PROPERTY,* and NO *STAMPS*."

BY SPRING OF 1766 Parliament repealed the Stamp Act. The very printers and newspapers that would have been taxed hardest had hastened its premature end. The Post Road's lines of communication had united the colonies with unpredictable strength, and a common identity had emerged across northeast America.

Nowhere was this cultural transformation more apparent than in Providence, which celebrated the act's repeal by firing one hundred eight skyrockets and downing thirty-two "patriotic" toasts. The place that, a few years earlier, thought a dancing school might cause the same degree of debauchery as a brothel, now threw a grand ball with "the most brilliant appearance of ladies this town ever saw."

Providence had been Rhode Island's first colonial settlement, but by the middle of the eighteenth century it trailed Newport as its most important. By 1761 Providence's streets were "almost impracticable to pass" and its courthouse, destroyed in a fire, had not yet been rebuilt. Most of the town's inhabitants, which numbered a few thousand, were tucked into two main squares near the Providence River. Newport published the colony's only newspaper. As a result, Providence remained largely isolated from the rest of New England until a young journeyman printer set up shop along the Post Road, on modern North Main Street, in 1762.

William Goddard had been born to the post office and reared in the print shop. His father, Giles, had served as postmaster of New London; when Ben Franklin toured the post roads in 1753, Giles's office was the first that Franklin encountered east of New York. Two years later this connection no doubt helped William land a job in Franklin's newly established New Haven print shop. There, as a fifteen-year-old apprentice to James Parker, Goddard traveled the Post Road to Middletown, Hartford, and New London, estimating the cost of delivering the news to these towns. Goddard also spent a few years working for Parker in New York. By the end of his apprenticeship, William Goddard had worked in one of America's most important print shops, and its absolute busiest post office. For his next act Goddard chose to fill one of the Post Road's biggest news holes.

Goddard's shop accelerated his new town's development as a mercantile titan. He printed almanacs that, for the first time, calculated the tides specifically for Providence—a great complement to the booming shipping industry controlled by the Brown brothers. His *Providence Gazette* offered a brand-new tool of trade: advertisements. Shipowners notified merchandisers of sloops with room for freight; landowners made farmers aware of new lots; tavernkeeper James Sabin called for outstanding tabs. A February 1763 issue announced the need for a local brazier and clockmaker, and by fall one of each had relocated all the way from Boston to fill the commercial voids. Within three years of his arrival Goddard's success had spawned an entire new industry: paper milling.

As was the wont of colonial printers, Goddard also became the town's postmaster. He published the post rider's schedule and listed each tavern along the Post Road—from George Burns's in New York to Richard Olney's in Providence, and on to Boston. By summer of 1767 the rate of travel demanded a stagecoach service that left Olney's tavern—also on North Main Street, beside the newly rebuilt courthouse—each Tuesday morning and returned from Boston each Thursday. Goddard's almanacs, owned by every household in town, benefited travel as much as they did commerce. His print shop became Providence's post office and center of communication.

From the start one of Goddard's greatest supporters was statesman Stephen Hopkins. A skilled writer who appealed to farmers as well as merchants, Hopkins used the *Gazette* to interrupt Newport's political hegemony. He stimulated pride in Providence from the very first issue, penning a multipart history of Rhode Island. Powerful Newport politician Henry Ward eventually swore off Goddard's paper because, said

Ward, the publisher slandered him in its pages "with the same Safety and Impunity that a Dog bays the Moon." From the *Gazette*'s launch until his retirement in 1768, Hopkins took three of five gubernatorial elections. Two years later—aided by Hopkins, the Brown brothers, and the *Gazette*—Providence raised more money than Newport to house the state college. Soon students were walking along North Main Street to what is now Brown University.

Through Goddard, Providence's political interest extended well beyond Narragansett affairs. While the Newport newspaper defended the Stamp Act, Goddard's *Gazette* railed against it. He released a special issue condemning the tax in colorful terms: "The American Horses are of too mettlesome a Breed to stand still under the Operation of Branding, and what whoever should attempt to apply a hot S to their Buttocks, would be in no small Danger from their hind Legs." When finances caused the *Gazette* to fold briefly, in 1765, Goddard joined John Holt in New York and secretly printed the volatile *Constitutional Courant*.

Goddard also printed a pamphlet, written by Hopkins, blasting the Stamp Act as unconstitutional. "The Rights of Colonies Examined," published in 1764, became widely read in America and England; unlike so many anonymous newspaper letters, it had been written—and written well—by a governor unafraid to publish under his true name. In it Hopkins also referred to the post office as a tax—a notion that had received little attention since Alexander Spotswood first mentioned it nearly fifty years earlier, but that would soon play a vital role, under Goddard's guidance, in the opening acts of revolution.

By 1770 William Goddard had moved south, but he left his print shop in the capable hands of his mother, while leaving Providence in a state of economic maturity and political awareness unmatched since the time of Roger Williams. England, meanwhile, still reeling from the aborted Stamp Act, was trying to reinstate its superiority however possible. In Rhode Island this effort took the form of stricter shipping customs. Many of the state's most popular goods—including molasses, staple of the thriving rum industry—were subject to duties that padded British pockets. For years such tariffs had been ignored, but in early 1772 Rhode Island was patrolled by an abrasive officer named William

Dudingston, who took his position further than those before him, and one day too far altogether.

On a routine customs check, Dudingston and his eight-gun ship, the HMS *Gaspee,* seized twelve hogsheads of rum. Local merchants roared, convinced Dudingston was abusing his power. Joseph Wanton, governor of Rhode Island, challenged Dudingston's authority, but the captain had already sent the confiscated rum to Boston. Hollering alone would not bring it back.

After dark on June 9, 1772, dozens of Providence merchants slipped down the Post Road to the corner of modern South Main and Planet streets and gathered in the tavern run by James Sabin. A ship captain had informed John Brown that the *Gaspee* had run aground on a sand-bar six miles south of Providence and was unable to free herself. Brown arranged for a number of boats to dock at Fenner's Wharf, across from Sabin's tavern. Their oarlocks, he ordered, should be muffled.

Toward midnight the group boarded John Brown's boats and slid silently south through the darkness. They were armed with everything from muskets to handspikes. Among the hundred or so, besides Brown, were Abraham Whipple, a West Indies trader and celebrated veteran; Joseph Bucklin, Providence restaurateur; John B. Hopkins, nephew of Stephen; John Mawney, a doctor; and young Ephraim Bowen, who had borrowed his father's gun for the occasion. As they approached the *Gaspee,* Dudingston hailed from the starboard gunwale, "Who comes there?" Whipple replied that he was the sheriff and had a warrant for the captain's arrest: "So surrender, God damn you." Bucklin turned to Bowen and whispered for the boy's gun, then fired toward the ship. If the *Gaspee* incident was truly, as it has been called, the Revolution's "first blow for freedom," then Bucklin made this first shot count—hitting Dudingston squarely in the groin.

The Providence merchants, urging one another not to use real names, boarded the ship, bound its crew, and took them ashore. The nameless men then prepared to set fire to the ship. Mawney attended Dudingston's wounds. He fashioned linen compresses and bandages, stanched the bleeding, and likely saved the lieutenant's life. Some of the raiders shuffled through Dudingston's papers and demanded compensation for the rum he had stolen. Eventually they moved the captain to a wharf in Pawtuxet Village. As morning neared, some of the men sat on a hill and watched the *Gaspee*'s flames welcome the dawn.

The precise medley of this mayhem differs based on the person giving the account. The final tally, though, remains the same: Providence had drawn English blood and come within an inch of killing a royal officer. The stakes had risen significantly.

If members of Parliament had remained skeptical of colonial unification after the Stamp Act, what happened next must have convinced them. Instead of bringing the offenders to justice, American leaders took offense that Britain wanted to try them in England. When England responded by convening a council of investigation in Rhode Island, this move too met with American discontent. Samuel Adams advised the participants, and Governor Wanton, to avoid any action that could validate the investigation, which he considered illegal. So one by one the excuses poured forth. James Sabin could not attend court because, as an insolvent debtor, he would be arrested. Instead he sent a letter with an alibi, saying he had been "attending company" during the evening in question. When the four men who made up this "company" were called to corroborate Sabin's statement, they too found reasons to evade the investigation. John Andrews couldn't make it to court because he suffered a mysterious "swelling in my hand, which hath rendered me unable to stir out of door." George Brown and a Mr. Hitchcock had other places to be. John Cole did not bother to make up an excuse at all.

Governor Wanton, though, was responsible for perhaps the most flagrant insubordination. He had received a personal letter about the *Gaspee* affair from high English authorities, and somehow its contents had spilled into the columns of a Boston newspaper, the *Massachusetts Spy*. In the letter, published clearly for all the Post Road to see, Britain's leaders characterized the incident as one of "high treason" and, beyond that, as "levying war against the King."

OF ALL THE PRINTERS and newspapers that united the colonies in rebellion, none had a greater impact than Benjamin Edes and his *Bos-*

ton Gazette, published from a shop a few steps from the Town House that marked the Boston end of the Post Road. The destruction caused to three hundred forty-two chests of British tea began here as a few bursts of craftsmanship emboldened by a bit of punch. It was in this office that the Revolution reached the summit of its progression—from threatening to violent to bloody to, one rainy winter day, inevitable.

Edes and his partner, John Gill, took command of the *Boston Gazette* in early April of 1755, and soon, in the words of deposed stamp officer Andrew Oliver, the country's second newspaper formed "the temper of the people." America's leading patriots spoke through its columns. John Adams, James Otis, Thomas Cushing, Joseph Warren, William Cooper, and Benjamin Church took turns "preparing for the next day's newspaper . . . cooking up paragraphs, articles, occurrences, etc, working the political engine." Paul Revere supplied many of the *Gazette*'s engravings.

Through it all Edes ensured that his incendiary writers fired with impunity. He and Gill published essays by Determinatus, Candidus, A Bostonian, A Chatterer, An Impartialist, A Layman, and Alfred—the many pseudonyms of Samuel Adams. When John Mein, a fellow publisher, tried to bully his competitor into revealing the identity of one particular writer, Edes told Mein he "never divul'g authors." (Poor John Gill bore the brunt of Mein's frustration the following day: two clubbings to the back of the head.)

In August of 1765, at the height of Stamp Act outrage, the *Gazette* published a four-part series by John Adams, later called "The True Sentiment of America," in which he implored the newspaper to "be not intimidated, therefore, by any terrors, from publishing with the utmost freedom . . . nor suffer yourself to be wheedled out of your liberty by any pretences of politeness, delicacy, or decency. These, as they are often used, are but three different names for hypocrisy, chicanery, and cowardice." Later that year a group dubbed the Loyal Nine congregated at Edes's shop one midnight and printed one hundred placards demanding that Boston stamp officer Andrew Oliver make a public capitulation. Oliver had agreed to resign in August, but had never done so officially. The rest of the Nine—merchants John Avery and Henry Bass, braziers John Smith and Stephen Cleverly, painter Thomas Crafts, distiller Thomas Chase, shipmaster Joseph Field, jeweler George Trott—dispersed the notices throughout town, and Oliver indeed gave up the office, this time for good.

Many of the *Gazette*'s articles took form over punch, wine, tobacco, biscuits, and cheese at the "apartment"—a Post Road tavern, kept by Chase, at modern Washington and Essex streets. When the *Gazette* scooped England's plan to send troops to Boston, Francis Bernard, royal governor of Massachusetts, complained that no government could operate if its confidential meetings were "canvassed by tavern politicians, and censured by news-paper libellers." At the height of its influence the *Gazette* published the Stamp Act before Bernard received an official copy, and, ironically, notified the governor that he was required to take a royal oath in support of it. By 1770 Thomas Hutchinson, Bernard's replacement, estimated that seven-eighths of Bostonians read the *Gazette,* and the *Gazette* alone. Edes and Gill even appeared on a list of primary American rebels, as "those trumpeters of sedition."

On November 29, 1773, this patriot brass mustered enough wind for an announcement in the *Gazette*:

> Friends! Brethren! Countrymen! That worst of Plagues, the detested TEA . . . is now arrived in this Harbour; the Hour of Destruction or manly Opposition to the Machinations of Tyranny stares you in the Face; every Friend to his Country, to himself and Posterity, is now called upon to meet at FANEUIL-HALL, at NINE o'Clock THIS DAY, (at which Time the Bells will ring,) to make a united and successful Resistance to this last, worst and most destructive Measure of Administration.

Five thousand people from miles around convened at Faneuil Hall—far more than it could hold. So the illegal gathering percolated down the Post Road to the corner of Milk and Washington streets, site of the Old South Meeting House.* The participants demanded that

---

*This same plot of land had been site of Governor John Winthrop's second Boston home.

Francis Rotch, owner of the tea-bearing ship *Dartmouth,* and James Hall, its captain, return the tea to England unopened as a sign of protest against the tax imposed on this popular good in May of 1773. Until Rotch and Hall complied the gatherers resolved to guard the ship; if the tea were secretly unloaded and dispersed to merchants, any hope of a political statement would be dashed. Volunteers for this round-the-clock armed watch were told to leave their names at the *Boston Gazette*'s office.

During the next nineteen days, Paul Revere, John Hancock, John Winthrop—great-great-grandson of the first Bay governor—Edes himself, and dozens more signed up to guard the harbor. By December 17 Rotch would have to unload his tea or have it seized by customs officials. The morning before this deadline Edes dispersed another notice requesting an assembly at the Old South Meeting House. At the stroke of ten, nearly seven thousand people, many from as far away as twenty miles, trudged through cold rain down the Post Road. That Samuel Phillips Savage was made moderator of the proceedings—he lived in the Post Road town of Weston, some fifteen miles west—reflected the extent to which the countryside was steeped in excitement.

The meeting lasted all day. Rotch had gone one final time to beg Governor Hutchinson for permission to discharge the *Dartmouth,* tea intact, back toward England. As the 5 p.m. deadline passed, the Old South filled with tension. Some wanted to disband immediately, but the group was determined to sit tight an hour more.

Conspicuously absent from this decision was Benjamin Edes. He and a number of friends had gathered in his parlor, a few steps from the print shop, where for some time they dipped into the publisher's punch bowl and watched young Peter Edes refill it. At some point during this other, much smaller Boston gathering, Edes no doubt consulted a roster of names he had secured in a desk drawer. Toward dark Edes and

---

When John Davenport moved from New Haven to Boston and was made minister of the First Church, his appointment upset some church members so much that they broke off to form the Old South Church, upon the elder Winthrop's former lot. An impressive Meeting House replaced the church building in 1730.

his guests shuffled—stumbled, maybe—down the street to the *Gazette*'s office. After a change of clothes, they finally made their way down the Post Road toward the Meeting House around a quarter to six. A candlelit glow hovered inside the halls of Old South as Edes and his cohorts, now dressed like Indians, converged on the Meeting House through the damp dusk. They reached it about the same time Rotch delivered the bad news that his ship would not be allowed to quit the harbor.

That's when all hell—or, in the colonial parlance of one witness, "the inhabitants of the infernal regions"—broke loose. "Who knows how tea will mingle with salt water?" cried one. "A mob! A mob!" cried another. After Sam Adams uttered his famous understatement—"This meeting can do nothing more to save the country"—the crowd joined the costumed mob on the streets and descended toward the docks.

Henry Bass was there, as was Thomas Chase. Robert Davis the importer and William Hendley the mason had come from their homes on the Post Road. Samuel Sprague had left his two-story house on the Post Road and climbed a chimney to blacken his face with soot. And Thomas Melville, who got some tea leaves caught in his shoe, and Josiah Wheeler, who did the same, and whose wife swept them into the fire when they fell from his boots after he returned to his home on the Post Road. And surely countless others, among these supposed Tea Partiers, their identities protected from punishment inside a desk drawer locked by Benjamin Edes, never to be divulged.

On which list, most likely, was also the name Paul Revere, who by the following day had cleaned himself off enough to ride a brief account of the evening along the Post Road to New York. The express message was signed by Samuel Adams, using his true name. He thought, continuing in understatement from the night before, that Manhattan's Sons of Liberty might like to hear about the "interesting event."

ON THE DAY of the Boston Tea Party, William Goddard's own mind bobbed with the flotsam of rebellion. He had concocted a scheme whose success, as he saw it, meant nothing less than the country's freedom. But in spite of the idea's importance—or because of it—Goddard sketched his thoughts only briefly in a note to John Lamb, one of New York's leading Sons of Liberty. The remaining details he shared with the post rider, who was to explain to Lamb the "Plan I am forming to give you a firm Opposition to a certain unconstitutional Act of Parliament now operating in the Colonies."

Public opinion of the post office, like imported English wine, had soured steadily for almost a decade by the beginning of 1774, at which time it turned to vinegar. The Stamp Act had sharpened colonial views on taxation, and the post office, though it benefited the American people, carried parliamentary spoils with each letter. The end of the franking privilege had made it difficult to find competent postmasters, or even warm bodies to fill the role. In New York, the Sons of Liberty hijacked the mail before it reached the postmaster, and no one dared confront them.

Post riders began to look out for themselves. They accepted private errands and jammed their pouches with items that earned no postage and delayed the true mail. Some, in a poor show of appearances, simply taped a legitimate letter to these rogue goods, invariably damaging it. Others, while on duty, also drove herds of oxen. "I find that it is the constant practice of all the riders between New York and Boston to defraud the Revenue as much as they can," a royal Post Road surveyor reported in late 1773. Whereas England had seen the post office as a tax for years, Americans were just beginning to do the same—and to react accordingly.

Parliament, meanwhile, had turned on the man who had made the American post worth fretting over in the first place. Ben Franklin's predictions had been correct: lower postage rates had indeed increased revenue. Despite all the sabotage on its highways, the colonial post office made England £3,000 a year by 1774. That January, while Franklin was in England, word of the Boston Tea Party reached the homeland. British leaders, directing their anger toward the nearest patriot, dismissed Franklin as postmaster not two weeks later. Any royal agent considered "too much of an American" would be replaced with someone willing to put British postal interests ahead of colonial rights. "How safe the correspondence of your Assembly committees along the continent will be through the hands of such officers," Franklin wrote to Thomas Cushing, "may now be worth consideration."

The safety of patriot correspondence was truly a prime concern. As far back as the Stamp Act, groups composed of Sons of Liberty, newspapermen, and various public figures had formed what became known as committees of correspondence. New York's committee dated back to the 1765 meeting at George Burns's tavern. Virginia, feeling the need to commiserate with New England after the *Gaspee* incident, formed a correspondence committee that included Patrick Henry and Thomas Jefferson. By 1774 Boston had compelled nearly every town in Massachusetts to assemble these "dangerous" and "illegal" groups, as Governor Hutchinson called them. The idea, in the words of Marlborough's leadership, was that "each Town, assisting and writing like a band of Brothers, may banish Tyranny from our Land."

Operating under vows of secrecy, these committees updated one another on popular sentiments from their particular locales. But the unprecedented number of urgent and covert letters pouring along the post roads were handled by postmasters who, if not unequivocally anti-American, were at least beholden to the throne for a salary. Political notes arrived with broken seals—a violation that, with proper permission, was within the postmaster's rights. "Our secrets are in the hand of Government and at its pleasure," New York's committee wrote to Boston's, "our News Papers in a time of public danger may be stopped."

These were the factors rumbling through the brain of William Goddard on December 16, 1773, and across the lips of the post rider he sent to meet John Lamb. Goddard's idea, quite simply, was to replace Parliament's postal structure with American parts. The system would remain the same, but towns would pledge to hire only loyal, "constitutional" post riders and postmasters. In addition, offices would share the revenue; unlike within the British system, the money spent by Americans on the post would go toward aiding the American post.

Of course the plan's success required the participation of every colony. So, in February of 1774, driven by a single-mindedness that would have made Francis Lovelace proud, Goddard set out on a tour of the Post Road to discuss the plan further. Goddard quickly won New York's approval with the support of Lamb and his old colleague, John Holt. They agreed, however, to endorse the idea only on the condition that Boston did too.

Goddard left Manhattan with a letter of introduction written by New York's committee, and hurried along the coastal Post Road. In Connecticut he stopped briefly in New Haven and New London, but spent longer in Rhode Island. There he collected another letter from the committee in Providence. Even Newport, the town that formerly held him in contempt, thought the plan important enough to back.

Boston was fairly blown away. Goddard arrived in mid-March, and within days was invited to lay out his entire scheme before the committee of correspondence. The post office's role as a public service, they reasoned, had blinded them to its true function as a tax—they might just as soon print political essays on stamped paper or toast liberty with excised tea as send their rebellious correspondence through the British mail. "The necessity of substituting another office in its Stead must be obvious," Samuel Adams and company concluded. "We wish success to the Design."

Soon Boston newspapers ran pieces favoring the idea; one called the British post office "the foundation of and precedent for" the Stamp Act, the tea duty—and every other tax ever levied on America. Adams prepared subscription cards with the heading "The PLAN for establishing a New American POST-OFFICE." No sooner had Boston subscribed than some convinced merchant donated £50 to the service. Paul Revere granted Goddard's idea the second-highest superlative available at the time: "I think it is one of the greatest strokes that our Enemies have mett with," he wrote, "(except the late affairs of the Tea)."

As the plan neared universal consent in New England, Goddard told Lamb he wanted New York—and, more specifically, Holt's print shop—to be the central office. But Goddard's mission did not end exactly as he would have liked. He traveled south to lobby for his system through the summer of 1774, but when the first Continental Congress met in the fall, it held off adopting the plan officially. Goddard's pushiness may have offended some; or, as a group of Philadelphia merchants put it, "America had enough upon her hands without meddling with the affairs of a Post Office."

At the second Continental Congress, the following year, Goddard's crusade finally intersected with Benjamin Franklin. There, the gatherers indeed ratified the constitutional post and, unanimously, named Franklin the first American postmaster general. Franklin donated his $1,000 salary to soldiers wounded in battle, but his generosity did not extend to Goddard. Franklin's precise vendetta* is unclear, but when it came time to appoint a deputy, he chose his son-in-law, Richard Bache, and relegated Goddard to surveyor, third-in-command. Goddard never recovered from the blow; three decades later he still recalled Franklin's "sinister plan" with the rage of the scorned.

On an April day shortly before this heartbreaking decision, however, Goddard's plan executed its main objective to perfection. The morning after Paul Revere rode into history, another set of constitutional messengers made their way along the Post Road with word that fighting had erupted in Lexington, Massachusetts. The first rider left Watertown on April 19, 1775, "near 10 of the Clock." He dashed toward Worcester so quickly that, when he got there around noon, his white horse promptly fell dead. Within days towns all along the Post Road in Connecticut and Massachusetts learned about the fighting. At Fairfield the first rider encountered a second one, who had traveled the southern branch, "by way of Providence," to inform everyone that "the Action Continued." They stayed, these constitutional riders, just long enough for committees of correspondence to copy down the alert, then clamored off into the wilderness.

By April 23 the details had reached New York. The stone mile mark-

---

*A number of reasons may have contributed to Franklin's decision. He might have felt just as much ownership of the idea; while overseas he suggested a nearly identical "Method to Starve the Post Office which hath always been given as a president [*sic*] for taxing the Colonies." He might also have felt disrespected that Goddard's rampage began while Franklin technically remained head of Britain's colonial post. What's more, Goddard had rankled Franklin by publishing malicious items about his friends.

ers of Franklin's conception, first placed on Manhattan in 1769, now escorted the rider along the Post Road, guiding him over McGown's Pass inside present-day Central Park, guiding him beyond the Bull's Head tavern in the Bowery, guiding him into the heart of the city. When John Lamb heard the news he and a few other patriots erupted in riot. They flew flags and beat drums. They busted into a government arsenal, stole a thousand weapons, and distributed them in the streets. They seized the mail and furiously opened letters to learn whatever else they could. "They received the news with avidity," noted a royal official. "They had wished for it for a long time."

The war had begun. The post had arrived.

Chapter 5

The General and the Blacksmith

O N A B R E E Z Y fall morning in 1783 the road that had brought
New York the news of war now brought George Washington
to its conclusion. A ceremonial guard led by General Henry
Knox—the corps of dragoons, the artillery, the light infantry—advanced
Washington. The British in their scarlet brilliance, looking far more
polished than the tattered victors, advanced Knox. George Clinton, the
governor of New York, rode beside Washington at the anchor. There
was no need to hurry: Clinton had just shaken a lengthy illness, and,
northwest winds aside, November 25 had dawned clear and pleasant.
Anyway, this was the type of ride to savor. It was the day the defeated
would evacuate Manhattan, and with each step of his gray horse Washington reclaimed the Post Road as American soil. Of all the routes he
traveled during the Revolution, none could grant the general a greater
sense of vindication.

They left Day's tavern and turned sharply south toward the stone
marking eight miles to City Hall. On a modern map they closely followed St. Nicholas Avenue as it approaches the northeast corner of
Central Park from One Hundred Twenty-fourth Street. Soon the party
reached a bridge over two tributaries that converged at the foot of a hill.
At their left an inlet of the Harlem River ripped along present-day One

Hundred Seventh Street. To any birds gazing down from the gusty sky that day, the Post Road and the inlet would have resembled an arm, bent just slightly at the elbow, reaching toward the river.

Across the bridge the Post Road climbed the hill to avoid the inlet and the swamp marsh south of it, and squeezed between two large rocks. At the crest of this pass, tracked today by Central Park's East Drive, the pair of leaders trotted past a stone tavern run by Mrs. McGown. Easing downhill they came upon the Seven Mile stone just west of Fifth Avenue, near modern Ninety-eighth Street. Near present-day Ninety-fifth they met the crossroad that stretched west across the island to Bloomingdale Road—the early sketch, more or less, of modern Broadway.

From here Washington's course was mapped by memories best forgotten. Near Third Avenue and Sixty-sixth Street, just south of the Five Mile stone, he reached the former site of Dove tavern, also used as a British artillery camp, where a young American spy named Nathan Hale had been executed. At the fourth stone, about modern Third Avenue and Forty-fifth Street, he came upon the small path that slipped off the Post Road toward Turtle Bay. Soon the road ascended Inclenberg, a hill known today by the surname of its wealthy landowner, the Quaker Robert Murray, whose handsome house sat atop the flat peak.

It was right about here that the British had charged into Manhattan seven years earlier—the last time New York had been an American city. Here too where, on that frustrating fall day, Washington had momentarily abandoned hope of winning the war.

GEORGE WASHINGTON HAD known the British would attack Manhattan on Sunday, September 15, 1776, but not precisely where. The night before, Washington had moved his headquarters to a mansion in Harlem Heights owned by Roger Morris. The Georgian-style wonder had no equal on the island. English brick lined the exterior. A vast portico greeted all entrants. Inside, standing out from the nineteen rooms, was an octagonal drawing parlor with a high ceiling and a marble chimney. A location at One Hundred Sixty-first Street and St. Nicholas Avenue, just east of the Post Road, made the new base highly accessible to Ebenezer Hazard, postmaster of New York, who kept an office on the premises.

Though advantageous from a military perspective, the stately grounds might have caused Washington some personal discomfort. By this time Morris, a loyalist, had fled to England, and his wife and family to Yonkers. But Washington had pursued Mrs. Morris in the summer of 1757 when she was still long-necked, large-eyed Mary Philipse. To him, back then, she had been Polly. That July a mutual friend informed Washington of a rival suitor. "You know him," wrote Joseph Chew of Roger Morris, "he is a lady's man." Chew promised to let Polly know "the sincere Regard ~~you h~~ a Friend of mine has for her," but the effort was in vain. The following January Morris and Polly wed.

Lost love aside, Washington had enough on his mind on September 15, 1776, with the British threat. Around nine he took the Post Road south toward Harlem, the likely site of attack. From a landing point near the mouth of the Harlem River, perhaps at Morrisania, the British could swing up to King's Bridge, where the Post Road departed Manhattan island across Spuyten Duyvil creek. By holding this bridge the enemy could cut off any egress to the mainland. The morning sun beat hot upon the plains. Washington feared the Americans could not save New York, but his permission to leave Manhattan had been granted by Congress only days earlier.

At that time, "New York" referred not to the island as a whole but to its southernmost tip. Most of Manhattan's population was packed within a mile or two of this point. Here too, at the Post Road's terminal, were stationed several thousand troops commanded by General Israel Putnam at Fort George. Washington wanted these men—a significant contingent of the American forces—to retreat eleven miles up Manhattan to Fort Washington, a far more secure position near One Hundred Eighty-third Street, and a far more feasible position for a mainland retreat. The move had been delayed, but Putnam's men merely needed, in the estimation of General Nathaniel Greene, one more day.

Meanwhile Washington had lined Manhattan's eastern shore to keep the British from securing the "Main Road," or so he called the Post

Road. In 1776 the Main Road remained the only avenue to span the entire island north to south. Bloomingdale Road, the west side's major highway, grounded to a halt in Harlem Heights. Two major crossroads connected these primary routes at approximately modern Forty-second and Ninety-fifth streets. If British commander William Howe captured the Main Road and stretched his men west along one of the crossways, preventing Putnam's troops from reaching Fort Washington, the war might end.

The brigade protecting the Main Road, however, was rather unworthy of its awesome task. Seasoned troops had been placed in Harlem at the anticipated spot of attack. The lines farther downtown consisted of young men from Connecticut with little combat experience. Their provisions were severely strained; one soldier was so thirsty that, according to witnesses, he stopped at a brook and literally refreshed himself to death. Another soldier recalled bread as hard as musket flint; some inside the shallow trenches—bereft of heavy artillery and guarded by meager breastwork—might have considered whether to put it in their mouths or pelt it at the enemy. Several hundred sick rested behind the front. Morale was so low that many men, figuring the British would loot the town soon after seizing it, raided homes themselves.

Before dawn on September 15 five British warships settled into Kip's Bay, which in Manhattan's slimmer youth nuzzled near modern Second Avenue at Thirty-fourth Street. The ships lined up neatly, their broadsides facing the shore, stretching north from Kip's Bay to Turtle Bay. Come daybreak they rolled one hundred sixty-four cannons into position. A wind whipped toward them from the southwest. A gambling man, assessing which was more likely to beat back the pending assault, might have laid equal odds to the Main Road's defenses and the southwest wind.

Into this tableau, around eleven in the morning, crept the first of several dozen barges filled with British infantry and Hessian grenadiers. Washington, it seems, guessed well about the likely point of attack, but Howe had changed course at the last moment, and the landing would instead take place at Kip's Bay, a few miles south of Harlem. To cover the troop landing, the five warships sprayed the flimsy Main Road guard with cannon fire and grapeshot. Smoke billowed, shots thundered, dirt rained, Hessians hymned. These senses filled the air breathed by hungry, tired, newly enlisted, inadequately armed young men—and sent to each brain the simplest of commands: Run.

The scamper was contagious. Soon American troops, infected with fear, scattered toward the Main Road a third of a mile west. A few soldiers ducked into a house, downed a few shots of rum, and dashed north toward Harlem. Guns, knapsacks, coats, hats—anything that could be jettisoned for speed—cluttered Manhattan's escape route. Before long the American commanding officer, and anyone else remaining on that side, had retreated.

The British proceeded more deliberately. Their plan after climbing the rocky shore was to fork three ways. The Hessians, bayonets out, would charge south toward the fort. Charles Cornwallis and his men would secure Murray's hill, "an advantageous piece of ground about 3½ miles on the great Road from New York to Kingsbridge." The light infantry would gather a bit north in the fields near Forty-second Street. The attack would unfold slowly: landing four thousand troops, even without the slightest hindrance to progress, takes time. British flatboats dropped off men, returned through the smoke, and scooped up more. Howe and a few other generals spent the intermission eating cakes and drinking Madeira wine, courtesy of Mrs. Murray.

Washington, meanwhile, had bolted south as soon as he heard the first cannon roar. Along with Brigadier General Thomas Mifflin and some aides, he had reached Inclenberg and was near modern Lexington Avenue and Forty-second Street when he encountered the fleeing American troops. The sight left the general shocked and embarrassed. He tried to call them to order, but they swept around him and continued north, as streaming water slides around a rock.

Beating downriver, then, Washington met Putnam, who had hurried uptown upon hearing the blasts, in the crossroad to Bloomingdale, near present-day Fortieth Street and Park Avenue. Washington demanded composure. He screamed for an end to this "scandalous conduct," and even threatened his own troops with a sword. Suddenly a few dozen British appeared and chaos reigned anew.

Washington, in a mad fury, slammed his hat to the turf and won-dered aloud if the war could be won with such men. Dismayed, and likely tired from both ride and tirade, the general slipped into a coma of abjection. Though the enemy was nearly within reach of gunfire, he sat still in his saddle, unarmed, making no move to withdraw. Nathaniel Greene later described Washington, at this moment, as having "sought death rather than life." Finally an attendant grabbed the general's reins and led his horse away.

Toward midafternoon the sky burst into heavy rain. By evening the Union Jack waved above southern Manhattan.

BRIGHT AND EARLY the next morning Washington detailed the previ-ous day's events in a letter to John Hancock, president of the Conti-nental Congress. Safely back at headquarters, he described the scene in terms that, if outwardly tempered, bubbled with innuendo. The British now controlled most of the island and had spent the night within strik-ing distance of Harlem Heights. "I should hope the enemy would meet with a defeat in case of an attack, if the generality of our troops would behave with tolerable bravery," Washington wrote. "But experience, to my extreme affliction, has convinced me that this is rather to be wished for than expected." His mind so thoroughly distracted by the looming danger, the lingering disdain, or otherwise, Washington forgot to sign the note.

Despite the general's bleak summary, the greatest loss of Septem-ber 15 was one of British opportunity. After his momentary breakdown Washington had established a blockade, directed by Colonel William Smallwood, just south of McGown's Pass. Given its narrow course, the pass was the most strategic spot along the Main Road for a small front to beat back a direct approach into Harlem. At the same time General Put-nam had charged back downtown after meeting Washington and rallied the troops for an immediate retreat. With the Main Road captured the troops raced up the west side of the island and reached the Heights just before the British, deflected by Smallwood's brigade, appeared at the western end of the crossroad near Ninety-fifth Street.

The call could not have been closer. Piles of valuable artillery and provisions had been left downtown in haste. Casualties and prisoners numbered in the several hundreds, in the reports of Howe, or merely the several, in those of Washington. Either way, defined by what it might have been—colossal defeat—the effort had sprung hope into mind.

The following day, September 16, the British indeed attacked Harlem Heights, from a point just southwest of Day's tavern. Washington's men fought with renewed confidence, however, and though on the great scoreboard of war it went down as a loss—the Americans would surrender Fort Washington by mid-November—the battle preserved, and even fattened, long-term morale. "I consider our Success in this small affair, at this Time, almost equal to Victory," wrote George Clinton two days later. "It has animated our Troops, gave them new Spirits, and erased every bad Impression." They now think of nothing, he said, but winning.

And so, seven years later, Washington paraded down the one road that, for an instant, would have seemed the least likely course to guide a victory parade.

Past Inclenberg and the Three Mile stone, inward toward modern Madison Square Park, then slightly back east down the Bowery, Washington and Clinton pulled to a stop in front of the Bull's Head tavern, just below modern Canal Street. Crowds filled the scene in powdered wigs, white ruffles, flowing dresses, silks and garlands. Sprigs of laurel poked from hats, and black-and-white ribbons—the Union cockade—hung over left breasts. Among the throng, surely, was publisher John Holt, who had returned to the city and restarted his paper just three days earlier—now calling it the *Independent New-York Gazette*. Knox had gone down to Bowling Green, where a mass of citizens, some on horseback and some on foot, waited to join the procession. He led them back to the Bowery, fashioned them into a prescribed order, and began the march of triumph.

New York looked every bit the part of war-torn city. Buildings remained charred from a massive fire set just days after the battle in 1776. The British occupants had not paid taxes for public works—trash went uncollected, lamps unlit, pumps unrepaired, streets and roads untended. Such debris sat this way for months; by spring of 1783 tens of thousands of British had sailed for Nova Scotia, England, or elsewhere. Many ended long legacies in Manhattan: The great-granddaughter of Mathias Nicolls—secretary under Francis Lovelace—left in May for Scotland with her husband, John Loudon McAdam, who in a matter of decades would invent a road-building method that still bears his surname. Many of the Americans who had fled in exile at the beginning of the war refused to return until the British evacuation was complete.

At Cape's tavern, formerly kept by George Burns under the name of City Arms, the people of New York issued a statement of thanks to Washington: "we look up to you, our deliverer, with unusual transports of gratitude and joy." Farther down the Main Road, at the fort, the American flag would be raised, making the reacquisition of Manhattan official. But the British, bobbing solemnly in boats off the shore, had managed one final mischief. They had removed both the halyard atop the flagpole at Fort George and the cleats used to climb it. Their colors remained, nailed into place, taunting in the breeze.

A young sailor, John Van Arsdale, threw himself up the pole to right the situation. Van Arsdale had much to begrudge the evacuees. On the day Kip's Bay was attacked, as his family loaded their things to leave New York, a cannonball ripped a wheel off their wagon. His leg had been wounded in battle. At one point he had even been held prisoner. The British had greased the pole, however, and with each attempt up, Van Arsdale slid back down. Finally a ladder arrived. He reached the few remaining cleats near the top, hoisted himself the rest of the way, and strung up the American flag. When Washington was told of the incident, back at Cape's tavern, he might have flashed a sympathetic face.

If it comes without frustration, he knew, it cannot be redemption.

ON THE ONE-YEAR anniversary of Evacuation Day a far smaller party huddled outside Cape's tavern for a Manhattan evacuation of its own. It was five in the morning, likely dark, perhaps cool enough to see one's breath. One by one the travelers, who numbered six at most, hoisted themselves into a covered carriage. They took a seat on one of the wooden benches and squeezed their luggage underneath—no more than fourteen pounds apiece, if they wanted to avoid the surcharge. When all was fastened into place Talmage Hall climbed the driver's platform behind the four harnessed horses. The reins snapped, the wheels creaked, and the first successful New York–to–Boston stage-coach headed up the highway Washington had paraded down the year before.

Presuming they kept schedule, the travelers ate breakfast at Fort Washington before exiting Manhattan island at King's Bridge. They crossed the Bronx on a rough road and entered the farms of Eastchester and New Rochelle, New York. Stone fences let each owner know which wheat and rye and Indian corn was his neighbor's, and which was his own. In Mamaroneck the passengers stretched. The stagecoach interior was not particularly comfortable. Bumps often sent the heads of travel-ers against the roof, and during the next stretch of highway, east of Rye, there would be bumps aplenty.

For here the stagecoach entered a truly terrifying segment—described by one contemporary passenger, a Frenchman, as "stair-cases of rocks." Traveling the Main Road from New York to Boston a year later, John Quincy Adams agreed: "The roads from Rye," he wrote in his diary, "are some of the worst I ever saw." Spring suspension had not yet arrived, and the carriage body jounced against a hard leather strap that kept it from crashing through the wheels. Across the Connecticut border the horses tiptoed above a steep drop into a valley. The stage-coach had double leather curtains, typically drawn in rain, and it might have struck the fancy of a few of these travelers to draw them now, rain or shine, and ride on in blissful ignorance.

That first night the travelers slept in Talmage Hall's own tavern in Norwalk. They had traveled fifty miles, and would have to wake before dawn to do it again. The following day they ferried across the Housa-tonic River. Jacob Brown, the driver for this next stage, met them on the other side and took them to New Haven for the night. Along the way they passed through Fairfield and a Connecticut coastline still recover-ing from British destruction.

The next day, a Saturday, introduced some much-needed serenity into the adventurous trip. The ride north through the Connecticut River valley was tame; the landscape, in the words of Quincy Adams, "enchanting." White onions dotted the vast greens of Wethersfield. Cattle lowed across the meadows of the river valley. Triangular pieces of wood dangled from the necks of hogs to prevent their escape through fences. Women and girls wore calico gowns. The entire pastoral scene, remarked the French traveler, "is really the Paradise of the United States."

By nightfall of November 28 they reached Hartford. There would be no travel on Sunday. Instead, no doubt, the day was spent in prayer— a portion of which might have been dedicated to the ferry and the horses that had, so far, held firm to their course.

Sometimes, after rising in the wee hours, stagecoach travelers read the newspapers over a breakfast of coffee and boiled meat. The New Haven paper of that particular week—for newspapers at that time ran weekly—told of strife brewing in Europe. The Hartford paper contained an essay on the Articles of Confederation and a brief story their driver likely hoped they would not see, about a stagecoach down south recently robbed of $4,000. The current *Massachusetts Spy* called for newspaper subscriptions past due and gave notice of newly printed almanacs for the year 1785, complete with a full roster of post roads from Boston to Georgia.

Stone walls generally ran along either side of official post roads. In marshy regions sometimes a "corduroy" road, made by placing heavy logs crosswise atop layers of bough, guided the way. A few decades would pass before macadam pavement appeared; "paved" sections of road, if any did exist at this time, referred to those layered with gravel. Still, most were dirt. Far more effort went into making tavern signs than into road maintenance. Each one represented the marriage of three minds: the artist who painted the sign's image; the joiner who framed the white pine panels in post-and-rail construction; and the smith who fastened the heavy hardware that allowed the signs to lure travelers on the post road from high above, as billboards lure modern travelers on the expressway.

North of Hartford the rural countryside became a rolling vista of white houses surrounded by orchards outlined by picket fences. In Palmer, Massachusetts, thirty miles after hooking sharply east at Springfield, they lodged at the tavern of Major Aaron Graves. Many tavernkeepers, with their tight connection to travel and the mail, grew to be well known by the country's leading patriots; Palmer's other inn was kept by the Scott family, whom John Adams once called "Zealous Americans." These and other tavernkeepers, no doubt, regaled the weary travelers with stories of the men who had just won the country's freedom.

From here the Main Road grew rocky once more. It curled north along the Quaboag River, tracking the base of low mountains, and followed the humming water east. Soon it entered a deep, raw forest, as though a portal into the past. "The traveller is well recompensed for the fatigue of this route," noted the Frenchman. Only a few scattered houses reminded one of civilization, of "the perpetual contrast of savage nature and the efforts of art," whose balance time tipped toward the latter. On Tuesday, December 1, they met the western-bound coach in Brookfield, swapped places, and continued on in Reuben Sikes's care to Worcester, where they spent the night.

At five the next morning, Levi Pease began the last leg of the great weeklong relay that represented, at the time, the very swiftest of inland transportation. It ended that evening at his Boston inn, near the corner of modern Tremont Avenue and Temple Street, a block west of the Main Road, underneath a sign with "New-York" painted in big letters, and a picture that looked just like the group pulling to a halt, in miniature.

JUST WHY LINKING northeast America's two great capitals occurred to Levi Pease, blacksmith from the backcountry, will never be certain. His craft put him in contact with carriages—but the leap to stagecoach entrepreneur, from there, seems as likely as Magellan's leaping to global navigation after taking a bath. Pease did not settle on the Main Road until his business was of it. By then he was pushing fifty. Only his itinerant role in the Revolution hints at a man fluent with the region and easy on the move. Whether those duties were the cause or the symptom of

Levi Pease's becoming, in the words of one newspaper upon his retirement, "Father of the New England Roads," is a debate best held within the taverns he came to know so well.

The Pease family were settlers of Enfield, a Main Road town on the Connecticut River between Hartford and Springfield. Nathaniel Pease, a distant relative of this founding clan, was made highway surveyor in 1736. His third son, Levi, was born three years later. At some point the whole family moved to Blandford, Massachusetts, twenty-five miles west of Springfield. It was here that Levi was living when fighting broke out in 1775.

The most incendiary region leading up to the war, New England hosted very few of its significant contests. The British held Boston for less than a year after the battle at Lexington, a period rife with looting and disease. During this time, as far as Americans were concerned, the Main Road ended at the gates of Roxbury, upon the neck, where General John Thomas and his men rained cannon fire toward the head of the Bay. Most patriot rebels fled before the British occupation. Benjamin Edes sneaked into Watertown, loading his printing supplies on a boat moored along the Charles. His son had less luck. He was captured in the old print shop in June of 1775, and was soon joined in jail by his father's former partner, John Gill.

On March 17, 1776, the Americans reclaimed Boston. They unbarred the Roxbury gate and found the Main Road covered with iron crow's-feet—the English army's idea of a parting gift. In early April Washington traveled the southern branch of the Main Road to meet his troops in New York, the next likely place of attack. The battle for Manhattan that fall marked the end of major fighting between New York and the Bay. A few lesser confrontations did occur. A thousand men torched New London under the guile of Benedict Arnold. Norwalk, Fairfield, and New Haven were plundered one summer. A fight to reclaim British-controlled Newport was called on account of a storm. But these outbursts, though occasionally costly at a local level, bore little impact on the war at large.

Still, the New England soldier had plenty to do. In April of 1776 Pease was made an adjutant, and though he left few records of his movements, it is possible to track his activity through the two generals he assisted. His first role came that summer, when he served as messenger for General John Thomas. For his valor in regaining Boston, Thomas had been given command of American troops in Canada—considered at the time a vital position. Alone, under cover of darkness, Pease shuttled posts to and from the general. Most of the notes written by Thomas at that time described soldiers stricken with smallpox; the replies expressed concern that the general would catch the disease. Later in life Pease recalled drifting in stealth past enemy lines, facing the white moon from inside a boat rowed softly by hand, mastering a delicate balance of patience and haste.

In early June, with Pease at his side, Thomas indeed died of illness. Soon, likely at Ticonderoga while under General Philip Schuyler, Pease caught the eye of Jeremiah Wadsworth, who hustled flour and wheat to Schuyler's men. Wadsworth soon became commissary general in charge of feeding and outfitting the eastern forces; eventually he stocked the whole American army. Pease joined Wadsworth's team of agents who scattered across the countryside. They loaded their saddlebags with cash and struck deals with farmers and merchants. Tents and clothing flowed west from Boston through Hartford, the likely course following the northern branch of the Main Road.

Wadsworth was wildly successful; under his care, Washington wrote to Lafayette in 1779, the American troops were "better clad and more healthy than they ever have been since the formation of the army." As the French allies neared the shores of Rhode Island in 1780, Lafayette turned to Wadsworth for provisions. Wadsworth, in turn, told Pease to secure horses to pull wagons. The French intended to drag their weapons to Yorktown, Virginia, by land; from Rhode Island to New York they almost certainly traveled the coastal Main Road. Pease followed to Yorktown and continued his role at the site of the war's conclusive battle.

Come 1783 Pease had settled with his family in Somers, Connecticut, ten miles east of his native Enfield. By then he was forty-four years old and had five children. Times were hard, especially for the working class, as Shay's Rebellion would soon bring to the young country's attention. Continental money had been swapped with such abandon that it was nearly worthless. (One day Pease met a farmer who had sold him horses for Lafayette during the war, and the man still had all the money from the exchange; no one would accept it.) Pease resumed his role as blacksmith and kept an inn. The poor economy; the fresh ideas of freedom; the anecdotes of war, brimming with excitement—these topics would have monopolized the tavern chatter, and stamped home an existence both provincial and uncertain.

IF THE IDEA of a full-blown passenger service on the Main Road between Boston and New York was not entirely novel for 1783, it was still uncharted cultural terrain. The only earnest prior attempt had come in 1772. It failed miserably. Nicholas Brown, a carriage maker in Hartford, announced that he would carry travelers between Manhattan and the Bay, "through that beautiful part of the country of the upper Post road." Jonathan Brown agreed to do some of the driving, but the partners had trouble attracting patrons. The Browns may not have made any trips at all until late July. Even then they had only enough interest to go twice a month, and by fall they went no more.

Any number of problems might have plagued the Browns, but most likely they underestimated the sheer breadth of their enterprise. In the late eighteenth century, packet boats were the closest thing to long-distance mass transit. The service was regularly scheduled, but winds made actual travel time highly variable; reaching New York from Providence might take three days on Long Island Sound, or it might take nine. Neither could the sea accommodate those wishing to travel just part of the way. Privately owned carriages remained by and large a thing of the future. They were familiar sights among the wealthy in large towns, but within the confines of these towns they stayed. Travel in general was a rare affair; long-distance travel by land, rarer still.

So what the Browns perhaps took as a business opportunity was actually an attempt to overhaul the speed of life. The public would have to grow comfortable with a culture of transportation that, to the extent promised, simply did not exist. "A journey to New York was not then such an occasion of pleasure," recalled well-known Bostonian Josiah

Quincy. "The stage-coaches were intolerable, and the passage through the Sound"—by which he meant the packet boats—"still worse." Guiding a group of travelers across two hundred fifty miles of relative wilderness, with upward of a dozen stops, introduced an entire scope of intricacies. The driver unable to rouse travelers in the wee hours; the innkeeper late with a meal; the smith who did a shoddy job; the rock in the road more jagged than it looked—countless minutiae threatened to topple the whole line.

As a result only very short stages succeeded in the day. A few local carriage lines supplemented packet service on Long Island Sound, but the most extensive of this smattering ran from Providence to Boston, a mere fifty miles. In midsummer of 1783 another stage line appeared, run by Jacob Brown.* Brown's satellite coach scooped sea travelers at New Haven, drove them to Hartford, continued on to Springfield, and reversed course back south. Each segment took a day to complete. His first advertisement appeared in a Hartford newspaper. Before long word would have drifted a bit east, into Somers, Connecticut.

Jacob Brown's shuttle is the logical inspiration for Levi Pease's leap into action, and considering their later partnership, it seems possible that the two exchanged thoughts early on. But Pease schemed grandly from the start, and it is a testimony to the size of his vision that his first recorded business move was to Boston. Sometime before fall Pease took his plan to the Main Road's eastern end and turned onto modern State Street. There he found the premier hackney coach stand in Boston— and the man running it, John Ballard.

The scene around this stand would have been abuzz. Boston's population, at twelve thousand, was busily recovering its prewar size of nearly double that. Hackneys, freight carts, and wagons laden with farm goods congested the streets. Coach lines to Providence left daily. Traffic was deemed such a public danger that laws required horses drawing vehicles to stay at a "common walk." As the locus of this hurly-burly Ballard was unquestionably qualified to assess Pease's plan. The advice he gave that day, after rejecting an offer of partnership, left no room for

---

*No apparent relation to the aforementioned stagecoach Browns.

doubt: The time might come when the public would support a stage line from Hartford to Boston, Ballard told Pease, "but not in your day or mine."

Pease would not be discouraged. He returned to Somers and approached Reuben Sikes, a fellow blacksmith, as a partner. The new team spent the remaining summer of 1783 preparing their business. They acquired coaches and horses. They fitted shoes themselves and handled whatever repairs they could in their own shops. They set the price at four pence per mile. Eventually they mapped a course from Hartford, through Somers, toward Boston. By using his own tavern, in Somers, Pease would surely save money—though the decision also meant traveling a fair distance off the Main Road. In October they took ads out in newspapers, and the dream became real.★

At first Ballard appeared prescient. Few people came to ride the stagecoach, and sometimes none came at all. Still, Pease set out as advertised. Many Mondays, promptly at six o'clock, he left from the Sign of the Lamb in Boston, and sixteen hooves crackled for his ears alone. By evening, as he neared Martin's tavern in Northborough, the noises of night would have joined this symphony. At some point, guided by slivers of silver light, he must have recalled his army days, drifting faceup in the boat, clutching a letter from General Thomas. Then, as now, he rode on in solitude, with little to do but hope at the moon. His friends and family begged him to give up; at least, they urged, only set out when the carriage has travelers. But if Pease ever flagged in the frustrating darkness he remained certain by day that once the service proved reliable, the passengers would come.

Soon enough they did. The service was publicized regularly by the well-known printer Isaiah Thomas, who had moved his Boston newspaper to Worcester during the Revolution. In exchange Pease stowed bundles of Thomas's *Massachusetts Spy* inside his coach and carried them on his routine trips to the Bay. By spring of 1784 Pease had shifted the

---

★The elder Reuben Sikes, a legislative deputy from Somers, disapproved of the partnership, to no avail. The first Pease coach ad ran on the same page as a legislative notice that Reuben Sikes Sr. was the representative from Somers, as though the parent was attempting one final warning in print.

route away from Somers back to the Main Road. It speaks to the highway's superiority at the time that this alteration shaved a whole day off the trip. Coaches left simultaneously from each terminal town and exchanged travelers in Spencer, Massachusetts, doubling the passenger load. The Boston headquarters moved from the Sign of the Lamb tavern to the Sign of the Lion.

By May Pease had made arrangements with Jacob Brown to connect the service to New Haven. From there travelers could hop a packet to New York—for the time being. Full service to Manhattan, going all the way by land, would start "as soon as possible." "Soon" arrived that fall. Pease reached an agreement with Talmage Hall, whose own line ran from New York to Norwalk, Connecticut, and the conglomeration was complete.

As the summer of 1785 cast its warm gaze on the Main Road, it found all four proprietors running their own taverns at critical stops along the route. Pease now kept his Sign of the New-York Stage beside the Boston Common. Reuben Sikes had moved out of his father's shadow and into a tavern at Wilbraham, Massachusetts, just east of Springfield. Brown took a New Haven inn across from Yale.

But Hall—Hall made the most elaborate shift of the bunch. He leased a private house in uptown Manhattan, some ten miles from Cape's tavern. It was a house of patrician, renowned on the island, capable of hosting genteel galas, which Hall promised to arrange at "ten minutes' notice." One particular room, with a memorable octagonal shape, would suit a handsome party. For Talmage Hall had made a stagecoach stop of the old Morris mansion. And so the former military headquarters of George Washington, once used by the general to halt the invasion of Manhattan, would now welcome outsiders into New York, and welcome them in style.

WHILE THE PEASE establishment was defeating all naysayers up north during the summer of 1785, the Continental Congress down south decided that America's mail was broken. Postal business, newspaper delivery in particular, had proliferated in tempo with the move toward independence. The literal bulk of this information surge was now straining post riders throughout the country. Complaints had been filed about their "very considerable delay." In at least one instance, national security had been threatened; a bundle of mail stolen from a post office was found abandoned in a meadow, the seals on letters sent by members of Congress split open. The young government could ill afford to have its communication network compromised. A committee was formed to investigate the troubling trends. The postmaster general, Ebenezer Hazard, was called upon to answer.

In some senses the irreconcilable rift between Benjamin Franklin and William Goddard led to Ebenezer Hazard's gaining control of the American mail. When Franklin left for Paris in the fall of 1776 he promoted Richard Bache to postmaster general. William Goddard, never able to shake his disgruntlement at being overpassed in the system he created, left the office in a huff, and Bache placed Hazard in the vacant position. When Bache retired in 1782 Hazard succeeded him. At the end of June 1785, when Congress called for bids "for the transportation of the several Mails, in the stage carriages," it was Hazard who would orchestrate this move—the largest postal overhaul since the days of Francis Lovelace.

On the surface, transferring the mail from post rider to stagecoach seemed a simple switch. Post riders only existed to carry the mail. Stages, on the other hand, already traveled the same routes as these riders in the natural course of their work. Riders had a single bag slung over their shoulder; stagecoaches could squeeze letters anywhere the bulky carriage body had room. And whereas solitary riders were susceptible to hijack, stagecoaches had relative safety by numbers.

But coach lines were private businesses. In his very first advertisement Levi Pease declared, in the *Connecticut Journal,* that "the greatest attention will be paid to the Passengers." Patrons already awoke at the crack of dawn and spent several grueling days on the road. What would they think of sharing a bench with wet newsprint, or waking even earlier so that the mail could be sorted at a few extra stops? For Pease and company to take on these paper passengers they needed compensation. That much they made clear in their "exorbitant" contract proposal to Hazard:

to carry the mail between Boston and New York they wanted as much as the post office paid its riders, plus over a third more.

Hazard, on a personal level, had reason to dislike stagecoach lines going into these negotiations. He thought poorly of tavernkeepers, equating their success with society's moral decay, and had seen the rise of the stagecoach industry only strengthen their contemptible position. When he received the offer from Pease and Talmage Hall in July of 1785, Hazard reacted with disgust. He was quick to point out to Congress that it was the only proposal he had received on the Main Road. So while Pease had offered "the best terms," they were technically "also the worst."

Hazard's insinuations could not dampen Congress's desire to see stagecoaches wheeling the mail from Maine to Georgia. The New York–to–Boston communication corridor, in particular, was too important to the country's welfare—important enough to command more money for mail delivery than the rest of the stages from Portland, Maine, to Philadelphia combined. So Congress forced Hazard to accept the terms, and come 1786 Pease's carriages were delivering the mail three times a week in summer, and twice in winter. The deal netted Pease about $2,500 a year and, perhaps more important, conferred upon his growing venture a sense of national prestige.

Hazard considered this defeat merely the first in a lengthy fight. He pounded away at the stagecoach mail service, session after congressional session. Some of the beating was deserved. Stage lines refused to adjust their schedules to meet post office needs. As a result, Hazard protested, the "Mail arrives as irregularly as formerly and even more so." On one occasion Talmage Hall reached New York and brought each traveler home before delivering his mail bundles. Hazard also suspected poor attention to the mail's safety, though "no actual Damage can be proved." Still, as early as fall of 1786, Hazard asked Congress for permission to revert back to using post riders.

Congress would have none of it. To the country's leaders, the matter of coaches carrying the mail went beyond the mere duty of delivery. Transportation and communication, at that time, were symbiotic entities. If one evolved into a superior state, the other followed by necessity.

Stagecoach travel, though still in its infancy, had clearly improved the country's mobility. Hazard, like the Brown brothers before him, was mistaking the fundamental structure of community for a simple taxi gig. It was precisely this urge to expand localities outward, toward the national level, that formed the true intention of Congress—not just to have the mail transported by stage, but to encourage, in a wider sense, "the establishment of stages to make the intercourse between the different parts of the Union less difficult and expensive than formerly."

Hazard persisted undeterred. When it came time to renew contracts for 1787, Pease requested a significant raise to meet the rising cost of the service. He now asked roughly $4,000 for the Boston–to–New York route—five times what the post office had paid lone riders. Hazard doubted these terms were as necessary as Pease claimed, instead choosing to portray stage lines as inflexible profiteers. He called out Talmage Hall personally as a detriment to the mail, insisting "it is not probable that he will perform better in the future." He prepared a letter to Congress detailing his complaints, and, "while I am writing," claimed to receive from Pease an updated contract proposal demanding an extra $226. "Such work sending the mail by stage makes!" Hazard wrote to a friend in exasperation. By year's end his intransigence had won out, and Hazard was allowed to contract with riders or stagecoaches—whichever he deemed "most convenient."

The change hit hard along the Main Road. Some stage drivers, finding a legal technicality, carried the mail for free to spite Hazard. But in doing so they were expending great effort on a weighty, nonpaying customer who took endless round-trips. Piece by piece the line broke down. Pease put his Boston tavern up for sale. Hall left the Morris mansion in New York and soon quit the stage business altogether. Soon the leg between Manhattan and New Haven was halted entirely.

Coming in 1788, the timing of the change could not have been worse. Whether or not to ratify the Constitution was at the front of minds, and on the front pages of newspapers, from New Hampshire to Georgia. Acceptance of the union was far from a certainty, and people, being people, wanted to know what other people thought. The post riders demanded more money to carry newspapers, which were as numerous and cumbersome as ever, and soon they stopped delivering the news with the mail. Enraged printers, in turn, unleashed their anger in Hazard's direction.

In midsummer of 1788 the "new arrangement in the post-office" caught the eye of George Washington. Upon learning that coach lines had been interrupted in New England, and elsewhere, Washington wrote to the statesman John Jay of the regrettable situation. It was axiomatic, Washington thought, that improvements in travel meant improvements in social dialogue; for a young republic these should be seen as a mark of progress. To deny the people their newspapers at such a time was cause for great concern. To do so because the postmaster general begrudged stagecoaches with an "inveterate enmity" was beyond Washington's powers of comprehension. If Hazard had any "candid advisers," Washington wrote Jay, "they ought to counsel him to wipe away the aspersions he has incautiously brought upon a good cause."

Unfortunately for Hazard his only counsel was a right eye that smarted whenever he worried, and if that anatomical stress flare offered advice during this period, Hazard was numb to it. Hoping to supercede Hazard's authority, Levi Pease stated his case directly to Congress in a formal petition. Calling himself "the first who established a line of Stages on the great road between New York & Boston," Pease said he carried the mail not to profit but simply "to defray the expence of an institution so advantageous and desirable to the citizens of the United States." The details Pease offered—including a willingness to name nineteen post riders with known violations—were likely more than an eager Congress needed to take action.

Without even hearing the postmaster general's side, a congressional committee ordered Hazard to reestablish Pease's contract. For "not enough favouring the stages in carrying the mails" Congress secretly tried to remove Hazard during the fall of 1788. Though this undercover impeachment failed, when it came time for President George Washington to appoint the first postmaster general of the United States, he deemed one Samuel Osgood more convenient.

Hazard, distraught, wrote a letter to a friend comparing himself to Adam being marched out of Eden. In that case Levi Pease was leading the march back into paradise, and when George Washington's presidential tour of America brought him to New York in October of 1789, the general followed behind, parading through Hartford and across the northern branch of Pease's so-called Great Road—the blacksmith's chosen road into Boston.

Chapter 6

Setting the Business in Motion

THE AUTUMN OF 1789 witnessed the Great Road in all its loosely pebbled splendor. Three weeks after George Washington traveled it during his presidential tour from New York to Boston,* someone underbid Levi Pease for the mail contract on the highway. The complexities of stagecoach travel had impressed themselves upon the country's leadership, however, and doubting that another could fulfill so heavy a task, the postmaster general thought Pease should win the job anyway. He "is the only person that will keep up a good line of Stages between this"—the New York post office—"and Boston," Samuel Osgood advised George Washington. The president, having just completed a firsthand examination of this good line, agreed.

From the time of Washington's tour to the time of Levi Pease's death, in 1824, culture rolled on to the beat of the stagecoach empire. The young were weaned on its wheels, nourished by its taverns, educated by its letters; they came of age hungry for speed and at home on the road. In his first State of the Union address to Congress, in January of 1790, Washington called "facilitating the intercourse between the

---

* It was in honor of the first president's tour in 1789 that those parts of the highway leading into Boston—once quartered as Orange, Newbury, Marlborough, and Cornhill streets—united as Washington Street.

distant parts of our Country by a due attention to the Post-Office and Post-Roads" a national priority. By the end of this era, in the words of one Boston newspaper, "a complete consolidation of the interests and feelings of the people of the United States" had nearly arrived.

Postal contracts, though by no means lavish, gave coaching lines the financial cushion they needed to thrive. In Pease's case, they provided a means to upgrade his entire outfit. He bought carriages with spring suspension to ease the ride. He brokered business transactions between the capitals, chaperoning bundles of cash and promissory notes between Manhattan and the Bay. He swallowed up the Boston-to-Providence stage line, expanding his dominion on the Great Road to its coastal branch. He even seems to have created the concept of "limited" travel in 1793: four-person express coaches that, for a tiny bit extra, made the whole trip in three and a half days.

In time the Pease influence trickled down the Eastern Seaboard. When the mail failed to run smoothly between Baltimore and Philadelphia, in 1799, Joseph Habersham, then postmaster general, asked Pease to "set the Business in motion." In short time Pease whipped every detail of the line into shape—the mail chests that doubled as seats; the words "United States Mail Stage" in roman capital letters; even the paints used to mix the green coach body (Prussian blue and yellow ochre). Altogether, Habersham later reported, the Pease-tailored route was faster, safer, and more efficient than any in the entire postal system.

The result was a faster, safer, and more efficient lifestyle than any the country had known. Blacksmith shops sprouted along the Great Road, as frequent breakdowns called for roadside service. Farm wagons wheeled into general stores to barter oats, butter, and cheese for snuff, linens, liquors, and other everyday essentials, all sold side by side. Livestock swarmed the highway thirty to a drove on their way to the country's premier abattoir, the Bull's Head tavern, in the Bowery neighborhood of Manhattan. Inns buzzed—and so did the heads of stagecoach drivers who downed New England's customary noon toddy before returning to the busy road.

The British naval blockades that lined the Atlantic coast during the War of 1812 only fed the highway fury. Where newspapers had once notified merchants of ships arriving into port, they now glibly told of wagon fleets, those "new, fast sailing, inland Boston and New York packet[s]," arriving into town in the care of Captain So-and-so. Teamsters hauled crates and barrels in canvas-covered wagons—at least four hundred a week, recalled Worcester resident Isaiah Thomas, rolled along the Great Road from the Bay toward New York. Some continued all the way to Savannah.

By that time personal carriages had grown more common as well. Bridgeport and New York were among the country's early carriage centers. New Haven led the way under James Brewster, who went to work one day after his stagecoach broke down while passing through the town, and never left. Full-sized coaches stood beside lighter buggies, phaetons, rockaways, and chaises. By 1811 New Haven had nine carriage shops, each of which spawned an economy of carpenters and painters and assemblers of its own.

As travel improved, communication followed in step. By the summer of 1792 Congress had granted Washington's wish, establishing the official post office and routing the post roads from Maine to Georgia. The nineteenth century dawned upon a complex network of stage, post, and combined stage-post routes. The mail now reached Boston six days a week, and a letter leaving there at 11 a.m. on a Monday in summer arrived in New York by noon Thursday. New towns sought inclusion with such alacrity that postmasters general, orchestrating from afar, had to rely on veterans like Pease not only to set the business in motion but to keep it going.

By the dawn of 1824, the speed of life had changed. Travel by stage between New York and Boston now took only thirty-six hours, and the Great Road was busier than any in the country. When Pease died in January of that year, asleep in his home in Shrewsbury, forty miles west of Boston on the Great Road, one writer thought youths would be astonished to learn that, before Pease, the mail had gone from Boston to New York on horseback, and had taken a fortnight each way.

But as all empires discover too late, the crest of success is also the cusp of decline. During this same period, from Washington's inauguration to Pease's death, innovations occurred along the Great Road that would change transportation for a century to come. One came about through Pease's own efforts: in a general sense, by building a culture bent on speed; and in a particular sense, when he petitioned the Massachusetts legislature to build a new kind of road, called a turnpike.

IN THE FRESH young years of the republic, even the very best of roads were not the sleek gray carpets found today. Methods of road maintenance—or, as one contemporary called it, "road-destroying"—had advanced little since colonial times. Some stretches of road were nicely covered in gravel, but dirt highways remained the norm. Oxen dragged plows over the path. Large stones were plucked out by hand. The rest of the loose soil was piled into the center with the idea that travelers, over time, would tamp down the mounds into even strips of earth. No great tool yet existed for uprooting tree stumps. More likely those called out to work on the roads used the stumps as natural seats for taking frequent breaks, for drinking rum, or as the starting line for the spontaneous footraces that characterized a hefty chunk of a good Road Day's work.

The entire operation had an amateur feel for good reason: the highway surveyor method of road maintenance had carried over from early colonial life and spread outward from the Northeast. Once or twice a year, typically in summer, most of a town's male population converged on the highway, shovels in hand, for annual road duty. Many sent a substitute, or simply paid the small absentee fine. Despite the public need for better roads, the quality of this effort improved very little over time; in a system where the dilettante leads the uninterested, completion is the goal and progress the delusion.

Certainly Americans wanted better roads, and as the stagecoach accelerated the speed of life, this desire increased. In general, though, people were reluctant to pay taxes for roads they might not use themselves. (Lawmakers were also hesitant; whether the constitutional right to "establish" post roads meant the physical act of constructing these roads was a lingering interpretative debate.*) The creation of turnpike companies massaged this overriding cultural soreness. Small business groups offered to maintain a particular stretch of highway. In exchange, states granted them the right to place tollgates every few miles, and to collect various fees for each type of traveler wishing to use the road.

In Massachusetts, the first such effort grew from Levi Pease's frustration with a part of the Great Road running east from Springfield. Past Wilbraham, the road became terribly rocky through Palmer and Warren toward Brookfield. After passing this segment on his ride in 1785, John Quincy Adams remarked in his diary, "I cannot recommend the roads of Massachusetts as a model." Part of this segment, beginning at a bridge a quarter mile from Major Graves's tavern, had been cause for dispute before the Revolution. It marked the boundary between Palmer and newly incorporated Monson. Each town, in gracious New England manner, had politely deferred road maintenance to the other. Several decades later this long-neglected stretch was slowing down the Pease stage line.

Pease petitioned the governor of Massachusetts, Samuel Adams, for the right to improve this winding, mountainous stretch "on the great road leading from Springfield to Boston." Adams approved the plan of this eminent group—among its thirty-one cosigners were Congressman Dwight Foster and future governor Levi Lincoln—and in summer of 1796 the First Massachusetts Turnpike** was born.

Soon turnpike fever swept the country.† New England's roads were considered the nation's best around the turn of the nineteenth century, and the Great Road held out longest against the changes on the strength of its centuries of use. Some segments remained unchallenged for

---

*Article I, Section 8, of the U.S. Constitution grants the right "to establish Post Offices and Post Roads."

**This First Massachusetts Turnpike in no way relates to modern Interstate 90, which is also called the Massachusetts Turnpike, though the roads do run very near each other in Wilbraham.

†The National Road, stretching west from Cumberland, Maryland, came to symbolize this era—rather ironically, as it was the only turnpike built with public money.

decades. But in the end no road was immune to the rush. There were dollars to be made now in movement, and investors flooded state governments with proposals similar to Pease's. Most of the public accepted the era cheerfully; if nothing else it meant the end of yearly road duty. When occasionally a landowner contested a turnpike's path, the state invoked eminent domain; compensation was issued, and construction resumed. After the eye of the storm—a fifteen-year blitz beginning around 1795—New England had laid out nearly enough miles of road, if placed end to end, to touch the sands of the Pacific.

Some of the turnpikes merely dusted off the old highway and presented it to the public with the promise of more dustings to come. In Greenwich, Connecticut, turnpike owners did little more than set up a tollgate. Elsewhere companies made small adjustments—ironing out a twist here, leveling a hill there. In Boston, a straighter Washington Street was extended out toward Dedham alongside old Centre Street. Just south, in the region between Dedham and Providence, the Great Road frequently snaked around the new turnpike; in one brief stretch they intersected thirteen times. Where the new pay roads met the old free ones, people often circumvented the tollgates (a practice called "shun-piking" that, in one humble opinion, would have been more cleverly termed "spurn-piking"). Such evasions grew so routine that Massachusetts had them outlawed.

Other segments were guided by a blind desire for straightness equated, often erroneously, with speed. The Boston and Worcester turnpike represented a most extreme case; there, in many places, the turnpike was laid several miles from the old highway.* Yet even in these instances the Great Road provided the inspiration for this highway evolution. In its original petition to the General Court, for instance, the Worcester turnpike company argued that "the great road or highway leading from Boston to Worcester is extremely crooked, hilly and in many places, narrow and inconvenient."

Even when the mentality of directness won the day, the Great Road

---

*On a modern map this difference is essentially the space between U.S. Route 20 (the old highway) and Massachusetts Route 9 (the new turnpike), from Boston to Worcester.

remained heavily trafficked. By one count the old highway between Boston and Worcester actually carried three times as many travelers as its neatly engineered counterpart. A federal report concluded that although the turnpike from New Haven to Hartford saved several miles of distance, the natural advantages of the old course—and its passage through several established towns—made it the more efficient route.

For these reasons, and many others, turnpikes failed to make money in the end. Few turnpike companies in New England reaped any sort of profit at all. A decade into its existence the New Haven–to–Hartford turnpike had earned little more in its entirety than it had cost to build a single mile. None achieved the type of modest success—typically twelve percent a year—that would have them revert automatically to state-owned public roads, though as each corporation folded, they became these anyway.

The most significant of the Great Road's new limbs connected Manhattan with the mainland along the present-day Boston Road in the Bronx, and the story of its creation merits some deeper explanation. Before the Revolution the patriot Lewis Morris, an eventual signer of the Declaration of Independence, had sought permission to build a toll bridge across the Harlem River, almost exactly where the modern Third Avenue Bridge exists today. (Morris lived in a region of the Bronx that still goes by the name Morrisania.) A branch road toward his bridge would severely duck the old approach from New England onto the island over King's Bridge. The diversion would pay off twice: once when the thankful traveler deposited a coin at the gate of the new bridge, and once again down the line, when the value of Morris's land increased.

Come 1790 Morris was ready to revive the idea of this bridge when the proposal caught the ear of the state's new attorney general, Aaron Burr. Burr offered to finesse the bill through to passage, and when he was finished, Morris earned the right to build his bridge, and the task of laying out the new road fell upon three commissioners—two of whom, Joseph Browne and John Bartow Jr., were Burr's close in-laws. In March of 1790 the bill indeed passed.

Some evidence suggests that Burr intended to purchase the land through which the new road passed, and profit as its value soared. Back in the fall of 1789, Burr had represented the heirs of Joshua Pell, a loyalist whose 146-acre farm had been confiscated after the war by the state. The following February, Burr bought the plot in question—dubbed The Shrubberies—for use as a summer home. The Shrubberies resided "on the post road" as it passed through modern Pelham, beginning near "the gate of the Boston Turnpike Road," precisely where a new road would branch toward Lewis Morris's new bridge. Burr soon transferred this land to his stepson, Augustine Prevost, for ten shillings—essentially gave it away, perhaps to distance himself from its acquisition.

A few years later Lewis Morris sold his rights to the toll bridge to John Coles, who soon undertook its construction. In summer of 1800 the Westchester Turnpike Company established its "Western Gate" near The Shrubberies and extended the new highway from Pelham to the "Eastern Gate," near the Connecticut line. When the city laid down fresh milestones in 1801, this new Boston road became the route of record between New York and New England.

And so the second generation of the Great Road had emerged near both ends of the original highway. By 1809, well-known Worcester resident Isaiah Thomas was referring to the "old road for Boston," and when a couple New York newspapers spoke of the "old Boston Post Road" several years later, the antiquation was official.

The changes rooted in the Old Boston Post Road had encouraged its rivals, but the resulting shifts in the traffic grid had not altogether diminished its significance. While turnpike investors nursed the road's physical development, another class of innovators—less directly related to roads but no less reliant upon transportation—were planting the seeds of American industry along its course. Two of the country's most formative manufacturing efforts were conceived on the old highway. The result was a proliferation of domestic goods that required superior avenues of delivery—superior even to the turnpike roads, whose death knell they sounded with a locomotive whistle.

To put it a bit more precisely, the Industrial Revolution led to the railroads that made all highway travel temporarily passé. To be even more precise, this revolution sprung from two acts of international espionage. And to be more precise still, the perpetrators of these twin heists found asylum along the Old Boston Post Road.

THROUGHOUT THE EARLY stagecoach years, industry shared the road with Levi Pease and company. Wagons along the coast carried raw materials to any of the nine ironworks in Fairfield. Buttons flowed from New Haven, hats from Stonington. Providence produced candles, soap, and enough nails to supply the country. Along the northern branch, Worcester and Leicester made much of the textile machinery used by primitive cotton mills. A corridor of weaponry stretched south along the highway from the first federal armory, in Springfield, to Simeon North's small arms shop in Berlin, Connecticut, then over to Middletown, and finally down to the gun plants in New Haven run by Eli Whitney.

On a meaningful scale, however, manufacturing did not yet exist. For decades following the Revolution northeast America clung to its agrarian roots. A few concerned leaders understood the importance of domestic production—even before the war Ben Franklin had stressed that industry raised real estate values and attracted money to a region— but in general Americans kept their taste for British cloths, and kept growing the farm goods used to barter for them. A booming new connection with the Far East, led in part by John Brown of Providence, solidified this preference for imported items.

It was John Brown's brother Moses who became one of the first enterprising men to grasp that America's economic independence depended on shifting the eyes of investors away from the high seas and onto the mainland. He needed to look no farther than Newport, whose maritime influence had fallen considerably since the war. The town's houses, shops, and trade were in ruin; by 1788 its seaside splendor had already been described by one contemporary traveler as "ancient."

Moses Brown realized that Rhode Island was quickly exhausting its agricultural expansion. The state still had plenty of interior waterways, however—the rivers, streams, and falls often followed by the early highway's course. At the time, English textile producers exploited these natural power sources to turn the heavy machines that spun raw cotton and wool into yarn. This much Americans knew. But they did not know how, and the British throne took measures to ensure they never would. Anyone caught leaving the United Kingdom with the parts, models, even drawings to re-create this machinery—known for its inventor as the Arkwright system—spent a year in prison.

That is not to say no one tried. The highly sought Arkwright system inspired some grand conspiracies, and at one point five American recruiting agents operated out of England. In 1787 a man named Thomas Somers smuggled over some of this textile intelligence. The Massachusetts legislature financed full construction of the plans, but Somers had pilfered an inferior model, and even this he seemed unable to recall in all its intricacy. The close of the 1780s found two thousand machines spinning yarn in America, mostly by primitive hand power. British textile manufactures, meanwhile, were operating 2.5 million water-whizzing spindles.

Knowing that better technology would benefit everyone, most New England mechanics shared their information. So while his brother's ships set sail for the exotic linens of the Far East, Moses Brown weaved along the Old Boston Post Road, consuming every bit of knowledge he could about the American clothing trade. He talked with mechanics at struggling outfits in Worcester, New Haven, and New York. He befriended Thomas Somers and studied his models, despite their inadequacies. He toured the Hartford wool factory owned by Jeremiah Wadsworth, which had furnished the brown suit George Washington wore to his inauguration, in a flourish of patriotism.

In the spring of 1789 Brown purchased the best devices he could find. He hired mechanics and woodworkers. He bought cotton. Eventually he bought a site for his mill on the Pawtucket River, just north of Providence along the Old Boston Post Road.

The challenges facing someone in Brown's position were nearly insurmountable. Without an expert to steady the wobbling spindles or adjust the speed of the pairs of rollers, even the best early textile machines produced only inferior yarn. Meanwhile England deliberately undersold this poor American product; the British were willing to take a loss, Brown wrote, "to break up the Business." He was convinced that only better machinery and a superior machinist could save American textiles. By fall things looked so bleak that Brown, finding the whole enterprise "much more arduous than I expected," handed the reins to his son-in-law, William Almy, and another relative, Smith Brown.

And then, out of the blue, Moses Brown received a letter from New York.

SAMUEL SLATER was born into an English farm family. One day his father was mortally injured falling off a load of hay, and before he died he arranged for a neighbor, Jedediah Strutt, to take on fourteen-year-old Samuel as an apprentice. Strutt preferred one of the elder Slater boys— but it was Samuel, his father insisted, who had a "decided mathematical genius." Strutt acquiesced, and soon Samuel was working beside the man building a cotton factory for his partner, Richard Arkwright.

At twenty-one Slater saw an interesting notice in an English newspaper. The Pennsylvania legislature had awarded someone a handsome sum for building a carding machine—a key component of the Arkwright system. No doubt thinking he could do just as well, if not better, Slater boarded a ship in London in fall of 1789. He passed through customs by presenting himself as the son of a farmer. He kept one incriminating document carefully concealed—his indenture to Strutt would serve as a résumé in America. Right before the ship embarked he left a letter for the post, explaining to his mother what he had done. He arrived in New York in November of 1789, about the time Moses Brown was losing confidence in his cotton affairs.

After a few weeks at the feeble New York Manufacturing Company, Slater was already looking for something more. He had nearly gone to Philadelphia to track down the source of the announcement, when he received a tip from the captain of a New York–to–Providence packet line. Acting on the lead, Slater sent a letter to Brown declaring he could replicate Arkwright's famous machinery. In Brown's frank reply—"we hardly know what to say to thee"—he admitted that his attempt to construct a power spinner had failed. He had little to offer Slater besides what the ambitious immigrant was looking for: the chance to etch his name in history as builder of "the first water-mill in America." In January of 1790 Slater left for Providence.

As the hub of Rhode Island's land and sea transportation routes, Providence was well on its way to becoming the commercial center of southern New England. When Slater arrived it would still be several months before Rhode Island ratified the U.S. Constitution—it finally did, by two votes, after Providence threatened to secede from the state. Going north from Providence, the Old Boston Post Road skirted a swamp in the Moshassuck valley and stayed on high, dry ground. In Pawtucket the road became modern Main Street toward the falls of the Blackstone River. Brown brought Slater this way and left him that first night at the house of a woodworker. Incredulous at fortune's smile, Brown told the employee to grill the young man through the night. In the morning, having passed this mental test, Slater was escorted to the mill.★

Working sixteen-hour days, Slater needed only a few months to re-create most of the Arkwright spinning frame. His aide, the man who had interrogated him, was bound to secrecy; the building was locked; the windows were covered. By spring, Brown had seen enough to lock Slater into an official partnership. The carding machine, which prepares the cotton for the water-powered spindle, took the rest of the year to complete. It has been stated, rather mythically, that the solution to Slater's carding struggles came to him in a dream. In reality he took to the Old Boston Post Road for answers, eliciting the help of Pliny Earle, an accomplished machinist in Leicester, Massachusetts.

When Slater did finish he had created a masterpiece that would become the envy, and the emulation, of textile entrepreneurs across America. In the eighteen months before Slater's machine was finished Brown's company produced some forty-five hundred yards of cotton yarn; after its completion they nearly doubled that in half the time. Slater's mill spun more cotton with seventy-two Arkwright spindles than a competitor did with six hundred thirty-six lesser ones. In his 1791 report

---

★ The site known today as the Old Slater Mill is actually a few hundred yards upstream from the mill Slater visited in 1790. After Slater's initial success an improved mill—the present-day Old Slater Mill—was built, in 1793.

on American manufacturing, Alexander Hamilton, by then Secretary of the Treasury, spoke at length of Pawtucket's "celebrated cotton mill." He called it the country's first and praised its broader impact on domestic production. In a previous draft of the report Hamilton was even more effusive about the mill's "superiority of advantages."

Over the next twenty years industrial knowledge, capital, and workers flung outward from Providence along the Old Boston Post Road. When mechanics left to form their own companies they went north to Attleboro, Massachusetts, and south to Kingston, Rhode Island. From these and other spots they trickled off the old route into Connecticut and beyond, and soon southern New England emerged as the clear manufacturing center of the American cotton world. Of the twenty-seven mills operating in the region by 1809, most had been started by former Almy and Brown employees. When the turnpike movement reached Providence, culminating in new highways to Boston in the early 1800s, the improved roads only enhanced the factory's success. After all, Hamilton had said in his 1791 report that good roads "arc the principal of the means, by which the growth of manufactures is ordinarily promoted."

IN THE YEARS after 1792, as cotton mills expanded at explosive rates, the Napoleonic wars began to alter the complexion of American business. For a while the fighting in Europe enabled neutral American ships to trade with both England and France freely, and profitably. This favorable climate failed to last. By midsummer of 1812 rising tensions once again brought America into war with England, and any seafaring interests still lingering afloat quickly ran aground.

So it became clear to many former merchants what Moses Brown had known for years: for America to remain truly independent, it would have to supply itself with the rudiments of daily life. The dangers of an economy built on foreign trade landed with a crash upon the shores of Boston. The Bay's tight circle of sea merchants had settled into a golden era, but as war approached, even this gilded sphere began to set its speculative gaze inward. By 1811 Patrick Tracy Jackson, who had made a fortune trading with Calcutta and Havana, knew the days of lucrative imports were nearing an end; instead, he wrote in June, "we must endeavor to make the goods at home." When Jackson's brother-in-law, Francis Cabot Lowell, wrote to him from England about the rising value of cotton, in the fall of 1811, Lowell had reached the same conclusion. By that time, Lowell had decided to pirate Britain's prized remaining textile tool before returning to the Bay.

Without question the foundation for a successful clothing industry had landed on American shores with Samuel Slater. But another crown technological jewel kept American textiles from competing on a global scale. Water-powered spinning mills indeed produced high-quality cotton yarn. But the process of weaving this yarn into cloth remained a household task, done slowly and by hand. What Slater's power spindle had been to yarn, the power loom was to finished cloth. This second secret remained trapped across the Atlantic. The English government, which made £1.5 million a year on the invention, intended to keep it there.

So even though Francis Lowell, Boston businessman, informed British customs officials in the early summer of 1812 that he and his family had merely traveled to England to ease his wife's failing health, he surely understood why they rummaged through his belongings. Perhaps the unwitting release of Samuel Slater had heightened the senses of these officials, for they searched Lowell a second time before he left the country. Again they found nothing. When the Lowells were halfway home the War of 1812 broke out officially. A British frigate captured their ship and diverted the family to Nova Scotia. From there Lowell hired a private boat at great cost to reach Boston. No matter what he ended up spending, though, it was a small price to escape Britain's grasp—for the third time in a single trip—with the plans that would take American industry to the next level.

Exactly what Lowell observed on his lengthy trip abroad can only be guessed; he committed just about everything to memory. Just how much time he spent around factories in Manchester and Edinburgh is unknown, but it was extensive enough for him to acquire, within months, the type of complex mechanical knowledge that a decade of mill management had etched into the mind of Samuel Slater. Eventually he met fellow Boston shipping prince Nathan Appleton in Scotland and divulged the full extent of his plan.

Upon reaching Boston, Lowell went immediately to work. By February of 1813 he and P. T. Jackson had received permission, with a few others from the old merchant circle, to start the Boston Manufacturing Company. Holed up in a storeroom-turned-laboratory, Lowell built a wooden model of the power loom—reconstructed into mahogany from wisps of memory. Friends and relatives struggled to understand the shift in lifestyle. "I most sincerely hope this manufactory in which he is engaged may prove lucrative," wrote one of Jackson's sisters after discovering that the partners planned to live at the new mill site. "I had no idea that it was a thing that would decide their future destination."

Come September, Lowell had finished his blueprint. A month later well-known engineer Paul Moody agreed to build the machines. For months Moody constructed the power loom in secret. Not even Appleton, one of the first investors,★ was allowed to see it before its completion.

Finally, on a fall day in 1814, Lowell brought Appleton to view the finished structure. They entered the new brick factory's basement and watched for hours as the waterwheel whirled and purred—taking in the "beautiful movement of this new and wonderful machine," Appleton later recalled, "destined as it evidently was, to change the character of all textile industry." The chosen site had once been a paper mill. It was situated at a point along the Charles River where the falls plunged ten feet. Waltham, Massachusetts, had only a thousand residents then, and much of its income came from nine taverns kept on the Old Boston Post Road, which ran straight through the center of town.

ON MAY 14, 1815, the Boston Manufacturing Company's first load of cotton cloth traveled by wagon from Waltham toward the Bay. The ten-mile trek began at the intersection of the highway and a path that led

---

★More than half of the first stock issue, set at $100,000, was taken among Lowell, Jackson, Appleton, and two of Jackson's brothers.

north from the mill at the river, a path today called Moody Street. Following present-day Main Street eastward, the wagon coasted through the exceptionally level course known as Waltham Plain. Near the end of the plain the wagon hopped across Beaver Brook—so named by the first John Winthrop when he traveled the highway and found several dams along the water.

Continuing east, the wagon crunched atop sandy soil, the Charles River on its right, until it reached Watertown. By 1815 the old highway had evolved enough to offer two main choices into Boston. The first, following the very oldest course, entered Cambridge and ran south on present-day North Harvard Street toward Coolidge Corner and Leverett Pond. The second crossed the Charles before reaching central Cambridge and headed down modern Galen Street, where it curled southeast on Washington Street into Brighton, running straight into Brookline Village, where it merged with the original route.

Once the wagon left Brookline it veered northeast in the direction of today's Fenway region and Harvard Medical School. (At that time the medical school held classes above an apothecary on present-day Washington Street, a bit farther into the city.) The wagon dashed abruptly east, breaking off Huntington Avenue on its way to the Roxbury Crossing. Right about here, near the intersection of modern Roxbury and Centre streets, the wagon passed a conspicuous rock on the side of the road. This was the "parting stone." It marked the point where the Old Boston Post Road's northern route, toward Waltham and eventually Springfield, diverged from its southern branch, toward Providence and the coast.

After crossing the still-thin neck of modern Back Bay the wagon arrived at the only shop in Boston that sold American cloth—the store run by the Bowers family, on modern Washington Street. There, among India cotton, muslin handkerchiefs, silk shawls, and other foreign linens, Mrs. Bowers found room for the Waltham material, and the historic delivery reached an end.

This was the trail, in its broader significance, blazed by the Boston Manufacturing Company for the modern American factory to follow. Lowell's industrial vision went far beyond one lumbering wagon. Never before had all stages of cloth-making—from gathering the raw material to shipping the finished product—mingled beneath a single roof. Each of the Waltham factory's four stories specialized in a particular aspect of cotton production: carding on the first floor, spinning on the second, weaving on the third and fourth. Beneath it all, the ceaseless river drove the wheels that turned the gears that set the business in motion.

Soon the reality of power loom–or–perish swept through northeast America. In 1817 the Boston Manufacturing Company made its investors a stock dividend of seventeen percent. By 1822 three cotton mills were running in Waltham, powered by five hundred workers. "The Waltham manufactory is the largest, and probably, the most prosperous in the United States," declared one of the country's leading newspapers. Francis Lowell did not live to see this success—he died in August of 1817—but P. T. Jackson was already planning the company's expansion north to the city that still bears the Lowell name. At the time of this move the Waltham factories made enough cotton cloth each year to stretch from Boston to New York twice on the old highway, and fall just shy, on the rebound, of the Shrewsbury home where Levi Pease breathed his last.

As the first quarter of the nineteenth century neared a close, American industry had clearly passed its own parting stone, but it left the city of its birth at a critical crossroads. Boston had led the factory charge, but its transportation system was in danger of being surpassed by New York's great link to the West, the Erie Canal. As each day passed, and that monumental project neared completion, the "old" sobriquet attached to Boston's main highway grew less affectionate and more worrisome. New England had sparked the Industrial Revolution with two mathematical minds borrowing English breakthroughs. It would take one more such man to lay the tracks that brought prosperity to the palace of Boston—to make the city a bellwether of transportation instead of just another stop along a forgotten road.

Part II

The Railroad as Highway

The streetcar went up the Post Road, along the Long Island Sound shoreline to the Connecticut border. In Greenwich, Connecticut, they transferred to another car. This took them up through the cities of Stamford, Norwalk and then to Bridgeport, the burial place of Tom Thumb. . . . They stopped for the night in New Haven, Connecticut. . . . The car slowly swung through the narrow streets of Hartford, the clapboard houses of the city seemingly close enough to reach out and touch. Then they were on the outskirts and racing along north to Springfield, Massachusetts. . . . In Springfield they bought bread and cheese and boarded a modern dark green car of the Worcester Electric Street Railway. Tateh realized now that he was going at least as far as Boston.

—*E. L. Doctorow*, Ragtime

A railroad is now regarded as a necessary highway for every community.

—*Henry V. Poor*, Manual of the Railroads of the United States for 1873–74

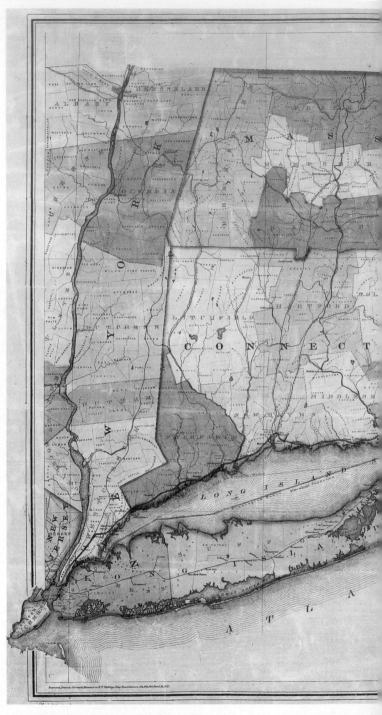

Library of Congress, Geography and Map Division

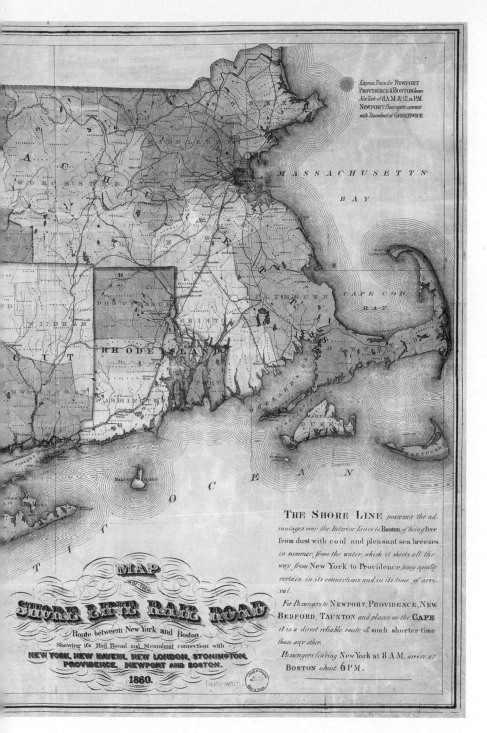

Express Train for NEWPORT
PROVIDENCK & BOSTON leaves
New York at 8 A.M. & 12.15 P.M.
NEWPORT Passengers connect
with Steamboat at GREENWICH

THE SHORE LINE *possesses the advantages over the Interior Lines to* Boston *of being* free from dust *with* cool *and pleasant sea breezes in summer, from the water, which it skirts all the way from* New York *to* Providence, *being equally certain in its connections and in its time of arrival.*

For Passengers to NEWPORT, PROVIDENCE, NEW BEDFORD, TAUNTON *and places on the* CAPE *it is a direct reliable route of much shorter time than any other.*

Passengers leaving New York *at* 8 A.M. *arrive at* BOSTON *about* 6 P.M.

MAP
OF THE
SHORE LINE RAIL ROAD
Route between New York and Boston.
Showing its Rail Road and Steamboat connection with
NEW YORK, NEW HAVEN, NEW LONDON, STONINGTON,
PROVIDENCE, NEWPORT AND BOSTON.
1860.

Shore Line railroad service between New York and Boston,
paralleling the coastal course of the Old Boston Post Road, in 1860

Chapter 7

✥✥✥

The Great Boston–New York Rivalry

O N A LATE- OCTOBER day in 1825 a leading citizen of Boston sat in his print shop at the corner of Congress and State streets, near Faneuil Hall and the Long Wharf, chugging through the New York papers with contempt. He was a scientific thinker with a keen civic sense—a calculating man, whose gears turned for the public good. From his home near Boston Common his likely walk to work had taken him past the corner of Washington and State, terminal of the old highway to Manhattan. Two blocks later Nathan Hale had entered the office of the *Boston Daily Advertiser* and set the day's type. A puff of steam rose to his brain. He felt the pulse of a city at the junction of past and present; he recognized the error of Boston's ways and envisioned the course of its salvation.

In the fall of 1825 the eyes of the nation gazed squarely upon the other end of the old highway, at New York, following a new sort of trail that stretched north along the Hudson River then west from Albany to Utica to Buffalo and the Great Lakes—the trail of the wondrous Erie Canal, freshly carved into the earth. Foreign trade had diminished considerably with the rise of American industry. Domestic production now ruled the day. By bringing New York Harbor within the reach of the expanding Western states, the Erie Canal would make New York the logical center for commercial exchange across the growing country.

111

Boston had been an early industrial leader, but transporting goods by land remained expensive—often prohibitively so. Manhattan's great canal enabled Providence merchants to send three tons of freight to Lake Erie for what it would have cost them to haul a single ton forty-five miles up the turnpike to Boston. Springfield companies funded by Bostonians faced a peculiar dilemma: they could shuffle goods over to New York for half the cost of looping them to the Bay. Passenger travel had surged with the turnpike movement—indeed, more stagecoach lines traveled through the Bay than through anyplace else in the nation—but no network of roads, not even one as heavily trafficked as Boston's, could handle the new influx of industry.

If one believed Levi Lincoln, the governor of Massachusetts, physical roads were nearing obsolescence anyway. Common highways have their advantages, Lincoln declared in 1825, but these advantages are "incalculably" surpassed by "navigable canals." Sixteen years earlier Lincoln's father of the same name, then governor himself, had proclaimed traditional roads the "convenient and unalterable" highways of commerce and industry. Now it seemed that transportation was not founded upon the hard rock of earth after all; rather, it tread more efficiently atop artificial waterways.

Across New England, towns urgently branded the land with their own fluid avenues. New Haven broke ground for a canal that would parallel the Connecticut River. Hartford, as though challenged to a duel, soon announced a project to widen the mighty Connecticut. Each such effort steered the spoils of early-nineteenth-century commerce toward Manhattan. Even Worcester positioned itself favorably, teaming with Providence to dig a canal across the mainland. "Boston, the metropolis formerly of New England, had almost ceased to be the commercial metropolis of her own State," Nathan Hale later recalled.

Soon Boston's anxiety presented as jealousy, and before long it blossomed into full-fledged bitterness. In early 1825, Massachusetts assembled a team to survey the Bay's own canal. By then the emerging rivalry with New York had grown so fierce that Governor Lincoln would hardly address it by name. Instead, he referred only to the enterprising spirit of "a neighboring state" when discussing Boston's leap into action.

Lincoln encouraged the Boston canal's "speedy accomplishment" in June. But on October 27 the survey remained unfinished, and the lead story in Boston newspapers was the Erie Canal's inaugural run. When the boat reached New York a "grand aquatic display" had taken place at City Hall. Afterward Dr. Samuel Latham Mitchill had ceremoniously poured out waters from several sacred rivers—the Ganges, the Nile, the Amazon, the Thames, the Seine; fourteen in all—"as an emblem of our commercial intercourse with all parts of the world." A special invitation had been sent to President John Quincy Adams, the Bay's own son.

Nathan Hale was acutely aware of this entire situation when he finished pressing the *Daily Advertiser* on October 28, 1825. One day earlier he had dutifully recorded New York's celebration, in all its excess splendor. Now he couldn't help but take a shot at Mitchill's theatrics, saying they cast "an air of ridicule" over the entire affair. He composed himself, however, and in the very next column resumed his typical measured tone. He told readers about an emerging form of transportation making great strides in England. Thomas Tredgold's treatise, so important that it was reprinted in America the same year it appeared overseas, had convinced Hale that such a system could spread across Massachusetts for half the price of a canal. "We infer, therefore," he wrote, "that the rail road is far better adapted to the country between Boston and the Connecticut river."

TODAY ANY MENTION of rivalry between New York and Boston elicits an immediate update on the positions of the Yankees and Red Sox in the American League East. In the early nineteenth century, however, the competition between these capitals was over transportation—a game with far greater implications than the contests confined to Fenway Park and Yankee Stadium. Its rosters included powerful state legislators. Its fan base extended to every single person who intended to purchase a commercial good. Its pennant meant nothing less than control of the nation's booming industrial trade.

When Nathan Hale embraced railroads as the Bay's antidote to New York's Erie Canal, the superiority of trains was far from certain. For much of the first half of the nineteenth century Americans remained in the dark about this experimental type of conveyance. Canals made sense; they harnessed the age-old act of shipping and relocated it inland. In contrast, railroads seemed fantastical and frightening. This was the case even before locomotives joined the discussion—early railroad cars were pulled by horses, acting more or less as familiar stagecoaches bound to strips of iron. As one Massachusetts lawmaker put it at the time: "What do we know about railroads? Who ever heard of such a thing?"

What everyone did know was that the means of transport had changed. The completion of the Erie Canal triggered a furious transportation race among America's foremost cities. Almost immediately, Hale later wrote, the unparalleled scope of the 364-mile canal put Boston, Baltimore, and Philadelphia at risk of becoming "provincial towns, dependent for all the principal operations of commerce on the port of New York." Something had to be done, and done fast.

In the end it wasn't done fast, but it was done well. By the summer of 1835, Boston had completed three railroads, making it the first train hub in the world and a transportation model for the growing country to follow. One of these roads, best known as the Boston & Albany railroad,★ loosely followed the old post road west toward Worcester, and then followed it far more closely into Springfield. It quickly became "the most important in New England, and one of the most so in the United States," according to a midcentury Senate report. "This work has probably exerted a wider influence, as the best illustration of what railroads accomplish for the advancement and welfare of a people, than any similar work in the country." Another of these roads followed the old highway's southern branch toward Providence, eventually earning fame, and infamy, as part of the New Haven railroad system.★★

Although stagecoach travel continued to grow through the Civil

---

★The use of ampersands in railroad company names, instead of the word *and,* has been adopted throughout for clarity.

★★The third railroad, the Boston & Lowell, was completed at the same time. Although it didn't follow the Post Road, it had the old highway to thank, in a sense, because the manufacturing success at Waltham had led to the expansion into Lowell that eventually brought the railroad to that city.

War, the highways between New York and Boston took a backseat to these rail lines for the better part of a century. The inadequacy of traditional roads certainly inspired alternative transportation; manufacturers looking to increase their industrial capacity were among the Bay's earliest railroad supporters. But Boston's growing resentment toward Manhattan played as big a part. At one point this competition grew so petty that a Bay State lawmaker moved to change the boundary language in a railroad bill from the "Easterly line of the State of New York" to the "western line of Massachusetts."

These forces ensured only that an alternative mode of transportation would emerge. Its precise form would be for civic leaders to decide. The choice between railroad and canal was not at all clear—Philadelphia authorized a canal to the Ohio River in early 1826 that was quickly outmoded—and Boston nearly chose wrong. It took the steady push of a newspaper editor who just happened to possess a nose for engineering to conduct these inspirations onto the proper track.

The printer Nathan Hale will never be as well known as his patriot uncle of the same name, but by some measures of success in life he probably should be. For decades Hale edited Boston's first daily paper, when papers were still the efforts of solitary men, and when such men still carried on their shoulders the conscience of the public. By convincing Bostonians to embrace a railroad over a canal he not only made the city the first true railroad hub in the world, he averted a potential disaster of historic proportions. He was president of one of these railroads, the Boston & Worcester, for nearly twenty years. When his railroad work was done he shifted attention to another civic problem, and in time Boston stopped drinking from wells and had a system of pure water.

Giving life over to a greater cause, it seems, was the burden of being a Nathan Hale. The railroad Nathan Hale was named for the patriot Nathan Hale, who had been hanged as a spy by the British in 1776. Growing up, the patriot Nathan had been close to his brother, Enoch, the railroad Nathan's father. ("You complain of my neglecting you," the patriot Nathan wrote to Enoch in early June 1776, from the battlefields. "It is not, I acknowledge, wholly without Reason.") So pained was

Enoch by his brother's death that he rarely gave voice to the memory of the fallen, except through the name of his first son.

The earliest indication of this son's keen social interest was a thesis he wrote at Williams College, in 1804, on civilization's recent advances. In it Nathan Hale made clear that intellectual progress must be encouraged, however unfamiliar its form. Such an effort meant denying the common belief that technology corrupted morals, and embracing science. He bade farewell to the days when lightning was considered the magical "anger of deity," and instead sought to harness the earth's natural powers. He praised new observations on the solar system, new understandings in electricity, new applications of chemistry to medicine. In short, he exalted man's ability to stand alone at the edge of the unknown, and conquer it for the public good.

After college Hale taught math at Exeter Academy, in New Hampshire, and several years later he left for Boston to study law. There he edited a journal on politics and history—the spark, perhaps, for his future in letters, though his father had a lasting interest in spelling and language. At some point Hale joined the *Boston Weekly Messenger,* and in spring of 1814, near age thirty, he bought the *Daily Advertiser*. At the time it was the only daily newspaper in Boston. "Newspapers ought to be illuminators of the public mind," he informed his readers upon taking over; as such, "the office of an editor is one of great importance and responsibility."

In his middle years Hale combed his hair to one side and let his sideburns curl well below his ears. These bushy hedges framed his solemn eyes with a touch of whimsy. A large nose peeked above thin lips and a round chin. Behind a rather broad forehead he possessed "the greatest amount of valuable knowledge, endowed with the largest capacity of usefulness," said the statesman Edward Everett many years later. Feeding this endowment were the world's newspapers, used to populate the *Advertiser*'s own foreign news section, and the world's books, sent to him in blind hope of an influential review. In this manner he would have learned of George Stephenson's work with locomotives; England's construction of the Stockton & Darlington rail line; and treatises on railway transportation by the likes of Nicholas Wood and, of course, Thomas

Tredgold. All of these texts expanded Hale's "capacity of usefulness" in the middle 1820s.

In this period it was typical for Boston families to display a decanter of wine in their main parlor, ready and waiting to quench a thirst. In the Hale household, propped beside this warm greeting, was a model railroad, ready and waiting to quench a growing curiosity. (In another room, instead of playing with toys, the Hale children built their own locomotives out of pulleys and rollers and whalebone springs.) Hale explained to company the wild potential of this peculiar contraption. As Nathan Hale's son, future author E. E. Hale, later recalled, these guests responded with faces that implied "it was a pity that so intelligent a man as he should go crazy."

THE ERIE CANAL celebration in fall of 1825 touched off a mad rush of railroad propaganda by Nathan Hale in the *Boston Daily Advertiser*. In early November, as if to contrast Manhattan's spectacle, Hale plastered his front page with furious details of the formal opening in England of the Stockton & Darlington railway. This line's basic function was to move coal from Darlington twelve miles to Stockton's port along the Tees river—similar in purpose, if not quite in scale, to sending goods from Boston Harbor to the Connecticut River.

At the Stockton & Darlington's maiden run, some twenty wagons carrying workmen, coal, and hundreds of passengers were pulled by a locomotive called simply *Locomotion,* as though its inventors had exhausted their genius on its creation. When the engine first surged, those in attendance "fled in a fright," fearing an explosion. By the end, though, some fifty thousand onlookers witnessed the "steam horse" pass from town to town. The crowds grew so dense that one man, pressed onto the track by the swollen masses, lost a foot. All told, George Stephenson's train towed eighty tons at a speed averaging nearly ten miles per hour.

None of this information appeared in time to stop Boston's own canal survey. The engineer, Loammi Baldwin, had worked at full speed through the fall and had finished his report by the time Levi Lincoln addressed the state legislature in January of 1826. "The interests of the Commonwealth require its execution," Governor Lincoln declared of Boston's canal plans immediately upon reading the report.

A few details from Baldwin's incredible survey are worth a closer look—not to cast Lincoln's hearty approval as foolish, but rather as a reflection of just how desperate Boston's situation had become. The canal proposal contained two basic parts. The first described a potential route to the Connecticut River. This leg alone would cost three million dollars. The ending balance of the state's treasury in 1826 was $83,000.

Undeterred, the survey roared. West of the Connecticut the new waterway would tap the Hudson, giving the Bay access to the Erie Canal. To get there, Baldwin recommended boring four miles through the Hoosac Mountain. Such a task, if it had been technically possible at the time, was not what one might call easy. A contemporary engineer, consulted by Baldwin for his opinion of the Hoosac project, said that his own men had drilled through a mountain around the clock for eight months—and had successfully forged a tunnel all of four hundred feet long. ("The contractor," wrote the engineer, "made a good living profit.")

Still, Baldwin recommended the Hoosac tunnel with "no hesitation." The final bill for Boston's canal came to $6,023,172. "There must be a FIRST STEP, and this, as in all other momentous undertakings, is the most difficult, but at the same time, the most important and conclusive," Baldwin urged. "The work shall go gloriously on, until every section of the state is traversed by these new *Highways,* of intercommunication." His parting shot cut to the quick: Anyone still unconvinced by the greatness of these new "highways" need only look at New York and the Erie Canal.

Together Baldwin's report and Lincoln's endorsement were supposed to sweep the state into action. The Massachusetts legislature moved slowly, however, even when it had cause, will, and strength to act at once. It is not that they lacked confidence in Lincoln; he was elected by an overwhelming majority, and would hold the position for years. Perhaps the price tag was simply too high. Or maybe the idea of literally moving mountains in response to pressures from Manhattan was too great a blow to pride. "Those people, in the little seaport of

Boston," E. E. Hale later wrote, "lived and moved as if they were people of the most important city of the world."

Whatever the case, Nathan Hale took advantage of the delay. He hammered into the public mind the need for a railroad survey every bit as thorough as the canal report. A week after Lincoln's legislative address Hale printed a letter, ostensibly submitted by a reader, wondering whether the Stockton & Darlington railroad might offer a better model by which Boston could avert the "evil" of goods going to New York. Hale's editorial response seems intentionally coy: We cannot know for sure, he wrote, because the government has not funded a railroad study.

By summer a three-man railroad committee took up Hale's cause in the legislature. The trio feverishly collected information in support of a railroad, while Governor Lincoln called canals "preferable" to railroads, "even if they cost a bit more." That fall the railroad advocates got the break they needed. Thomas Perkins, a shipping magnate shifting his wealth into industry, had financed a tiny railroad to transport granite around the Bay. The granite project was hardly a precursor to New England's future railroad empire: The entire length of the road ran only three miles, and the cars were pulled by a single horse.* The system worked, however, and railroad advocates could now point to a model of success—in Boston's own backyard, no less.

By the time Governor Lincoln addressed the state at the start of 1827 his tone was too urgent to play favorites. Improved transportation was now a "pressing consequence," he said. Whatever mode the legislators ultimately preferred, they should prefer as soon as possible. "A neighboring State is alive to the subject of internal improvements," a group of concerned citizens told the government around this time. "And shall Massachusetts, whose Revolutionary lustre is equal to that of the brightest star in the constellation of liberty, be exceeded in the race of public utility?"

The day after Lincoln's address, Hale published the first of what became a series of articles—and, eventually, a separately published book

---

*The granite railroad from Quincy to Charlestown, Mass., is often considered the first in America to demonstrate the working principles of railroad technology.

of *Remarks*—detailing the findings of the three-man railroad commit-tee. The following month the state's House of Representatives approved the idea of a full railroad investigation. When the Senate demurred, the House sprang to life, distributing three hundred copies of Hale's *Remarks*. Two days later the Senate agreed to the proposition. By June complete railroad surveys had been authorized southward to Provi-dence and westward to the Connecticut River, following the general lines of the old post road.

IN THE EARLY days of 1827, as the Massachusetts legislature debated the railroad idea, Nathan Hale received a thank-you note from Gover-nor Levi Lincoln. He had read Hale's collection of essays on the railroad. "It is with great sincerity I add that my own opinions have been much corrected and informed by their perusal," wrote the governor. "They present . . . a better practical illustration of the subjects, in reference to our local situation and interests, than I have elsewhere met with, and the public cannot fail to derive great benefit from your labors." The short letter marked a shift in official position—away from New York's shadow, and toward the light of Boston's own mind.

Hale's *Remarks* are as convincing as Baldwin's report was flimsy. At times the mathematics Hale employs are overwhelming—he may have intellectually bullied some legislators into following his lead—but some of Hale's more digestible calculations bear repeating. The physics of rail travel eliminate all but one pound for every two hundred carried, he wrote. As in lifting weight with a pulley, the effort exerted during rail carriage is little compared to what it otherwise would have been. In practical terms, a single horse* would be able to transport on a railroad what a dozen did on turnpikes and highways.

For the sake of estimating savings, Hale supposed the railroad would follow the northern route of the old highway toward Worces-ter and Springfield. The Boston Manufacturing Company in Waltham

---

*Despite being well versed in locomotive technology, Hale based his work in *Remarks* on a railroad drawn by horses, so as not to frighten potential advocates the way the British crowd had "fled in fright" at the steam engine named *Locomotion*.

was still along this route, and it alone transported twelve hundred tons a year, he estimated. Another six thousand tons came from Springfield's industry. By lowering transportation costs all the way to the Connecticut River, Boston might stop goods from heading toward New York and "bring back to this city the business of those factories, which otherwise has left us forever." Canals also froze up in winter, so by choosing a railroad Boston could turn back the clock on "forever" by several months a year.

The railroad's most glaring advantage was that of passenger travel, something canals did not offer. In 1827, Hale wrote, a stagecoach carried a person from Boston to Springfield for about six dollars. It left at two in the morning and arrived by eight at night. The railroad could make the same trip in half the time while carrying forty passengers, with baggage, for $1.70 each. That price included the railroad's profit.

The bottom line was that a railroad track from Boston to the Connecticut River would cost just about one million dollars—one-third the cost of Baldwin's canal to the same point. The cheaper price and greater speed at which the railroad could whisk both people and property "will be not merely a convenience," wrote Hale, "but will produce an entire revolution in the business of this part of the country."

Not everyone was as thoroughly converted as Governor Lincoln. The rival editor of the *Boston Courier* called a railroad to the Connecticut River "as useless as a railroad from Boston to the Moon." A letter Hale received about this time illustrates the extent of the public's misunderstanding. The writer offered Hale a modest suggestion: a system by which a horse, running in place atop a conveyor belt, would propel the train at four times the animal's speed. "The grand principle is, the horse rides himself," wrote the man. The writer supported his point with a crude drawing of a horse standing atop train wheels twice its size—ready to usher Boston into the industrial age. Such was the novelty of Hale's proposed technology; such was his burden.

To combat these misconceptions Hale and his growing flock of supporters did whatever they could to bolster public understanding. With the help of Thomas Perkins, Hale opened a Railway Exhibition permanently on display to the public. When necessary he even withheld facts that could have damaged his case. After Peter Cooper unveiled his loco-motive, for instance, Hale praised the *Tom Thumb* steam engine in the *Daily Advertiser*—without mentioning that it had broken down during a race against a horse-drawn train, and lost.

By the time the official railroad surveys were completed, in June 1828, the situation was clear. The Erie Canal was handling so much traf-fic that New York's governor soon proposed a second one, running par-allel. Massachusetts could watch others prosper from the Erie's lucrative course, or it could build a railroad to reroute much of this business to the Bay. As surely as he had endorsed the "speedy accomplishment" of a canal three years earlier, Governor Lincoln now hoped that a railroad going west from Boston would be "speedily commenced."

The results of the survey, a two-part proposal on rail routes to Providence and the Connecticut River, convinced nearly everyone in the legislature as well. It estimated the thousands of freight tons, and tens of thousands of passengers, likely to use the system. It predicted social benefits from a "freer intercourse" throughout the state—so that the same solidarity John Adams had once found in a Shrewsbury tavern as a result of more efficient mail would now exist even more remotely. It showed that the entire rail line to Albany could be completed for just over three million dollars, or half the price of the disastrous canal.

Then, as though the board's survey had actually been a mystery novel the whole time, the report revealed that the state should pay for the undertaking. And as quickly as they had been converted the state's politicians were lost.

Soon the fabric of the entire commonwealth began to unravel. Towns on the Atlantic coast wondered what they had to gain from a railroad going inland. Stage lines and innkeepers mourned the loss of their livelihoods. One newspaper questioned how the state could justify spending the people's money for a project similar to turnpikes, when those had utterly failed.

The public debates raged for months on end. In January of 1830 the legislature reconvened for a final vote on the railroad's future. Argu-ments rattled the walls of the statehouse for weeks. One statesman's comments properly summarized the proceedings: "If the rail-road don't go to my house," he said, "it shall not go at all." Sure enough, the state-funded railroad project lost the vote. By that time the decision surely did not come as a surprise to Nathan Hale, but it remained a disappointment. When a representative from Ipswich introduced a bill for a state-funded railroad passing through *his* town, just days later, Hale's disappointment likely grew into anger. And when someone suggested the following month that perhaps the legislature had been too quick to dismiss canals, Hale began to feel "hopeless." Another representative announced that if Boston capitalists thought the railroad was so great, they should build one themselves.

In the end Hale did just that. Instead of a massive, statewide railroad system, Hale settled on a simple track from Boston to Worcester that could be built for far less money, and in the process prove railroads as a sound public investment. He kept interest piqued through his newspaper: the *Daily Advertiser* publicized the results of the celebrated Rainhill competition, in which George Stephenson's winning locomotive averaged nearly fourteen miles per hour over sixty miles. Finally Hale organized a group of investors and led the march for private incorporation. Nathan Appleton, P. T. Jackson, Thomas Perkins, and many others involved in manufacturing outside Boston as far off as Springfield—all these names and more like them officially formed the Boston & Worcester and Boston & Providence railroad companies in June of 1831.

It was summertime, and sunlight would wink off the gilded pinecone perched atop the statehouse cupola, onto the cobblestone streets of Beacon Hill. This had been Hale's own little railroad track: from the *Daily Advertiser* office to the new statehouse and back, past the old statehouse at the foot of the old post road. The people of these streets had always been set in their ways—they had continued to call the old highway "main street," long after its name became Washington Street, E. E. Hale later recalled. But since the days when John Oldham introduced the Bay to that same route, they had also known a good thing when they were shown it, and now a new sort of highway, a set of Boston Roads, would once again lead them west.

Within two weeks the entire Boston & Worcester stock—all $600,000—was subscribed. In August Hale was named president.

IN MIDSUMMER OF 1835 the first train crossed the Worcester sight line at half past ten in the morning. They had tried to make the full trip the day before, the people running the Boston & Worcester railroad, but a forward axle had broken down en route. A mechanic worked all night to repair it, and by morning it was running smoothly. It was just as well that the complete run had been delayed until the next day, for now two things could be celebrated in Boston on July Fourth.

For the rest of the holiday afternoon all four of the Boston & Worcester railroad company's eleven-car trains made two round-trips each, without a hitch. Three of the engines had been special-ordered from George Stephenson and shipped overseas. By this time he had invented more colorful names, and so the *Rocket,* the *Comet,* and the *Meteor* all shot out from the train depot near Washington Street. At some point it might have occurred to Hale that such machines were better suited, as the *Boston Courier* editor had so smugly suggested years before, for a track leading to the moon. A fourth locomotive, built right in the city, was called the *Yankee.*

As the trains entered Worcester, people from neighboring towns lined the track for miles just to catch a peek at the hissing steam engine. (At least one horse bucked wildly as the train passed by, though there is no evidence, as farmers had feared, that the steam engines frightened their hens out of laying eggs.) The railcars themselves were less of a spectacle. They seemed rather ordinary, with good reason. They had been built by Osgood Bradley, a carriage maker in Worcester, and had many of the features travelers had come to expect in a stagecoach, except that their rounded bodies looked unnatural atop the flat gear frame—a bit like an ark out of water.

During the ride conductors walked along planks outside the cars. They gripped an iron bar mounted above for support, collected fares, occasionally ducked sparks. In all, some fifteen hundred passengers rode that day. To many it must have seemed unreal—must have felt, in the words of one man upon his first ride into Boston, "like a dream."

But to Hale and his railroad colleagues, by then, it would have felt routine. They were on to bigger things than the forty-four-mile Boston & Worcester line. A few days earlier a group of important railroad figures had convened, in Worcester, to discuss a survey for continuing the road west. Once built, these tracks would nearly trace the course of the old highway as it approached Springfield. From there they would extend south to Hartford on a route whose survey had already been completed. Famed carriage maker James Brewster announced that his Hartford & New Haven line would soon be finished too, covering the rest of the Connecticut River. And after the Boston railroad reached New Haven, the newspapers surmised, "is it not absolutely certain it will be extended to the city of New-York?"

In the minds of those concerned with transportation along the routes of the old post road, it absolutely was. The directors of the Boston & Providence railroad, the one leading south from Boston, declared their "true policy" to be not of moving people and goods from the Bay to Rhode Island, but "of effectuating the most safe, cheap, and expeditious transit of persons and merchandize between Boston and New York."

And so the goal of everyone involved in Boston's railroad system at the time was clear: to move Manhattan toward the Bay along the highways of the future. One by one, over the next several years, the pieces to this puzzle were placed atop the earth. By the very end of 1844 Boston and New Haven were connected by rail, so that only one piece remained—leading from New Haven to New York—for the ultimate goal to be achieved.

Boston's major lead in the railroad race had not escaped the notice of those at the other end of the old highway. At one point in the early 1840s the Bay State had built twelve hundred miles of railroad to New York's twelve—and those drawn much of the way by horse. Soon New York businessmen began to worry, in terms the Bostonians would have found familiar, that "the movement of our enterprising neighbors" would tip the scale of trade back toward the Bay. "If New York has any thing to fear from rivalry," one man wrote of Boston's great railroad builders, pushing their projects ever westward along the line of the old highway, "it is from such men as these."

Chapter 8

Toward Union

ABEL T. ANDERSON met Samuel Sparks about a quarter mile north of Union Square, in New York City, on an autumn day in 1838. Here, at present-day Twenty-third Street and Fifth Avenue, the city's two main highways split violently, as though deterred by the structure before them. Upon a converted military parade stood a stone wall, seventeen feet high, surrounding a juvenile reformation center called the House of Refuge. At this abrupt divide Bloomingdale Road forked up the west side of the island—following the path of modern Broadway—and the Boston Road veered up the east. Anderson and Sparks turned east.

Together the two men made up the Street Committee of the city's Board of Assistant Aldermen. They walked through the grounds that, about a decade later, would open to the public in the more pleasant form of Madison Square Park. When they neared present-day Thirty-first Street and Lexington Avenue they walked straighter north a ways, perhaps another mile and a half up Third Avenue, though by that time they had probably reached a decision. They had come out that day to investigate a potential road closure, Anderson and Sparks, and on November 12 they filed their official Street Committee report. With that, the brief moment in history had passed, when the Boston Road was almost Broadway.

Exactly why Broadway and not the Boston Road became Manhattan's eminent thoroughfare is a bit of an unsolved mystery. Certainly Boston Road was the more compelling candidate up through the early part of the nineteenth century. During the colonial period, the Revolution, and the younger years of the new nation, the "High Road to Boston," as it was often called, swung along modern Park Row and Bowery Lane before continuing northbound—the only road to traverse the island in its entirety, from tip to top.

Today that distinction belongs to Broadway, but the precise moment for this transfer of power is difficult to place. The shift could not have occurred before 1795, according to city historian I. N. Phelps Stokes. In his seminal, six-volume history of Manhattan, Stokes marks that year as the date when Broadway's precursor, the Bloomingdale Road, was extended to meet the Boston Road, in Harlem Heights, as it climbed the island. John Randel, surveyor of the city's modern grid, recalled that as late as 1809 the Boston Road via Bowery Lane—and not a route via Bloomingdale—was considered "the principal road leading out of the city." A popular New York City writer from this era agreed. Felix Oldboy, who published "roadside rambles" for city newspapers under the name John Flavel Mines, went so far as to call Broadway "in reality an accident." "Originally it was supposed that the city's main artery of travel would . . . follow the old Boston Road," Oldboy wrote. "In point of fact, provision was made to that end."

Exactly what "provision" Oldboy meant is unclear, but quite likely his reference dated back to the spring of 1807—where any full examination of the Boston Road versus Broadway question must begin. At that time most of the city's ninety-six thousand residents lived well below modern Fourteenth Street. But the Common Council, New York City's municipal body, foresaw the day when the citizens of Manhattan would creep ever northward. So on April 3 the council authorized three street commissioners to survey and plan out nearly all of the island. (They felt no need to go north of One Hundred Fifty-fifth Street—certain that such a remote region would remain uninhabited "for centuries to come.")

The commission was a formidable one. Simeon De Witt had been George Washington's geographer-in-chief during the Revolution, and later became New York's state surveyor. Gouverneur Morris had engi-

*Bernard Ratzer's map of lower Manhattan, c. 1769, shows the island's
main highway—identified as the "Road to Boston"—as well as
"Broad Way," then unfinished.*

neered more complicated documents than a city outline; he had helped to frame, and later signed, the United States Constitution. The third commissioner, John Rutherford, seemed to have his preference—he lived at 219 Broadway—but as a group the commissioners appeared to favor the Boston Road: Their office was located right on the old highway, at present-day East Seventy-seventh Street.

The survey of Manhattan island commenced in two phases. The first was completed by 1811. It might have been finished earlier if John Randel, the surveyor appointed by the commissioners, had not been arrested so frequently during the course of his work for trespassing. (On March 24, 1809, the city finally passed a law permitting Randel to trespass upon and even damage property, if necessary.) In the end, Randel and the commissioners famously diced Manhattan into a checkerboard of east-west streets and north-south avenues. They reasoned that "strait sided, and right angled houses are the most cheap to build, and the most convenient to live in."

Their general layout differs little from the city's present-day look, with the notable omission of Central Park, which was designed decades later and officially completed in 1873. The commissioners did not care much for parkland. The Hudson and East rivers supplied residents with plenty of nature—made the island "in regard to health and pleasure . . . peculiarly felicitious," they believed. The commissioners did set aside one large green area, however. They reserved space for a 239-acre military training ground, spanning Third to Seventh avenues, and Twenty-third to Thirty-fourth streets, which they called the Parade.

The map that accompanied this original plan for Manhattan offers a striking indication of Broadway's mortality. At Tenth Street the commissioners intended to continue Broadway straight until it met the Parade at Twenty-third Street, between Third and Fourth avenues. There and then, Broadway would unceremoniously cease to exist. The street "destined to be trodden by more people than ever migrated through any other avenue of travel on the globe," as Oldboy put it, was, in the minds of the men who designed New York City's streets, destined to be swept neatly beneath the Parade's green rug, and forgotten forever.

Had things ended there, Broadway's destiny might have been

sealed, and the Boston Road's name might have endured. But the commissioners embarked on a second, more rigorous phase of the survey,
which took another decade to complete. It was during this second act
that Broadway's legacy gained new life.

Before considering this revival further, it's necessary to point out
the historical relationship between Broadway and the Bloomingdale
Road. Although Bloomingdale is generally considered Broadway's predecessor, the two roads began as distinct entities. Bloomingdale, a winding Native path, curled up the island's west side through the region of
that name, more or less today's Upper West Side; Broadway, straight and
precisely landscaped, toddled uptown from the southern tip of the island
in tiny steps, over many years. It wasn't until the nineteenth century that
any thought was given to connecting brief Broadway with the longer
road to Bloomingdale. For decades, such a thought wouldn't have made
sense. Toward 1810 Broadway ran only two miles total, barely reaching modern Tenth Street. Only a little more than a mile of this meager runway was paved. Along the unfinished portion "there were only a
few scattered buildings," John Randel later recalled. The Boston Road,
meanwhile, was populated through modern Houston Street—a half
mile farther uptown.

Had the first plan for Manhattan remained intact, Broadway would
have ended at the vast Parade, separated from where Bloomingdale
Road began its run up the island. But the commissioners, clearly no
friends of parkland, evidently reconsidered their vast apportionment for
the Parade during the survey's second phase, for in April of 1814 its estimated size slimmed significantly. The shrinkage left no place for Broadway to cleanly disappear at Twenty-third Street, so the commissioners
pulled it back to Tenth Street.

Though Broadway, in Randel's words, was still "made to terminate"
there, at Tenth, the change had created some complications to the grid.
At Tenth Street the straight Broadway and the looping Bowery began to
converge. Instead of allowing these roads to collide, the commissioners
covered their point of union—and so Union Square was born. More
important was the name they chose for the quarter-mile stretch leading
from Union Square to the Parade: Bloomingdale Road.

This had not always been the case. Earlier maps clearly considered this same stretch the Boston Road. In the late-eighteenth-century maps drawn by Bernard Ratzer, widely regarded as Manhattan's most complete early maps, the "Road to Bloomingdale" only appears north of the Parade region, or modern Madison Square Park. In Ratzer's 1769 map, everything south of this point was labeled the "Road to Boston." (See pp. 128–29.) By granting the name of Bloomingdale to this stretch from Union Square to the Parade, the commissioners had shifted Bloomingdale's influence farther south, so that it touched Broadway. Simply put, the move left open the possibility of combining the two roads into a single avenue with a single name.

While the commissioners fiddled with downtown Manhattan's configuration, some of their uptown changes also diminished the Boston Road's significance. The new grid enabled a traveler to take Third Avenue straight north from about modern Cooper Union, at the Two Mile stone, all the way to the Harlem Bridge. Across the bridge travelers could connect onto present-day Boston Road, in the Bronx, toward New England. Before long this gateway to Manhattan was the most traveled entrance into the city. In 1822, a year after Randel's map was published, new milestones were placed along Third Avenue. By early 1830 "the increasing Travel on the Third Avenue" demanded it be kept in better condition. So the Common Council recommended a new method of street maintenance, known as the McAdam plan. Third Avenue would become the first substantially macadamized road in the city, and soon, in the words of *Scribner's Monthly* magazine, it was "the finest drive on Manhattan Island." In spirit, purpose—everything but name— Third Avenue had become the new Boston Road.

All these factors, taken together, signaled a changing of the guard from Boston Road to Broadway, and if a precise date of closure must be chosen, it would have to be the final day of 1838. On December 31 the Board of Aldermen concurred with the opinion of Abel Anderson and Samuel Sparks, who had recommended closing the Boston Road south of Thirty-first Street. "This portion of the road," Anderson and Sparks wrote, was "no longer necessary."

Two months later the board of assistants received a modest petition.

After considering the request the board referred it to the Street Committee for further investigation. The petitioners thought it made sense "to change the name of the Bloomingdale road to the name of Broadway."

Three months later, the House of Refuge, in a sign interpretable as either approval or disgust, burned to the ground.

AS BROADWAY REPLACED the Boston Road in Manhattan toward the middle of the nineteenth century, the railroad was busy replacing it on the full route to Boston up to the Civil War. For nearly a century after Nathan Hale's successful railroad scheme—until the firm establishment of the automobile sparked a rejuvenated highway effort—rails dominated transportation between New York and Boston. They even came to be seen as the new highways: "The first substitutes for earth roads were canals," wrote Henry V. Poor, America's foremost railroad editor, in 1869. "The mode finally adopted was the *railway*."

Between New York and Boston these substitute highways paralleled the Boston Road—at first favoring the northern branch through the mainland, then later the course along the coast. In some places the railroad tracks fell a few miles from the old highway; elsewhere, particularly along the sound, they often overlapped. Following the development of these tracks can get tricky. They evolved not all at once but piece by piece, and though they typically took the name of their destinations, the unification or extension of a line occasionally caused confusion. The New York, Providence & Boston railroad, for example, began in Stonington, and for years the railroad between Worcester and Springfield was called the Western. But once again, suffice it to say that in spirit, purpose—everything but name—the railroad had become the new Boston Road.

For starters, the old highway influenced the course of early railroads in several ways. Engineers and railroad company leaders based their passenger and freight estimates on the people and goods traveling certain stagecoach corridors. The ability to acquire right-of-way beside an established road often determined the line a rail took. When investors sought to place rails where few major roads existed, they often found that sharp curves and heavy grades greatly raised the price of the project.

Some surveys were more direct in their homage; one segment of the Boston & Providence railroad, for instance, was intentionally made to follow the direction of the "old Post Road."

Before long, railroads also assumed the title of "post roads." Though the postmaster general initially forbade Nathan Hale to transport his newspaper on his railroad, Congress declared all railroads official mail routes in July of 1838. One of the first to suggest this shift was Boston postmaster O. B. Brown, who wanted rails to carry the mail between Philadelphia and New York because this slow stretch was delaying messages intended for his city. Right before the Civil War the post office experimented with night trains between New York and Boston. The letters traveled between the capitals in just nine hours. The following year the department adopted the change across the board.

The speed at which rails moved the mail quickly altered the entire nature of communication—particularly after 1845, when the post office drastically reduced its postage rates. Up to that time newspapers had been cheap to send, but personal letters relatively expensive. The difference was so striking that some people, instead of sending a letter, sent a newspaper with certain words crossed out to convey a new meaning. In one case a New Yorker sent a newspaper to John Garigo Smith of Boston: the middle name was actually an acronym for "goods all received in good order."

By 1851 rates were slashed even more. Personal letters, as opposed to business correspondence, now became the post office's primary purpose. Five cents sent a single letter up to three thousand miles, and this postage was discounted to three cents if prepaid—a practice that Congress encouraged by simultaneously approving the mint of three-cent coins. It was not until 1857, however, that prepaid postage was absolutely required, in the form of stamps. The very first of these displayed the heads of Benjamin Franklin on the five-cent stamp and George Washington on the ten.*

The days of taverns doubling as post offices were done. New head-

---

*This first series appeared in 1847, though prepayment by stamps was not mandatory for another decade.

quarters were built, specially designed to handle the rising patronage. Mailboxes appeared on the streets of Boston and New York by the 1850s. Early ones took the form of spheres built into streetlamps, as though the pole had swallowed a balloon and got it lodged in the throat. Before the Civil War had ended, home delivery had begun in the country's largest cities. Soon after the war's end, postal employees rode in customized railway mail cars, sorting letters on the move and accelerating the entire system of exchange.

Cities themselves were proliferating at pace. Populations spiked all along the railroad's course. In 1840, before many railroad lines had been completed, only nine towns in southern New England had a population over ten thousand. By the Civil War twenty-six towns had reached this point, with seven of the top nine populations appearing directly on the old highway.

Places where the train stopped felt an additional boost. As one of the first railroad depots, Stonington, Connecticut, grew 72 percent between 1830 and the Civil War. Stamford and Norwalk, both stops on the New York & New Haven, rose 104 and 96 percent, respectively, from 1840 to 1860—vastly exceeding even Connecticut's general population rate increase for the period.

Of course, those towns falling off the railroad's course experienced a reversal of fortune. Levi Pease's old home of Shrewsbury, on the old highway but not the railroad, grew only 11 percent in the three decades before the Civil War. Westborough, meanwhile, somewhat equidistant to Boston and a stop on the Boston & Worcester, soared 103 percent during the same period. Middletown, Connecticut, a primary Boston Road town but only a branch on the railroad, grew 20 percent from 1840 to 1860, while Meriden, a branch on the Boston Road but now a primary railroad town, exploded some 300 percent.

Such population shifts occurred across the growing country. Rail depots attracted manufacturers in need of freight access. Manufacturers attracted immigrants and a laboring class in need of work. As industrial production rose, markets expanded along the railroad line. Cities swelled in size and wealth, and the early cycle of urban centralization emerged. As downtown districts developed and, over time, overdeveloped, the wealthier classes, who had typically lived in the center of the action, sought more space toward the outskirts. When the New York & Harlem first left City Hall, in 1832, one newspaper said the railroad "will make Harlem the suburbs of New-York." During that decade New York's suburban population increased 130 percent, and Boston's 85 percent. These shifts in the dynamics of urban living often left pockets of poverty surrounding a downtown factory district, which spurred only more outward movement by those with means.

The idea of daily suburban commuting did not take off in earnest until after the Civil War, but its roots were clear as early as the 1840s in New York and Boston. Major railroads offered monthly commuter fares, but big railroads typically carried commuters at a loss because their rates were designed for longer distances. So intracity, horse-drawn rail lines cropped up to serve particular neighborhoods. The Third Avenue railroad, chartered in 1853, ran up through the Bowery to Third Avenue toward the Harlem Bridge "every four minutes from 6 a.m. to 8 p.m."—all for six cents a ride. Within three years a commuter village was building around Thirtieth Street, as a result. A similar line in Boston, called the Metropolitan, serviced Washington Street—and so the precursors of modern city transit systems stretched along the Boston Road.

In these ways, life transformed along the new highway just as the new highway itself had transformed from the old. The scale had changed, however. Quaint taverns, unable to accommodate all comers, swelled into hotels. Stagecoach lines, now too slow for long distances, became mere taxi services, shuttling railroad riders to and from each Union Station. Telegram wires, representing the very latest and fastest form of communication, stretched from town to town beside the railroad tracks. Social strata mingled unlike ever before. "The rich and the poor, the educated and the ignorant, the polite and the vulgar, all herd together in this modern improvement in travelling," wrote one early passenger on the Boston & Providence. The evolution of travel from rider to stagecoach had been a clear but modest progression. The leap from carriage to rail now pushed civilization toward unimagined levels of fluency.

The northern route of the railroad between New York and Boston had been finished for a decade when, in the final days of 1858, the rail line along the coast was completed. By the time this last piece was laid, the nation had reached the verge of Civil War. It came just in time too, this full Boston Road track, as it would soon play a pivotal role in the campaign of the man who would bring the country back together. But first it had to survive two early disasters that nearly crushed the railroad before it left the proverbial station.

A LIGHT RAIN sprinkled the New York & New Haven tracks the morning of Friday, May 6, 1853. In Manhattan, on Canal Street, a couple hundred people filed into the railroad depot just before eight o'clock. Many of the travelers were doctors heading home from the sixth annual meeting of the American Medical Association: Dr. Beech to Bridgeport, Dr. Welch to Hartford, Dr. Smith to Springfield, and several others all the way to Boston. The rest were a typical assembly of strangers: Thomas Hicks the artist; his companion, Miss King; the Parker baby, headed to its parents in Springfield, in the care of an aunt; Thomas White of Marlborough, Massachusetts; Priestly Young of Worcester; the clergyman and his wife; the lone sailor.

City law, at that time, forbade the use of steam engines downtown, so horses powered the first stretch of the trip. At the corner of Grand Street and Bowery an employee of the railroad stopped pedestrians until the seven-car train—the two baggage in the front, with five passenger behind—had passed. At Forty-second Street the horses were unhitched and the locomotive attached in their place. At Ninety-second Street the cars dipped into the Prospect Hill tunnel, and soon they had arrived across the Harlem River at Williamsbridge, where the train switched off the tracks owned by the New York & Harlem and onto its own.

The New York & New Haven cars chugged beyond New Rochelle and, in Mamaroneck, crossed an arched granite bridge above a stream that emptied into Long Island Sound. Just past Rye the track intersected the old highway to Boston at a ridge before dipping into the Blind Brook valley and continuing on to the Connecticut border.

A little before ten the morning express reached Stamford and made the first of its two stops before New Haven's Union Street Station. The next would come at Bridgeport. It was at Stamford, the newspapers later reported, that conductor Charles Comstock told Edward Tucker, the engineer, to "drive like hell" through Norwalk. Comstock had grown upset with two passengers who wanted to get off there. (The westbound express made the Norwalk stop, and possibly these men thought the eastern one did too.) By speeding through Norwalk, Comstock could be sure that the men didn't hop out of the moving train.

Coming east, the New Haven tracks descended a large rock ridge, navigated a curve, then straightened out just before crossing a draw-bridge that spanned the Norwalk River. A large red ball raised up a pole meant trains were clear to enter the draw; the ball was lowered when it was open for a ship to pass. The pole temporarily disappeared behind the curve then reemerged some five hundred feet from the bridge, W. E. Worthen, a civil engineer in New York, later testified. That left only a brief window of time for Tucker to spot the indicator. The three brakemen needed about eight hundred feet to stop a train going ten miles per hour, Worthen said. Several people later swore the express was going twice that fast, at least. The entire maneuver was a delicate one— the type best left to a veteran engineer. Tucker had been on the route only two months.

The drizzle had made the rails a bit slippery. "The train is going so fast," Thomas White told the doctor beside him as they rounded the curve, "that I am afraid we shall be thrown off the track." George Selleck, who owned a restaurant near the Norwalk depot, had seen the steamboat's smoke a few minutes earlier—and after he saw the whizzing train he knew what was coming and dashed toward the bridge. There, at about ten in the morning, Edward Tucker and George Elmer, the train's fireman, lunged out of the speeding engine moments before it hurtled past the bridge pole—its red ball lowered—and through the open draw. The two baggage cars followed the locomotive into the embankment, some fifty-five feet across, and the first two passenger cars plunged twelve feet into the river. The third snapped in half on the precipice.

Within an hour the first telegram had reached New York. Business ground to a halt as the concerned and the curious packed newspaper

offices for the latest details. By the time the *New York Daily Tribune*'s
reporter left the scene at nine that night, forty-six passengers had died.
Dozens more were badly hurt; many of them might have been lost but
for the preponderance of doctors on hand. Thomas Hicks and Miss
King were among the second car's only survivors. Priestly Young had
moved to a rear car to bird-watch, and the Parker baby also survived,
even though—or perhaps because—its chaperone did not. The clergyman and his wife lived, unlike the sailor, with whom they had traded
seats just moments before. None of the railroad employees—not Comstock, Tucker, Elmer, or any of the three brakemen—suffered more than
minor bruises. The wounds of their consciences would take longer to
heal, predicted Horace Greeley, the *Tribune*'s editor: "Better far to be the
victim," he wrote the next day, "than the author of such a crime."

The Norwalk disaster far outranked any catastrophe in the history of American railroads up to that time. The public's response was
a mixture of outrage and fear. Boston newspapers ran headlines like
"Railroad Murders." Patronage along the Boston Road was literally
decimated: trains once carrying two hundred travelers soon carried
twenty. By the time all the settlements were meted out, totaling some
$325,000, the New York & New Haven had lost the equivalent of two
years' profit.

Much of the blame fell on the company's leadership. "The grossest
and most criminal negligence has prevailed in the management of the
road," wrote Greeley just days after the crash, having changed his tone
from remorse to rancor. "Yes, Gentlemen Directors, it is upon you above
all that it rests!" The Connecticut legislature imposed mandatory stops
before all drawbridges and formed a railroad oversight commission. It
also passed a law prohibiting a person from serving as president of more
than one railroad—forcing the New York & New Haven's leader, Robert Schuyler, to step down as head of the New York & Harlem.

Hailing from one of the most celebrated families in New York,
Schuyler had been a rising superstar in the nation's rising form of
transportation. "Probably no road in this country has ever advanced
in public favor so quickly, or made money so rapidly since its completion," wrote *Scientific American* of the New York & New Haven, two

years before the crash. At one point Schuyler had been labeled "America's first railroad king."

Despite some behavioral peculiarities—Schuyler lived apart from his wife and six kids, and many friends thought him a bachelor—his pedigree as grandson of Revolutionary War hero General Philip Schuyler and nephew of Alexander Hamilton placed his reputation beyond question. So confident was the New Haven's board in their leading man that in addition to being president Schuyler was also the company's sole transfer agent. Every stock transaction went through him, and him alone.

But while Schuyler tended to avoid criticism on the strength of his legacy, the New York & New Haven had less than auspicious beginnings. The railroad's inaugural trip, on Christmas of 1848, serves as the best symbol of its mismanagement: the cars reached Williamsbridge, in the Bronx, only to find the junction with the Harlem track unfinished, forcing them to turn back toward New Haven. The impression of foul play also lingered in many New York & New Haven operations. The track's builder, Alfred Bishop, had been accused of shoddy work, particularly at the curve approaching the Norwalk bridge. And when Robert Schuyler resigned as president of the New York & Harlem after the Norwalk incident, George Schuyler, his brother, took over—a nominal change of leadership, and only half of one at that.

It was in the wake of the Norwalk disaster, during the New Haven's financial downturn, that Robert Schuyler began to perpetrate his massive scandal. According to the warrant for his arrest, Schuyler began to issue phony stock certificates within six months of the crash—though he was likely engaged in more moderate fraud from the start. By midsummer of 1854 at least a few parties were clearly on to his misdeeds. Between June 14 and June 28 the New Haven's stock plunged ten points, to 93. The next day Schuyler stopped coming to work, claiming a "dangerous hemorrhage of the lungs," and by July 3 the stock had sunk to 73.5. That same day Schuyler wrote a resignation letter to the board of directors. "Your attention to the stock ledgers of your Company is essential," he wrote, "as you will find there is much that is wrong."

After studying the books, which had long remained in Schuyler's sole possession, the New Haven directors discovered he had issued

19,540 shares of counterfeit stock between October of 1853 and the time of his resignation. At one hundred dollars each the phony shares defrauded the company, and the public, of nearly two million dollars. Among the hoodwinked was Cornelius Vanderbilt, whose illegitimate investment exceeded two hundred thousand dollars. Soon several hundred other supposed stockholders realized they held nothing but paper.

What the Norwalk crash had been to railroad accidents, the Schuyler fraud was to business scandal—entirely unparalleled for its time. For weeks Wall Street hung on the verge of panic. Stocks dove at home and abroad; creditors called in loans. A common refrain was sung: If a man as reputable as Robert Schuyler could perpetrate such a scheme, then no one's chief executive could be trusted. "The Schuyler fraud completely absorbs attention in Wall-street and, indeed, we may say out of it," wrote the *New York Times* on July 7, 1854. Soon stock prices fell on railroads from Pennsylvania to Michigan; directors everywhere raced to publish proof that their records were sound. Many even offered them up for inspection. Since the depression of 1837, declared the *Times* on July 10, a "darker day for public confidence had not been seen."

For a while the railroad's future was uncertain. Many felt the only way to recover public faith was "unhesitating" compensation for the victims; newspapers nearly begged for such action. But the New York & New Haven leadership faced a tricky situation. On one hand, by assuming wholesale responsibility for Schuyler's actions the company might go under. On the other, by divesting itself from one man's roguish conduct it would turn its back on the victims of the crime. In the end it took the latter course and acquired a villainous reputation that would follow it into the twentieth century. Placing the full onus of the stock fraud on Robert Schuyler, wrote one newspaper editorial, was no different than refusing to compensate the victims of the Norwalk crash "upon the plea that the conductor was negligent or reckless." One judge asked to review the case and offer his thoughts for the *Times* was "fully of opinion that the Company is answerable in some form for the acts of Schuyler."

At first the courts agreed. One of the earliest rulings came down in favor of the swindled. But it was a harbinger of the railroad's powerful lobby that the judge who rendered this decision was the only one in the district not disqualified for conflict of interest. A year later Judge George F. Comstock of the appellate court reversed the ruling. By calling the bad stock entirely worthless, Comstock essentially let the railroad off the hook with a brief invocation of caveat emptor. It probably surprised few people when, ten years later, Comstock showed up again in court regarding the New York & New Haven—this time as an attorney, representing the company.

Over the years, a sinister air hovered about the railroad, and few people trusted the company farther than they could throw a locomotive. "The late Schuyler frauds . . . have opened the eyes of the community to the corruption and evils of our railroad system," wrote *Scientific American* three months after the scandal surfaced. "Instead of our railroads standing out as spectacles of prosperity and good management, they appear before the world as objects of suspicion—bankrupt in character and confidence." In 1857, at the height of the railroad's legal storm, the New York & New Haven directors even tried to declare a stock dividend, though intense opposition prevailed.

News of Schuyler's death—apparently caused by "grief and mortification"—reached America in late 1855. He had absconded to Geneva with his family, supposedly unenriched by his actions, though at least a few people doubted both this claim and even his passing. A few years later Edward Tucker, the engineer of the Norwalk train, took his own life. He had not driven a train since, and it was said he had lost his senses.

One of the most important decisions in the lingering case, though far from the final, was set to appear in the fall of 1860. Week after week newspapers reported delays in the settlement. Come early November the trial remained unfinished. Finally the matter was concluded on November 5, 1860. Not only did Judge D. P. Ingraham rule in favor of the railroad, he ordered anyone holding fraudulent shares to hand them over to the court, which would stamp them "cancelled." Even the mighty Vanderbilt's stock was considered "null and void."

But the settlement, which could have sparked outrage, or at least heavy attention, was widely overlooked. A far more important decision gripped the public. The very next day, with the country on the verge of civil war, the people would elect the president tasked with saving the union.

RANGY, AWKWARD ABRAHAM LINCOLN crammed into a seat on the New York & New Haven's eight o'clock express train to Boston on the morning of February 28, 1860. He would not be going to Boston, however. In New Haven Lincoln disembarked at the depot and transferred to another train, the Shore Line toward New London. The steamboat ferry that carried the cars across the Connecticut River—a notoriously bumpy affair Dickens once described as being "beaten about"—surely jostled the six-foot-four traveler. At the Thames River this unpleasantness was repeated. Shortly across he transferred again, this time to the Stonington railroad, which, if the train arrived on schedule, put him into Providence's Union Passenger Depot at about a quarter past four. That left Lincoln about three hours to dine and make whatever preparations necessary before he returned to Railroad Hall for his highly anticipated speech.

For the next twelve days Lincoln's services would be at a premium across New England—and this was a bit strange, for in early 1860 the lawyer from Illinois was not considered a serious candidate for the presidency. Certainly not in the East. But his speech the evening before, at Cooper Union in New York City, had within the span of a day done much to transform Lincoln into a most-coveted speaker all along the Boston Road. By the time he headed back west, on March 12, he had given a dozen talks—six directly on the old highway—often using his time on the railroad to hastily alter a lecture he had prepared at great length and intended to deliver but once. By the close of this torrid stump tour several people had remarked to Lincoln that his "chances were about equal to the best" of winning the most important election in the young country's history.

The first and largest step toward this conclusion had occurred the previous night, in Manhattan. The foremost topic on the minds of the electorate was handling the spread of slavery. Stephen Douglas, the likely

Democratic candidate, thought states should decide for themselves whether or not to allow the practice. Lincoln, like many Republicans, thought the federal government had a say in the matter, and should use this voice to curtail its expansion. Unless someone beat Douglas that fall, slavery would certainly extend across the union, along a perforated line.

Lincoln spent months preparing his New York speech. The loose, frontier speaking style that had endeared him to Westerners would not play as well to the city's stiff intellectual audience. So Lincoln focused strictly on the facts. Douglas had argued that the framers of the Constitution would not have wanted the federal government to limit a state's rights to permit slavery. "Our fathers," Douglas had declared, "understood this question just as well, and even better, than we do now." Lincoln would take a counterintuitive approach to deconstructing this argument: He would begin by *agreeing* with his opponent's declaration, then proceed to prove, through rigorous historical examination, that the fathers who understood the question better than we, would have disagreed with Douglas's answer to it.

So Lincoln dug through archives, slowly documenting the voting records of the thirty-nine men who had signed the Constitution. As historian Harold Holzer points out, in his definitive study of the Cooper Union speech, the extent of Lincoln's solitary effort was astounding. Later on, two editors tasked with preparing footnotes for a published version of the speech needed three weeks and the help of several historians, including the esteemed George Bancroft, just to verify the facts. It was quite fitting, then, that Peter Cooper had buried beneath his institute a copy of the Constitution.

On Monday evening, February 27, thousands of New Yorkers paid their quarter and found a seat in Cooper Union's basement lecture hall, no doubt unaware that they hovered just above the very document their speaker would address. At nearly the last moment, and without Lincoln's knowledge, the speech had been shifted to take place here—the largest such venue in the city. The change had thrown him near frenzy. Typically Lincoln took a deliberate, almost osmotic approach to speechwriting, according to his close friend Ward Hill Lamon. He jotted down thoughts on strips of paper, carried them around in a pocket or beneath his hat, and, once moved, sat down to connect these scraps of enlightenment. Realizing that his new audience would be far different from the church-going one for which he had prepared, Lincoln revised furiously in his hotel room. As evening neared eight he too made his way to the redbrick building at Third Avenue and the Bowery, completed just the previous fall at the original site of the Two Mile stone on the highway to Boston.

The towering Lincoln, looking thoroughly unimpressive in a wrinkled suit, stumbled at first. But soon the magical logic of his work, hammered home by frequent repetitions, took hold. Bit by bit Lincoln chiseled away at Douglas's statement. In 1784, at the Congress of the Confederation, three men who would later sign the Constitution voted to prohibit slavery in the Northwest Territory. A fourth voted to allow it, but this act still opposed Douglas's theory that the framers did not favor federal oversight. In 1787, faced with the same question, three more future signers chose to deny slavery in the territory, a decision known as the Ordinance of 1787. Two years later, during the first Congress, a bill enforcing this ordinance passed unanimously. Thirteen new signers voted for it, and a fourteenth—President George Washington—signed it into law.

All in all Lincoln had found evidence that twenty-three men who signed the Constitution had taken a political action endorsing the federal government's right to control the spread of slavery. Twenty-one of these, a clear majority of the thirty-nine, had voted to actively stop such a spread. Of the sixteen signers for whom Lincoln could not find direct voting behavior—including "Dr. Franklin, Alexander Hamilton and Gouverneur Morris"—all but one were known to oppose slavery. It was reasonable to conclude, then, that of the thirty-nine men who signed the Constitution—men who "understood this question just as well, and even better, than we do now"—at least thirty-six would certainly, or very likely, agree that the government can and should interfere with slavery's expansion.

Lincoln's ninety-minute speech had a crisp charm. It was academic enough to earn the respect of a snooty crowd, and emotional enough to rouse patriotic squeals of approval. Its ending, in particular, drew admiration: "Let us have faith that right makes might; and, in that faith, let us, to the end, dare to do our duty, as we understand it." The audience responded with a flourish, and gave Lincoln many cheers. Afterward it was thought that this one talk alone recruited more people to join the Republican party than had previously existed in the whole city. Horace Greeley, editor of the powerful *New York Tribune,* called the talk "one of the happiest and most convincing political arguments ever made in this city," in an editorial the following day. "No man ever before made such an impression on his first appeal to a New-York audience."

AND SO EARLY the next morning Lincoln boarded the New Haven toward Providence with a substantially brighter aura of intrigue. Still, he remained more of a dark horse than a front-runner—after his speech the audience had also given three cheers for the Republican party's leading candidate, William Seward—but the seed for Lincoln's consideration had been planted.

Now, on the road, the expectations were raised in proportion with the stakes, and Lincoln faced the added obstacle of altering his words just enough to seem fresh, yet not enough to lose their flavor. The task would not be easy: four major New York newspapers—Greeley's *Tribune,* William Cullen Bryant's *Evening Post,* James Gordon Bennett's *Herald,* and the *Times*—had reprinted the speech in full. Before long it would be known across New England.

So he used his travel time, did Lincoln, to tailor certain points for his upcoming audience, and over the course of his tour the Cooper Union talk grew increasingly different. This series of alterations began on February 28, with his eight-hour ride to Providence. The typical Boston Road train of 1860 sat about fifty people to a car. Small squares above the windows provided ventilation, with the bad air flowing out the short stovepipes in the roof. Wire screens on windows kept out cinders. Stable springs kept the car from swinging much around sharp curves. The lighting was pretty poor, often one dim lamp per end of the train, but that would not have caused much of a problem in the daytime. The tall Lincoln's biggest discomfort, no doubt, was the low back cushion of his seat—a shared walkover designed to face either direction. Newsboys roamed the aisles, and quite possibly they provided for him the Providence newspaper he read for much of his ride.

Lincoln's paper of choice was the Democratic-leaning *Providence Daily Post*. On the second page, first column, of that day's issue was the headline that interested him: "Mr. Lincoln is Sent to Us." Like nearly all news articles of the day, this one made no attempt at impartiality. It portrayed Lincoln as an "unquestioned" abolitionist intent on converting the Rhode Island populace to his point of view. Perhaps then, as the Long Island Sound rolled beside him, Lincoln decided to omit from his Providence talk a potentially inflammatory section of his Cooper Union speech that had mentioned the radical abolitionist John Brown.

The *Post* then reached back to Lincoln's 1858 debate with Douglas and quoted his well-known "house divided" speech, in which Lincoln had questioned whether the government could survive with half the country enslaved, and half free. "In plain English—The UNION is a failure," the paper concluded. "This is Mr. Lincoln's doctrine."

By the time Lincoln arrived at Providence's Union Passenger Depot, his Boston Road reading had helped him formulate a plan of attack. He had dinner and, with his lean frame swimming in a loose frock coat, made his way back to the brick station. When it was first built, in 1848, Providence's Union Depot had been the largest in the country. The station, designed by an architecture student at Brown, had a pair of towers, octagonal pavilions at the end of both wings, and, on the second floor, a lecture hall that, around seven in the evening on February 28, 1860, stretched whatever bounds of capacity the young student had conceived.

Lincoln began by mentioning the parts of his 1858 speech that had appeared in the *Post* that day. The true meaning of these words, he argued, was not quite what the paper would have its readers believe. On the contrary, his belief that "this government cannot endure permanently, half slave and half free" was consistent with his current view: that stopping the spread of slavery would sufficiently derail it.

With that, Lincoln led back into the heart of his New York talk. He repeated the powerful facts he had stated the night before, and soon won over the audience in Union Depot just as he had won it at Cooper Union. "He strives rather to show by plain, simple, cogent reasoning that his positions are impregnable, and he carries his audience with him, as he deserves to," the *Daily Journal,* a Republican paper, wrote the following day. More impressive was the reported reaction of the *Post*'s editor, Welcome Sayles: "That is the finest constitutional argument for a popular audience that I have ever heard."

The next morning Lincoln rode the Boston & Providence to the Massachusetts capital. After giving a few talks in New Hampshire—his son, Robert, was attending Exeter Academy there—Lincoln arrived in Hartford on March 5. Here he incorporated a new wrinkle, inspired by an experience he had while riding the rails along the Sound a few days earlier. While making his way toward Providence Lincoln had taken a seat beside Cassius Clay, a well-known Republican statesman. No doubt the two had plenty to discuss. Clay, though a Southerner, had become adamantly antislavery after the economic panic of 1837. (At the time, it should be noted, many opponents of slavery were more concerned with its impact on free-labor economics than its moral iniquity.) He too was a potential candidate in the upcoming election; in fact, Clay had immediately preceded Lincoln as a speaker at Cooper Union.

During the course of the ride Lincoln noticed a peculiar growth on the neck of the man sitting in front of them—accentuated, as it would have been, by the train's low-backed seats. The growth, Lincoln told Clay, represented all the complicated facets of the slavery topic. For one thing, it was certainly unpleasant. Yet the way around this unpleasantness was anything but clear. Remove it and the man might bleed to death. Keep it and death would arrive anyway, if a bit slower. Lincoln relayed this incident to the audience in Hartford. The Democrats, he said, would like to hang such an "ornament" around everyone's neck. In that case the disease would soon spread to the entire country, and everyone would be faced with the decision of not whether to die, but how quickly and by what means.

Out of New York, now, Lincoln used this sort of country charm a bit more liberally. He still finished with the rousing "right makes might" chorus, for instance, but added "Eternal might," appealing a bit to Connecticut's more religious nature. The result, in the words of the *Hartford Courant,* was "the most convincing and clearest speech we have ever heard made." In a larger sense Lincoln was becoming exactly what the Republican party needed: a candidate who could tug on Western hearts without losing a grip on Eastern heads.

Lincoln's Hartford speech also inspired a grassroots movement that would become critical to the 1860 election. Not ten days earlier, a small gang of young Republicans had escorted none other than Cassius Clay to the lecture hall where he would speak. It was evening, and the group carried torches to light the way, but occasionally some of the oil dripped from these torches onto their clothes. So as the group passed Talcott and Post's Dry Goods Store, at the corner of Pratt and Main streets, a few young men grabbed some black cloth to protect against the drips. Draped around their shoulders as it was, the dark material resembled a cape, and a trademark uniform was born.

After Lincoln's speech these same young men, dubbed the Wide Awakes by a city editor, still wearing black capes and carrying torches, marched him back to his hotel. That very evening they held their first official meeting in a building on Hartford's Main Street. By midsummer the underground movement had gone national in a big way: some four hundred Wide Awakes clubs, sporting half a million similarly costumed members, spanned the Northern states. It was later felt that the Connecticut Wide Awakes had supplied the difference in the state's gubernatorial race, which the Republican candidate, William Buckingham, won by a mere 541 votes. The movement made such a difference in the general election that, come fall of 1860, the original Hartford chapter of the now-expansive group was invited to parade beside Lincoln at his inauguration.

Next Lincoln took the Hartford & New Haven railroad to the latter city, where he spoke on March 6. There, at Union Hall, he gave a similar speech that so moved Yale's professor of rhetoric that the scholar accompanied Lincoln on his special train, the following day, to Meriden. The professor was not the only one to make the trip; the Hartford & New Haven became a bona fide Lincoln bandwagon. Some six hundred Republicans hopped on at various stops along the line. By the time the train reached Wallington the cars were so packed that a hundred people were left behind at the depot.

In Meriden, before a raucous crowd three thousand strong that had braved the snow and mud, Lincoln displayed a final wrinkle to his adapted speech. He said that when the Republicans had beaten the Democrats in recent Illinois elections, many of the defeated party sang "Farewell, Old Connecticut." At this the audience erupted in cheers for "Lincoln and the Union"—the name of William Seward was not to be heard. "The effect of last night's meeting will be long felt," reported the *Hartford Courant*, "and whenever hereafter we see the name of *Lincoln*, warm remembrances will be awakened in the hearts of thousands."

Lincoln was not quite a Boston Road memory yet. He rode the Shore Line train back to Providence for a speech in the nearby town of Woonsocket, then circled back along the Sound toward Bridgeport for his final talk, on March 10. Immediately after this speech the exhausted orator, hungry for home, boarded a New Haven night train back to New York. From there he would leave for Illinois, but not before strolling around the city one final time with James Briggs, the man who had originally invited Lincoln east. By then, in the words of the *Providence Daily Journal*, Lincoln was "as much of a favorite in New England as in his own State."

Back in Manhattan, Lincoln and Briggs walked past the New York City post office. The office, formerly at City Hall Park, along the original high road to Boston, had moved into an old Dutch church downtown. The temporary structure was far from ideal. Briggs turned to Lincoln. "When you are President," he asked, "will you recommend an appropriation of a million dollars for a suitable location for a post-office in this city?"

The question, powerfully presumptuous just ten days earlier, was posed without any sort of qualification. A few months later Briggs's pronouncement proved half-true, when Lincoln earned the Republican nomination. At that time politicians did far less campaigning than they do today—and it is a consequence of this practice that, in hindsight, makes the speeches Lincoln delivered along the Boston Road even more significant. After his final stop, in Bridgeport, Lincoln gave a grand total of zero public talks until he was elected president.

Chapter 9

Barnum, Morgan, and New England's "Invisible Government"

EVEN BEFORE THE official outbreak of the Civil War the old highway played a role in the country's growing hostilities. Like many places in the Northeast, cities and towns on Long Island Sound and the Connecticut River became havens for escaped slaves. Boston in particular housed a great deal of Southern refugees. Many hid in a room above the office of the *Liberator,* an abolitionist newspaper run by William Lloyd Garrison, on Washington Street. Some slipped out of the Bay, crammed into the false bottom of a market wagon, to a well-known house belonging to Israel Brown, half a mile north of the post road in Sudbury, Massachusetts. Others rode Nathan Hale's old railroad to Worcester, where they were protected and, when necessary, passed along farther north.

Though distant from the action, the Boston Road played several important cameos once the fighting began. Toward the fall of 1861 some fifty soldiers from Guilford and New Haven, led by soon-to-be-major-general Joseph Hawley, hopped the Shore Line railroad to Saybrook to disrupt a "peace flag" ceremony. The announcement of a draft in 1863 ignited a terrifying riot along Third Avenue that engulfed Manhattan for days. Word of success at Gettysburg that summer reached Lincoln through the intercepted telegram of a reporter from Norwalk, who was wiring Horace Greeley's *New York Tribune* with the scoop.

Even victorious general Ulysses S. Grant had roots on the old route. A direct ancestor, Matthew Grant, was a founding settler of Windsor, Connecticut, and the town's early records and plots place his residence immediately north of the Meeting House along the old highway. To top things off, when the Union finally captured Confederate president Jefferson Davis, reportedly disguised in women's clothing, P. T. Barnum offered the Secretary of War five hundred dollars to display Davis's "petticoats" in his American Museum at the foot of modern Park Row, where the old high road to Boston broke east toward the Bowery.

None of these individual instances, however, approached the railroad's overall impact as a conduit of arms and armies. This role began at the war's opening charge. When Lincoln called for seventy-five thousand men following the events at Fort Sumter, it was the Boston Road rails that whisked the first regiment toward Washington to defend the capital, arriving at a time of great vulnerability—and in doing so carried them into the war's first fatal skirmish.*

In response to Lincoln's request some seven hundred volunteer fighters gathered in the streets of Boston on April 16, 1860. Around one o'clock this hastily assembled crew left Faneuil Hall and marched through the city, escorted by hoards of cheering citizens, toward Boylston Hall, at the corner of Washington Street. By evening of the seventeenth the Sixth Massachusetts collected at the railroad depot. Shortly after seven the nineteen cars passed beneath Washington Street on their way west toward Worcester, and war.

At every stop along the Boston Road people gathered in great numbers as a show of solidarity. Thousands watched the troops transfer to the Western's tracks at Worcester, and again to the New Haven line at Springfield. No fewer than twenty-five hundred people met them in Hartford, despite their arrival at two in the morning. The train hurled on through the night, and when it arrived in New Haven near dawn

---

*One Union soldier was killed during the evacuation at Fort Sumter, in a flag-saluting mishap. The volunteers from the Sixth Massachusetts were the first to die by hostile fire, though not technically by the guns of Confederate soldiers.

three thousand people offered up coffee and sandwiches. By sunrise of April 18 the Sixth Massachusetts was making its way down to the Manhattan ferry that would take it to New Jersey, and on toward Washington.

At ten thirty in the morning on April 19—the anniversary of the Battle of Lexington no doubt in the minds of the Massachusetts men—the train bearing the Sixth regiment reached Baltimore's President Street Station. In the words of its mayor, George Brown, Baltimore was "a border city with divided sympathies." The troops had hoped to pass through undetected, but the city's arrangement of north- and southbound depots required detaching the steam engine at President Street so the train could be drawn a mile to the station on Camden Street. Simply put, an inconspicuous movement was out of the question.

By the time seven horse-drawn cars had crossed the city, the rioters had assembled in full force. A wild confrontation ensued. Shots flew from both sides. Stones rained onto the streets from nearby warehouse windows. Eventually the mile of mayhem ended, and the exposed companies joined their comrades at Camden Street. As the train staggered off, "the panting crowd . . . almost breathless with running, pressed up to the car windows, presenting knives and revolvers, and cursed up into the faces of the soldiers," reported the *Baltimore Sun* the following day. All told, four soldiers and twelve citizens were killed in the conflict, with dozens more injured on both sides.

After the Baltimore riot, Lincoln and the rest of Washington temporarily lost contact with the Northern states. Mayor Brown, fearing another fiasco when more troops crossed through his city, arranged for parts of the railroad track to be dismantled. The move cut off the Northern mail, and because many of the telegraph poles had been torn down in the mob's attempts to block the track, those were severed too. For a few crucial days Washington and the Northeast remained incommunicado. The reserve troops expected from New York and Rhode Island could not reach the desperate president, who in turn had no way of informing anyone of his growing desperation.

For nearly a week the only thing defending a capital on the verge of capture was the Sixth Massachusetts. When Brigadier General William A. Aiken reached Washington at nightfall on April 24, having been sent with a note of support from Connecticut Governor Buckingham, he was the first messenger spotted in three days. Aiken found a dejected Lincoln sitting beside a telescope aimed at Arlington Heights, Virginia—a possible point of attack. "What *is* the North about?" Lincoln asked Aiken. "*Do* they know our condition?" Between the loss of rails and mails and telegraph wires, Aiken assured the president, they did not.

Finally the famed New York Seventh regiment arrived, by a circuitous ferry route, at noon on April 25, and Washington could rest secure. Once the rail lines were repaired three of the soldiers killed in the riot were packed in ice and shipped back to Boston for a proper burial. The fourth, Charles A. Taylor, was buried in Baltimore by mistake. Taylor had pushed past the crowds along Washington Street when the Sixth regiment arrived, and enlisted at Boylston Hall. Eventually his musket was returned to Boston, where it was displayed for many years in the statehouse. It was an Eli Whitney model, the musket, from 1861. The ramrod was missing, presumably lost while Taylor was reloading, for his gun had been fired.

Whitney arms from New Haven were just some of the many that supplied the North during the years of battle. Samuel Colt had begun to fill orders before fighting commenced—for the South. In March 1860 his Hartford revolver factory sent the Virginia militia half a million firearms along the private tracks Colt had constructed from his warehouse to meet the Hartford & New Haven. The rifled muskets made in the Springfield armory became the Union soldiers' basic weapon. At peak operation the factory finished three firearms every five minutes. After the New York draft riots Governor Buckingham stored Connecticut's arms in the homes of loyal men in Stamford, Norwalk, and other places along the rail line.

The outbreak of war initially hurt the Boston Road rails, in particular the New York & New Haven. Its receipts fell to depths unmatched since the Norwalk crash of 1853. But by early 1862 the war spurred a flurry of income, and by year's end the railroad had grossed record profits. Most of the several hundred thousand troops supplied by New England during the course of the fighting would have reached the field over train tracks running at least part of the way beside the Boston Road. The profusion of young men who fled towns by rail during the drafts, many of whom jumped out of guarded compartments, caused companies to add extra passenger cars.

With its heightened patronage the railroad began to see itself as the monopoly the public had always feared it would become. Bids to open competing lines from New York toward Boston languished on legislative tables until "amicable arrangements" made them disappear. In the spring of 1862 the New York & New Haven forced more than a hundred wounded soldiers from Massachusetts and Connecticut to wait in New York until they could scrape together enough money to reach their destinations. Able to charge whatever it liked, this railroad's commuter fare in 1865 was double the going rate for gold. Such company policies maddened the public, but no amount of outrage could shift the New York & New Haven's essential location.

The railroad's increased profits did not translate into improved service, and this perceived injustice fueled part of the uproar. Of $6.5 million in income earned by Connecticut railroads in 1864, barely one-fifth was spent on track repairs. The entire state of Boston Road rail travel began to decay. Riding the trains ranged from bothersome to downright dangerous. Drunken soldiers, returning home on leave, damaged cars and irritated passengers. A wreck in the fall of 1864 killed or injured some sixty soldiers, and the following year at least fifty people died in accidents. When it became clear that the railroad companies themselves would not address the situation, the public turned to the Connecticut railroad commission—until it became clear that this regulatory body would not address the situation either, because the two were in cahoots.

During this period of unprecedented activity the railroad companies achieved a level of power they would not be content to relinquish after the war. The New York & New Haven, in particular, relished its elevated influence. Eventually it formed the critical piece in the great trunk line of the Boston Road system, known generally as the New Haven railroad, nursed into a powerful maturity by J. P. Morgan. By the time its directors were federally indicted in 1914, the New Haven railroad held such a tight grip on the country's psyche and economy that the Interstate Commerce Commission called it New England's "invisible government," and sought to crumble the mighty empire "for the welfare of the Nation."

Until that time, only one man had even come close to toppling the railroad that ran beside the old highway—a man less interested, at the close of the Civil War, in tackling corruption than in acquiring a certain Confederate leader's petticoats for display in his American Museum.

PHINEAS TAYLOR BARNUM'S lasting reputation is one of swindler and showman. True, his American Museum featured a mischievous exhibit that led patrons out an exit and made them pay full rate for reentrance. But such antics belied a political interest and moral rigidity typically ignored when discussing the Prince of Humbug's influence. In the course of his lifetime Barnum put himself in harm's way to support the Union, fought aggressively for woman suffrage, attracted some of the country's top manufacturers to Bridgeport, and even served that city for an efficient term as mayor. As a member of the Connecticut legislature in 1865 his unflinching standoff with the New Haven and the irresponsible state railroad commission made it illegal for a member of that committee to be employed by a railroad company. Barnum cut so deeply into the powerful company's core that his bestselling autobiography was banned from train vendors on the entire New Haven line.

There is a touch of irony in P. T. Barnum from Bridgeport taking on the New Haven. From the start Bridgeport threw itself entirely behind railroad projects. The town did not even exist in 1800. By 1836 it was petitioning Connecticut for incorporation as a city, so that it could use city taxes to fund a railroad north to Albany. By the time the New York & New Haven was finished, in the waning days of 1848, three railroads served Bridgeport. Its population leaped 191 percent from 1840 to 1860, and it housed many elite industrial operations, including the largest sewing machine factory in the country, Wheeler & Wilson.

In many ways Barnum was the exemplary railroad persona. With his home in Bridgeport and his primary business, the American Museum, in Manhattan, Barnum represented the railroad's early potential to unify city and suburb. He chose Bridgeport as his home, he later recalled, for "its nearness to New York, and the facilities for daily transit to and from the metropolis." Barnum's first glorious mansion, dubbed Iranistan, was visible from inside the New York & New Haven cars. In the fields beside the tracks Barnum positioned an elephant from the museum and instructed an employee to keep the animal "busily engaged in his work whenever passenger trains from either way were passing through." This plow-pushing pachyderm became an animated billboard—intended to linger in the minds of riders until they reached New York, by which time many were converted into patrons.

The American Museum itself was as much an emblem of the times as the railroad. More than 37 million patrons visited the museum between 1841, the year Barnum took it over, and 1865—surpassing the entire United States population in the latter year. Here, on the original high road to Boston, everyday tourists hobnobbed with the Prince of Wales, Henry Thoreau, and Henry James. Barnum's museum drew praise from scientists at the Smithsonian and Harvard, inspired aspects of Peter Cooper's Union, and funded marine expeditions for the man who later started the American Museum of Natural History. Of course, it still featured a "mermaid" that was actually the torso of a monkey sewn onto the tail of a fish, as well as little Tom Thumb, who eventually took his newfound wealth and moved back to Bridgeport, his original home, into a house right on the old post road.

Originally Barnum ran for a seat in the Connecticut House of Representatives* only to cast a vote in favor of the federal Constitution's Thirteenth Amendment. When this law to abolish slavery passed, unanimously, early in the legislative term, Barnum temporarily turned his attention to the issue of suffrage within his own state. He became

---

*Though Barnum considered himself a resident of Bridgeport, his home technically fell outside that city's limit, so he was elected as representative of neighboring Fairfield.

the most outspoken advocate for the enfranchisement of Connecticut's black men—giving a stirring ninety-minute speech in favor of the
change, and often ridiculing those who spoke out against it.★

These debates were held early into the session, and Barnum spent
much of the remainder of the term, it would seem, amusing himself
at the expense of his colleagues. In transcripts of the House debates,
reprinted daily in the *Hartford Courant,* hardly a Barnum comment
was recorded without being followed by the editorial "(Laughter)."
Barnum's extensive European tours had made him perhaps the most
famous American in the world, and it's highly doubtful other lawmakers took him seriously, at least at first. But apart from the slavery amendment and the general goofing around, attacking the New Haven railroad
became Barnum's all-consuming task.★★

The first battle came on the session's opening evening, when Barnum gave what the newspaper called a "humorous speech" to defeat the
railroad lobby's preferred choice for Speaker of the House. Over the next
few months Barnum kept up the pressure. When the railroad commission declared that the cars were comfortable, in its annual report on the
New York & New Haven, Barnum objected. As a frequent commuter,
he knew firsthand that as many as fifty people were often forced to stand
during the afternoon train from New York, because the company refused
to improve accommodations. He questioned why the report "glossed
over the facts" of the still-troublesome Norwalk bridge, and wondered
aloud if it had something to do with a member of the commission
employed by the railroad, a representative named Henry Hammond.

As the session wore on Barnum continued to expose Hammond's

★One day during this debate a group of opponents presented a "minority report" saying
that "negroes . . . are not capable of competing with white civilization." Immediately
following this report the legislature was invited to tour a local insane asylum, to which
Barnum piped up: "I move, Mr. Speaker, that carriages be procured for the conveyances of
the members who have just presented a minority report to the constitution."

★★ Barnum also made it a pet project to revamp the capitol building in Hartford. The
statehouse—still located exactly where the Meeting House had stood during the days of
John Winthrop Jr.—had been woefully maintained. Barnum's adamant stance that it must
be refurnished paid off a few years later when Hartford once again became Connecticut's
sole capital city. (It had split this duty with New Haven since 1701.)

conflict of interests. Somehow Barnum had coerced several New Haven lobbyists to confess to their attempt to pack the railroad commission with their own people. On the morning of July 6, 1865, Hammond failed to appear at the legislature. He had, quite suddenly, become "confined to a sick bed," incapable of attending. As the days rolled by and Hammond did not return, it became clear that his sudden illness would last for about the length of the remainder of the session.

Barnum introduced a regulation that would limit the New Haven railroad's ability to raise fares without also enhancing its service. The railroad's low commuter fares had encouraged countless families to populate Boston Road towns near New York, Barnum argued. Without a law regulating a fare increase, the railroad would now slam this expanding ridership with "exorbitant rates."

Eventually some state senators embraced Barnum's cause. They found that property values along the road, particularly in Stamford, Connecticut, had also soared as the population along the route rose and demand increased. In the decade leading up to the Civil War, aggregate wealth along the "New York road" more than doubled, to a reported $29 million. With this information in hand the Senate overwhelmingly passed Barnum's version of the railroad regulation bill, stripping the New Haven of its right to hike fares to unreasonable heights.

The House of Representatives, more heavily influenced by the railroad, was a harder sell. Eventually it agreed to take a vote. On July 13, members of the legislature filed down Main Street to the statehouse in Hartford shortly before nine. Reverend Gates led the men in prayer. As Barnum looked around he saw more bowed heads than usual. The statehouse halls teemed with railroad men from across Connecticut. When it was Barnum's turn to speak he looked around the room, "crowded with railroad lobbyists, as the frogs thronged Egypt," he later recalled, and saw the sort of scene upon which he had made himself an American icon: a packed hall, awaiting a show.

So he gave them one. Once again Barnum enumerated his arguments. He understood that more riders meant more railroad maintenance, which in turn created a need for higher fares. His problem had been the way the New Haven had deliberately enticed people to live along the Boston Road tracks with low commuter fares, and that now, with the hustle completed, these workers would have to pay whatever was asked for an essential daily service that had no true alternative.

A short while into his speech a messenger approached Barnum with a telegram. Barnum read the note, calmly laid it on the table before him, and continued speaking: "I am going to expose the duplicity of these men," he recalled having said. "I have had detectives on their track, for men who plot against public interests deserve to be watched. I have in my pocket positive proofs that they did, and do, intend to spring their trap upon the unprotected commuters on the New York and New Haven railroad."

Barnum then produced, from his pocket, telegrams from New York and Bridgeport. Together they offered the findings of Barnum's detectives. The New Haven directors had held a secret meeting the evening before, and voted to raise commuter fares twenty percent. The change would go into effect immediately. By doing so the new price would precede any decision made by the legislature—rendering its regulatory bill meaningless. To counteract this scheme, Barnum proposed that the legislature lock in whatever fare had existed on the first of July, predating the company's secret new agreement.

The railroad interests were stunned. Barnum struck for the kill. He called for a vote and, roused by the showman's fantastic intelligence, the bill easily passed.

Immediately afterward Barnum left the statehouse in a rush, but not before making one quick stop. He scooped up the telegram he had received during his talk—the one he had placed on the table—and handed it to a colleague, William Coe, an ardent supporter of Barnum's bill. Coe immediately relayed the note to the rest of the legislature. It was from Barnum's son-in-law, S. H. Hurd, who worked at the American Museum. The entire building had burned to the ground. Barnum had been handed this information, and delivered his winning speech anyway.

Just before Barnum boarded the afternoon Hartford & New Haven train toward Bridgeport, a writer from the *Hartford Courant* snagged him for a comment. He took the news of the fire "very coolly," the paper reported the following day, "remarking he 'didn't care, now that the railroad bill has passed.' "⋆

P. T. BARNUM served another term in the legislature the following year, mainly to spite the New Haven executives who wanted him gone, but never did repeat his success. "The state had better have been called the State of Hartford and the town of Connecticut," he said, after one unsuccessful battle with the railroad lobby.

By 1868, the nearly two million dollars of liabilities brought on by Robert Schuyler's stock scandal had been wiped clean from the New York & New Haven books. Immediately the railroad formed an implicit partnership with the Hartford & New Haven. Connecticut leaders, wary of a budding monopoly, refused to allow an official merger. So the railroads took advantage of a legal loophole—a "trifle that some careful friend nursed through the legislature," wrote the *Hartford Courant*—allowing connecting railroads to share management. In the spring of 1871, William Bishop, then president of this joint railroad company, gained a legislative seat from Bridgeport. In the summer of 1872 the thin veils disappeared and the New York, New Haven & Hartford railroad, sometimes called the "Consolidated" but typically just the "New Haven," was officially born.

All the while the railroad maintained an icy relationship with its riders. This tone is best captured by one executive explaining why the New Haven would not add a needed passenger train to the schedule: "If we put on that train it won't be a week before people will be crowding it; then we'll have to put on another." Meanwhile the population between New York and Boston, cornered in its transportation options, was exploding toward the end of the nineteenth century. The federal census of 1890 ranked Rhode Island first, Massachusetts second, and

---

⋆There doesn't appear to be a connection between Barnum's anti-railroad stance and the burning of his museum. According to the July 29, 1865, issue of *Harper's Weekly*, the fire "broke out in the basement, from the contact of the heated boiler of the engine with dry wood."

Connecticut fourth in population density. The era of centralization was in full swing. The majority of these masses now lived in cities, and the New Haven railroad served the region's major ones.

As the conglomerate grew in power and profit, it used the full force of its political influence to fight off proposals for railroads that would parallel its profitable route along the Boston Road. One such plan alone cost the company some $400,000 in "legislative corruptions" to defeat, reported the *Railroad Gazette*. It leased the Shore Line railroad, running east from New Haven to New London, gaining control of the railroad bridge across the Connecticut River. In time the Consolidated became a blue-chip stock—the kind padding trust funds throughout the Northeast. In 1889 a bridge built across the Thames River, in New London, gave passengers a ferryless ride between New York and Boston along the coast, and gave the New Haven company a seamless connection with the New York, Providence & Boston railroad, whose board members included J. P. Morgan.

The Morgan legacy along the Boston Road extends back to the country's beginnings. Miles Morgan, an ancestor of J.P., had been among the earliest settlers of Springfield, possibly coming from Roxbury as part of the group that followed William Pynchon along the old highway in 1636. Miles served many years as a highway surveyor. In that capacity, it seems quite likely he maintained parts of the early route that eventually stretched east from Springfield along modern State Street toward Worcester, and south along modern Main Street toward Hartford.

There Joseph Morgan, J. P.'s grandfather, settled in the early nineteenth century, operating the City Hotel on Hartford's own Main Street, near the center of town. He joined Nathan Hale and other early railroad advocates at the July 1835 convention in Worcester, where the goal of developing rail transportation between New York and Boston was publicly declared. Joseph bought one hundred shares of Hartford & New Haven stock, and later on his son, Junius Morgan, became a director of the railroad. In April of 1837 Junius's son, John Pierpont, was born, and soon the family moved to a house just west of the new Hartford & New Haven depot.

When the original Hartford & New Haven made its first run, in

1839, two-year-old J. P. Morgan had been among the passengers. When that road was completed through to Springfield, in late 1844, young J. P. was on that inaugural train too. Legend holds that at some point in his youth J. P. declared that the New Haven must one day have its own entrance into Boston. (At the time, New Haven riders connected to the Bay on the Boston & Albany railroad, from the west, and the Boston & Providence, from the south.) Years later, as he faced federal indictment for crimes committed as head of the New Haven, Charles Mellen recalled riding with Morgan between Manhattan and the Bay, hearing the country's most powerful businessman discuss the train in a tone "sentimental to the point at times of being whimsical." Morgan's roots along the road had been so strong, said Mellen, that he refused to remove the name *Hartford* from the New York, New Haven & Hartford company, even after the line's primary route traveled the coast through Providence, avoiding Hartford altogether.

In the fall of 1891 a death on the New Haven board opened a spot that was quickly filled by J. P. Morgan. In the year to come the New Haven unleashed an "aggressive campaign" to unify its hold on Northeast transportation, wrote the *New York Times* in January 1893. By then Morgan and William Rockefeller were reportedly the New Haven's largest shareholders, and the rumor on Wall Street was that "Morgan has more of his personal fortune in the New Haven road than anything else."

Right around this time it was announced that the president of a competing railroad, the Reading railroad, had made overtures to buy the Old Colony line. The jewel of the Old Colony was the old Boston & Providence, which connected the Rhode Island and Massachusetts capitals. If the Reading gained this control it could block the New Haven from reaching the Bay.

Immediately upon hearing this rumor, "potent influences" went to work, "silently, to protect the interests of the New-Haven and Hartford in New England," a large New Haven stockholder later told the *Times*. By early February the rumors had shifted—and now it was the New Haven that had scared off the Reading and reportedly bought its way into Boston. Playing coy, Morgan denied the sale: "There was something of a twinkle in his eye, however," the *Times* reported, "when he remarked, 'Why, it was only a day or two ago that some of the news-papers sold the Old Colony to the Reading people.' " Whether or not the boyhood legend was true, Morgan had secured for the New Haven railroad its own entrance into Boston.

IN THE FALL of 1903 Charles Mellen, new president of the New Haven, received a letter from Theodore Roosevelt, then president of the country, congratulating him on becoming head of the Northeast's most powerful train line. Roosevelt considered Mellen a good friend and an important railroad consultant to his administration. "I have leaned on you much in many ways, and I fear that (for your sins) I shall continue do so," wrote Roosevelt. "I believe in you, and I know how well you will do in the new place of high trust to which you have been called."

The New Haven's impressive growth over the last decade had cer-tainly made its chief slot a position of high trust. Immediately upon acquiring entrance into Boston the New Haven chopped time from New York by an hour and began track upgrades along the entire Shore Line—changes "the public has been constantly seeking," wrote the *New York Times*. Many of the improvements had come as the result of a meet-ing held in March of 1893 at the Manhattan home of J. P. Morgan. The participants had divided New England along the line of the Boston & Albany track, which paralleled the old highway between Springfield and the Bay. Everything south of this line was declared New Haven railroad territory. And by century's close, reported the *Railroad Gazette,* the New Haven held a firm "territorial monopoly."

Not firm enough for Mellen's taste. He had only to glance out his window on the ride between New York and Boston to find an emerging competitor more frightful than any of the rival railroads that had been beaten back since the close of the Civil War. This was the expanding, and increasingly connected, system of electric streetcars. The trolleys paralleled the New Haven along the shore, sidled the Boston & Albany across the mainland, and frequently traveled directly atop the old post road itself, all the way from New York to Boston. They offered flexible short-distance travel for mere pennies—a dangerous alternative to the New Haven, whose passengers typically rode only twenty-five miles per trip. It would not be enough to keep out the major railroad companies, Mellen later recalled. For the New Haven to thrive it would have to control "the entire transportation system."

Streetcars had evolved a number of times in the second half of the nineteenth century, beginning as horse-drawn cars, then powered by cables, and finally running on electricity. Originally these local lines connected town and country. Little by little they extended themselves, and soon trolleys became the quickest form of city-to-city transit. Streetcar promoters began to publish guides for the trolley tourist. The guides outlined how to reach Boston from New York for less than three dollars—a trip anyone could take with ease, to virtually any major destination, "both for business and pleasure."

Trips began at the corner of Park Row and Broadway. The intersection once dominated by Barnum's American Museum had, since 1875, been home to the majestic New York City post office. Travelers could take the streetcar up Third Avenue or the elevated trolley, which rained shadows, soot, and squalor onto the old highway as it made its way through the Bowery north, eventually reaching the Harlem River.

Across the bridge off Manhattan riders took a shuttle to the trolley in lush New Rochelle, where "we get a fine view of Long Island Sound, and also first enter the old Boston Post Road," according to one trolley guide from the time. "Along this, perhaps the most characteristic of New England streets, galloped in olden days the post, or rolled the stage-coach, from New York to the Hub," it continued. "This fine old road, extending all along the shore, keeps throughout a note of peace and pleasant order."

As closely as the trolley cars adhered to the old post road, their guides adhered to historical anecdotes about the highway. So moving east from Springfield the traveler was informed, rather accurately, of nearing the Old Bay Path that carried original settlers west and "followed substantially the present line of the Boston and Albany railroad." But approaching Shrewsbury one was told, quite erroneously, that here was Levi Pease's birthplace, rather than his resting place, and that Pease "started the first line of mail stages from Boston to New York, in 1784," some two years before he accomplished the task.

If inaccurate at times the guides successfully drew on the bucolic nostalgia that had pulled families from the city to the country in great numbers. The rise of the streetcar reflected the pattern of suburban migration that climbed toward the start of the twentieth century. Since the Civil War the public had wanted "facilities for getting quickly, cheaply, comfortably, from our homes to our work and back again," said the *New York Tribune*. Streetcars became these facilities, and because the streetcar largely followed the old highways, the old post road largely governed the suburban course between New York and Boston. Homes sprouted up along the lines. People filled the homes and piled into streetcars toward the city. Improved technology made riding more affordable. The prospect of more passengers lengthened the lines, and the process cycled accordingly.

Washington Street, in Boston, was a strong example. By the 1870s the Metropolitan streetcar ran about two miles along Washington from downtown Boston toward Roxbury. For decades this route carried most of the city's traffic. It brought enough people to and from Roxbury to warrant a car every eight minutes. In the streetcar's early years, the suburban scope was limited by the slowness of horse-drawn transportation. This range was expanded after trolleys became electrified, toward the end of the nineteenth century.★ By 1900 electric trolleys had extended Boston's suburbs some six, even ten miles, from downtown, with cars making the trip every fifteen minutes. Houses continued to crop up near rail stops—the well-to-do moved farther out, immigrants and the middle-class tucked in nearer to the city.

This social pattern, carried even further, created Rochelle Park at the other end of the old highway. The housing development was sixteen miles from midtown Manhattan. Aware that "business men among the

---

★ Suburban expansion owes much to the West End Railway Company of Boston, established in 1886. Frank Sprague, a native of the old post road, from Milford, Connecticut, and pioneer of electric traction, convinced leaders of the West End to electrify their streetcar lines. The West End became the first major urban transit system in the world to electrify its routes. Its success inspired an industry-wide shift, and by 1902 nearly 94 percent of the country's street railways ran on electricity.

park's future residents would want the most direct route to and from New York trains," wrote *House and Garden,* its designers located the grounds a ten-minute walk from the New Rochelle depot. Such efforts lifted New Rochelle from a tiny town of four thousand in 1870 to a genuine suburb—one of the country's wealthiest—nine times that size by 1920. Similar shifts led to a rise of suburban communities throughout the Northeast during the same period.

These were the sorts of movements—brief excursions from city to suburb, from home to work—that Mellen sought to capture for the New Haven railroad beginning in 1903. Nearly as soon as he was put in charge Mellen embarked on an aggressive strategy of purchasing streetcar lines throughout southern New England. Armed with J. P. Morgan & Co. as its lender, the New Haven spent some $73.5 million on trolleys in Connecticut, Rhode Island, and Massachusetts in Mellen's first four years alone.

At times Mellen used the Morgan firm to muscle a competitor into compromise, as he did with a proposed trolley connecting Boston and Providence. In other cases, as in his 1906 decision to purchase all the trolleys in Rhode Island, he reportedly sought Morgan's direct approval to act against the will of the New Haven board. To circumvent a Massachusetts law preventing railroad companies from owning streetcar lines, Mellen established dummy corporations to distance the New Haven from such acquisitions as the Springfield Railway system. Many of the trolleys were kept in horrible condition, arousing widespread public resentment.

Between 1894 and 1913 Morgan & Co. oversaw $333 million of New Haven transactions. Not all of the expenses came from trolleys. Steamboat lines were also gobbled up at exorbitant rates. Journalists were paid for favorable coverage. A Harvard professor was retained for favorable lectures. Millions of dollars were disbursed among contractors and a city official to secure rights to the New York, Westchester & Boston railroad, an electric line to suburban Westchester whose tracks would run right beside the New Haven's own, before it was even built. The bribes were camouflaged within the Morgan firm's "Special account No. 2."

Meanwhile the railroad's four main tracks between New York and New Haven underwent a massive conversion to alternating current wires. Once completed, in 1914, the upgrade would give the New Haven the most substantial electrified trunk line in the country; the passenger corridor between Manhattan's Grand Central Station and Stamford, Connecticut, was already more heavily traveled than any other at the time. If the New Haven was truly Morgan's "pet road," as the *Wall Street Journal* later wrote, then its electrification was his pet project. "The electrification delighted him beyond words," Mellen recalled. "He was like a boy about it."

By 1913 the New Haven's investments had reached an astronomical $417 million. No one could travel an inch between Boston and New York without Charles Mellen's whispering how fast, how far, and for how much.

In the fall of 1913 these efforts quite literally crashed to a halt. Several ghastly wrecks between New Haven and Stamford precipitated a stock dive that kept the railroad from paying a dividend to investors for the first time in forty years. Such an announcement from New England's "premier gilt-edged security" was front-page news: "Many persons of moderate means have all their money invested in New Haven stock," lamented the *New York Times*. At the height of the commotion Mellen resigned, but by the summer of 1914 he was back in the news with scandalous disclosures reported by the Interstate Commerce Commission, whose full investigation into the New Haven's affairs scaled all the way up the American business ladder to implicate Diamond Jim Brady, William Rockefeller, and, of course, J. P. Morgan.

The precise extent of Morgan's personal involvement in "the most glaring instances of maladministration revealed in all the history of American railroading" was never resolved. He died on the last day of March 1913, well before the commission commenced its scrutiny. The matter of who should rightly be called emperor, Mellen or Morgan, has been widely debated. The commission itself seemed certain that Morgan's obsession with monopoly—which Mellen repeatedly qualified as "beneficent monopoly"—had led to the New Haven's dictatorship over transportation in the Northeast. William Randolph Hearst, editorializing in his *Boston American,* espoused this belief, relegating Mellen to the role of "messenger boy." Others, including his authorized biographer, portrayed Morgan as the victim of posthumous betrayal at the hands of Mellen.

Mellen himself seemed conflicted. At one point during the railroad's investigation he compared the New Haven without Morgan to "a herd of cows deprived of the association of a bull." Yet when asked about the quest to conquer transportation he replied in the first person: "I came pretty near doing it."

The remaining clues to this mystery died with Morgan. His death did bring about a resolution to the question of why Morgan was so delighted with the track's electrification, however. It had been his dying wish, reported the *Wall Street Journal*—an unfulfilled wish, as Morgan met his end abroad—that his lifeless body would travel from New York to Hartford on the New Haven's electric tracks, borne "to its last resting place in Connecticut" along a road of peace and pleasant order.

The fall of the New Haven railroad, at the height of the Progressive era, reflected a cultural shift toward an egalitarian spirit. Manifested in transportation, this meant a movement away from the strictures of steel borders and toward the open highway. As the rails had made the country strong, so the free road soon would make the countryman. A year after the New Haven's collapse, a million automobiles would be produced— more than five times what had been made at the start of the decade. By then a new traffic pattern was in the process of replacing railroad *and* streetcar travel along the old post road, "for under its quiet elms dash daily a thousand motor cars," noted a trolley guide from 1914. "Its great days have returned."

Part III

The Nation's
Road Standard

❦

Times have changed along the Post Road, and the young men must change with them.

*—Grace Sartwell Mason, "Clarissa and the Post Road"
in* The Saturday Evening Post, *July 14, 1923*

Chapter 10

⚜

Colonel Pope and the
Good Roads Movement

A S THE RAILROAD network exploded during the nineteenth
century, connecting towns and cities all over the country,
the highways that had once performed this task were largely
neglected. The policy of highway avoidance trickled down from the
highest levels of government. When the turnpike era began, in the
early 1800s, Albert Gallatin, then Treasury secretary, had recommended
building a massive highway from Maine to Georgia. Such a road likely
would have followed the basic course of modern U.S. Route 1, along
the Atlantic Seaboard. Gallatin felt certain this highway would increase
the nation's wealth, and even went so far as to say it would secure America's liberty. But the $4.8 million road, he wrote, could only be built with
"early and efficient aid of the *Federal* Government." At the time many
legislators doubted that the federal government had the constitutional
power to make improvements at the state level. With few exceptions,
such as the National Road, it did not even try.

Unfortunately, neither did the states themselves. The colonial New
England method of road maintenance—the town's men gathering on a
few-mile stretch a couple times a year—remained largely in place. Many

173

other regions of the country even copied it. When the turnpike era failed, those roads reverted back to public roads. This meant even more local highway grooming. Or, in most cases, more highway lunching, smoking, and gossiping. The overall effect was habituated stagnancy. New Englanders liked to retell the joke about the hat sitting atop the muddy road—when someone stooped to pick it up, the person beneath said, "Hang on, I've got a good horse down here somewhere"—and by neglecting their highway upkeep, they could.

As more and more miles of railroad track appeared, the highway conversation was brushed aside, so that this inadequate approach persisted through the Civil War. "There is probably no public interest in which sound and intelligent legislation is more needed than in the enactment and revision of our road laws," reported the Department of Agriculture in 1868, after a survey of the country's roads. Texas's response to the surveyors epitomized the general highway disinterest: "Texas can boast of the best roads, with the least work, of any State in or out of the Union. Our citizens generally regard work as *unconstitutional*." So by the end of the nineteenth century the system of road maintenance that had changed little since colonial times had changed even less since the beginning of the railroad era.

The lack of effort was not due to lack of technology. Blake stone crushers for preparing small rocks, steamrollers for smoothing them atop the earth, plows, scrapers, watering mechanisms—all the tools existed. New York, Hartford, Boston, and other major cities laid excellent macadam streets with city taxes. Missing were personal vehicles that ventured outside city limits; the very notion of pleasure touring; the realization by farmers that better railway feeder roads would increase their efficiency and decrease wear on their wagons. Missing too were academically trained highway engineers. As late as 1889 none truly existed, wrote Nathaniel Shaler, who created the country's first specialized road program, at Harvard.

Even if these experts had existed at the time, few towns would have felt their services worth securing. For the country had the steel pulled over its eyes. A national tempo, set to the chugging tracks, was the most important factor in highway neglect—if steam railroads were the transportation of today, and electric railroads the transportation of tomorrow, then *some* railroads were the transportation of forever. The "astonishing growth of the railway system" was the "principal reason for this comparative neglect of the common roads," wrote J. W. Jenks, a leading political economist, in spring of 1889. "Then, too, though the railroads have not really lessened the importance of the wagon road, they seem to have done so."

This misunderstanding was so deeply ingrained that even the smallest request for road funding triggered sharp reactions by federal lawmakers. Such a request appeared in the halls of Congress in early 1893 as part of a larger appropriations bill. It was a line item granting the Secretary of Agriculture a paltry ten thousand dollars "to make inquiries in regard to the systems of road management throughout the United States." When a congressman from Texas noticed the item he balked at the notion of federal road oversight, and tried to abandon the clause, rather than please "a lot of 'cranks' in this country who are asking the Government to take the supervision of the dirt roads."

A national highway interest was emerging, however, and though its impact would not peak for many years, it had by this time gained enough support to secure this important first step. So, after a bit of contention, the highway item passed the House, and then the Senate. In time the resulting Office of Road Inquiry—today, the Federal Highway Administration—would unearth the old highways that had been lost beneath the railroad tracks between New York and Boston, and across the country.

The federal government's approval of road-related funds in February of 1893 is, by itself, a modest historic landmark. But the date becomes more intriguing when one considers that the first American-built gasoline car would not be completed until that fall. What initially raised the importance of highways, then—what pried people from the tracks and released them onto the open road—was not the automobile. The car would play a role. But to imply that the Model T marked the start of the movement toward good roads, as the Ford Motor Company did in 1927, was sorely revisionist.

Rather, the original push for better American highways came not from a Midwestern auto company but from an Old Post Road native who popularized bicycling—an ironically hefty fellow who lived in Boston, worked in Hartford, and shuffled in between. Largely forgotten now, Albert Pope ingrained the idea of independent travel into the nation's psyche with his Columbia bikes. He then nurtured highway interest into a feverish "good roads" movement, and, from there, into a faction of the federal government. He certainly knew all about the small line item that passed through Congress in early 1893; its passage was largely his doing.

IN MARCH 1846, when Albert Pope was not quite three years old, his family moved to Harvard Street, in Brookline, on a part of the original Old Post Road that curled down toward the neck of the Bay from Cambridge. His father speculated in real estate near the emerging lines of the horse-drawn street railways. Over the next five years Charles Pope bought many more lots, at least eight of them directly along the old highway, flipping them once their value rose. At first Charles succeeded. But in the nascent days of suburban expansion, so did many others. Toward 1852 Charles bottomed out. So Albert peddled fruits and vegetables up and down the Brookline streets to help support the family, and soon had several young men working for him.

Albert Pope's service during the Civil War included fighting for the Union under General Ulysses Grant at the Battle of Vicksburg. He achieved the rank of lieutenant colonel, but it might have been his tendency to assume control in the absence of his regiment's commanding officer that afterward led writers, colleagues, and friends alike to affectionately call him "The Colonel." A decade after the war Pope's shoe supplier business had become a sizable concern. He joined the Newton city council, a role that sent him to Philadelphia in 1876 to explore the Centennial Exposition. There he first laid eyes on a strange apparatus better suited to P. T. Barnum's circus act: the high-wheel bicycle.

By 1876 a brief American fling with the velocipede, that bicycle antecedent, had come and long gone. A French mechanic, Pierre Lallement, had brought the contraption to the United States in 1866. He was arrested, twice, for scaring horses while riding around the center green in New Haven. And though Manhattan flocked to the sport for a couple years—Charles Dana, publisher of the *New York Sun,* was a notable fan—the fad had faded by 1870. But the high-wheel was gaining popularity in England, and when Pope took a trip there to view the industry, he decided it was high time to try again in America.

In the summer of 1877 Pope invited an Englishman named John Harrington to his suburban Boston home. There, over the course of two months, Harrington constructed a bike at a cost of around three hundred dollars. He then taught Pope to ride. This was no easy task. It often took hours just to learn how to mount the high-wheel—planting one foot on a notch, propelling with the other, then vaulting into the seat. The Popes lived on Washington Street, in Brighton, at the time. Pope likely took some of those first lessons, and no doubt those first face-plants, along the Old Post Road that crossed the river onto modern U.S. Route 20 toward Watertown.

The experience must have been a rewarding one, for Pope acted quickly, and at great expense, to ignite the business. He imported forty-two high-wheelers from overseas. He acquired, through shrewd maneuvers, Lallement's original patent, so that for several years no person could sell a bicycle in America without paying Pope ten dollars. By 1882 he had forty other patents and a clamp on the industry. He traveled to Hartford in search of industrial aid, and convinced the Weed Sewing Machine Company to construct fifty of the strange vehicles in its spare factory space. To emphasize their American origin, Pope named his model Columbia.

By the early 1880s Pope had set up a retail headquarters in downtown Boston. If a tangle of metal or a stream of profanity could be heard above the buzz on Washington Street during the hours of 7 a.m. to 6 p.m., it likely emanated from the four-story building at No. 597. There, rattling over the general office, was the Columbia riding school. Downstairs Pope sold his products: the Standard Columbia, the Special, the Mustang, rubber tires ranging up to sixty inches for the six-foot-one man, waterproof cyclometers, sperm whale oil for headlamps, canvas shoes with extra rubber soles. Bit by bit an interested public left this store and rolled onto the old highway with a boundless new spirit: "For unquestionably," *Harper's* magazine declared by summer of 1881, the bicycle "bids fair to become as important a factor for enlarging the scope of personal travel as the railroad has become for the rapid collective circulation."

IN THE COURSE of twenty years, bicycling in America evolved from affluent hobby to instrument of liberation to national obsession to well-worn pastime. The extra corner rented by Pope in one Hartford warehouse mushroomed into a cluster of factories, a worldwide hub of agents and retailers, and a place of employment for thousands of workers. Soon it turned Connecticut's capital into one of America's richest cities. "It is safe to say that few articles ever used by man have created so great a revolution in social conditions as the bicycle," declared the United States Census in 1900. "Colonel Pope bears the undisputed title 'Father of the American bicycle,' and a great part of the credit for the extraordinary development of the industry was due to him."

From the start Pope made it his agenda to explode the common biases against his machine. The general notion—that bicycles scared horses, cluttered streets, endangered pedestrians, and required a gymnast's balance—lingered from the days of the velocipede. So along with bicycles Pope manufactured a mind-set. He invested heavily in publications. Early on it was his great fortune to secure, entirely by chance, the editorial services of a young S. S. (Samuel Sidney) McClure. In fact Pope first put McClure to work in his Washington Street training rink in July 1882.

The magazine they launched that fall, *The Wheelman,* which later merged into the more widely read *Outing,* was devoted entirely to the bicycling lifestyle. As antidote to the perceived difficulty of riding his machines, Pope offered cash prizes to doctors who published the best essays on bike riding's benefits to health. He also shelled out thousands of dollars in legal fees to fight laws banning bikers from streets and parks in Boston, Providence, Hartford, and other cities—spending $8,000 alone on a single battle to gain all-important access to Manhattan's Central Park.

Pope helped start, and frequently financed, the League of American Wheelmen, a national club whose expansive efforts raised bicycle interest from trend to passionate avocation. (An undated note that survives in some Pope correspondence suggests he might have had an even more powerful "sway over the affairs of the L.A.W." than is often attributed to him.) Through its publication of travel-sized bicycling guides the League cultivated a touring culture that harmonized with the growing urge for suburban retreat. One guide from 1885, printed at 597 Washington Street, describes a route west from Pope's old stomping ground toward Watertown and Waltham along the old highway. Later guides refer to the "old Post Road" directly. A Connecticut book from 1890 outlines a trip from New York to Boston via Hartford as Route 1, and from New York to Providence via New Haven as Route 2. At its peak the League boasted more than one hundred thousand members—nearly the 1900 population of all New Haven. About forty percent of this membership base lived in states traversed by the Old Post Road.

These guides, in many ways precursors of modern AAA books, went a long way toward fostering a sense of personal freedom. They were small enough to fit in a pocket, and they included foldout maps—a necessity in the age before widespread road signs. They listed thousands of League-certified hotels and inns where members could receive discounted rates. By the mid-1890s hotelkeepers everywhere kept a bicycle pump and repair kit close by.

Escapism ensued. Middle- and upper-class urbanites shed the crowded city for weekends in the wilderness. One League leader even wondered at the reemergence of quaint tavern inns "that marked the stopping-places of the old stage-coach, which, in the years following the Revolution, used to make the distance between Boston and New York in six days." But the difference was significant. Those six days had been spent boarding where Levi Pease pleased. Bike riders could travel as near or far as they wanted, unbound by predawn stagecoach awakenings, or even the more recent rigidity of railroad schedules they had grown to memorize.

The result, in the contemporary words of *Scientific American* magazine, "changed completely many of the ordinary processes and methods of social life." This became particularly true after the introduction of the safety bicycle in the late 1880s. Unlike the high-wheel bicycle, whose front wheel dwarfed the rear, the safety's wheels were the same size. This simple change, combined with pneumatic tires for a more cushioned ride, broadened interest in bicycling from sportsman to everyman. And soon, every woman. Riders numbered in the millions. Courtship habits changed; couples skipped church to ride together on Sundays. Ladies donned bloomers to keep from getting their gowns tangled in bike chains. The scandalous bit of exposed leg was acceptable to prevent accidents; but just why these short pants were being worn off the bicycle became cause for public debate.

Celebrities heightened the exposure. Mark Twain, then a Hartford resident, strolled down to Pope's factory and bought a Columbia with a dozen lessons in 1886. "I was partly to realize, then, how admirably these things are constructed," he wrote after the first of many spills. "Get a bicycle. You will not regret it, if you live." Diamond Jim Brady produced his own gold-plated, jewel-encrusted bike for the actress Lillian Russell, after Pope (and then Tiffany's) declined to make one for him. Theodore Roosevelt, then police commissioner of New York City, launched a "bicycle squad" to wheel down outlaws. It was not beyond the bounds of reality, at the peak of the bicycle's power, for Pope to envision a futuristic bicycle-railroad that whizzed between New York and Boston at two hundred miles per hour. By the time J. P. Morgan bought a bike at the 1896 Madison Square Garden trade show the luster had largely worn off.

Soon the focus shifted on to the particulars of bicycle touring. Highway conditions, maps, and preferred routes became party conversation. Riders everywhere shared a common obstacle—hazardous roads. Describing the bicycle route east from Springfield, for instance, one League guide suggests taking a train to Worcester. (Pope had been among those who compelled railroads to allow bicycles as acceptable luggage.) This portion of the tour, another book noted, was riddled with "ruts and loose stones"; its roads were categorized as "poor." By then Pope's second ambitious venture was already under way. "And the good roads are inevitable," remarked *Forum* magazine in August 1896. "They are coming in all directions, and they are coming because the bicycle is creating an irresistible demand for them."

In the closing decades of the nineteenth century, Albert Pope could often be found in a lecture hall somewhere, speaking to carriage makers or postmasters or boards of trade or even railroad executives—speaking, really, to whoever would listen—about the importance of road improvement. At the time his goal seemed far-fetched. It demanded, from the start, the kind of heavy government oversight that had been avoided for a century. But looking back at the Office of Road Inquiry that emerged in February of 1893, and the national interstate system this office finalized three decades later, the results bear a striking resemblance to what Pope had been proposing all along.

One of Pope's first such calls to action, in 1889, neatly captured his basic argument: "The invention of steam, and the development of the railroad, seem to have taken all our energies and resources, to the neglect of our roads and highways," he said. "The high point to be aimed at, is the recognition of the importance of the whole situation by the national government, and the establishment by Congress of a national system." Recognizing that many critics feared federal administration of roads, Pope envisioned a system in which most responsibility fell to the local level. At the top, a federal highway commissioner would provide general guidelines and supervision. In the middle, state highway boards would actually manage road projects. At the bottom, counties and towns would handle the details of road construction.

However logical such thinking seems now, it took years of effort to convince the public of the need for highway reform. But in Pope the Good Roads movement had a perfect driver. As one of America's eminent businessmen he had the platform to push an agenda. As the president of Pope Manufacturing Company he stood to profit from better roads, but as The Colonel he remained, in the public eye, a civic-minded patriot. (This was no ruse; when one of his retail stores burned, his first concern was not the quarter million dollars of lost merchandise but the Civil War memorabilia he had housed inside.) With each

Columbia bike that rolled off the shelf and onto the street, Pope had a growing means to support a struggling cause. By 1890 the Massachusetts Institute of Technology wanted to start a specialized "highway engineering" program, but it took Pope's five-year, six-thousand-dollar commitment to get it going. When he sponsored contests for scholarly essays on good roads, he offered prizes up to $500—matching an average laborer's annual salary.

In the League of American Wheelmen Pope also had a devoted advocacy group at his disposal. With his backing the League started *Good Roads* magazine in 1892. The association's president, James Dunn, adopted Pope's movement in his own talks and writings. At an annual meeting in 1891 Dunn tossed out an idea: Why not reconstruct the Old Post Road, in its entirety from New York to Boston, with the most advanced scientific methods, to serve as an exemplar for the country to follow? Pope must have approved of the suggestion, for he proposed something similar in one of his own talks: a state-of-the-art highway following "in general the line of" the New Haven railroad.

In July of 1892 the wheelmen took their influence to Washington. They drafted legislation for a National Highway Commission—a body composed of two senators, five representatives, and five presidentially appointed citizens. Though the bill was not passed before Congress adjourned it seemed poised for approval come fall. The League's pending breakthrough was significant enough to be described by the *New York Times* in an article: "What Bicycles Have Done."

To rally support, Pope requested letters advocating Good Roads legislation from powerful friends. He received responses from congressmen, cabinet members, military leaders, governors, and university presidents. John Wanamaker, the postmaster general, wrote to Pope that postal delivery could only expand at the rate of quality roads. Pope even coaxed a letter from the country's president, Benjamin Harrison, who told League members that "if wheelmen secure us the good roads for which they are so zealously working, your body deserves a medal in recognition of its philanthropy."

By that time the Good Roads movement had enough popular momentum to break its bicycling ties. In October, at a meeting of minds funded partly by Pope, the National League for Good Roads was formed. The National League began a furious race for support. State governors were offered board positions. Editors were pitched for publicity. Big shots were called upon to empty their pockets.* The *New York Times* agreed to house a Good Roads fund. Influential Senator Charles Manderson agreed to act as the new venture's political figurehead. Before long a powerful national advocacy network had been assembled to push Good Roads legislation forward.

Pope had been made an officer of the National League, but while that effort gained support he began making solicitations of his own. One such effort took the form of a congressional petition—a memorial in which Pope called for a Department of Roads, similar to the Department of Agriculture, to promote good road knowledge and advance road-building education. Acting independently from the National League, Pope printed fifty thousand copies of his petition and distributed them to post offices, news editors, and political leaders across the country. Within a few months 150,000 people had signed the petition, and newspapers from Boston to San Diego to Tyler, Texas, had endorsed the proposal. When it was finally presented to Congress, toward the end of 1893, the petition stretched nearly a mile. It wound around the tires of a specially made bicycle and was "wheeled to the Committee on Inter-State Commerce."

In addition to his general memorial, Pope sent a letter to every member of Congress, urging them to include a line item devoted to highway reform in the upcoming Department of Agriculture appropriations bill. Which brings things back to early February 1893, when the House of Representatives does just that: appropriates $10,000 for a highway program under the auspices of the Department of Agriculture. On March 3, 1893, President Harrison signed the bill into law on his final day in office. By fall of that year the Office of Road Inquiry had been established.

The long struggle for highway reform was far from over. As ini-

---

*Among the donors, who included several Vanderbilts and Thomas Edison, only J. P. Morgan appears to have "paid cash."

tially conceived, the Office of Road Inquiry was not authorized to actually build roads at all; even if it had been, ten thousand dollars could have constructed about three total miles. Still, a critical stage of federal acceptance had been achieved. As such, Nathaniel Shaler, writing in *Harper's* magazine in early 1894, acknowledged the beginning of an era: "The presentation of the great petition to Congress marks the last step in the effort of a number of men, of whom the most efficient has been Col. A. A. Pope, of Boston, to arouse the people to an understanding of the burden which their ill-conditioned highways impose upon them."

One aspect of the early Good Roads saga remains to be clarified. The National League often gets credit for the achievement of 1893, but it appears that Pope's solitary efforts were more influential. Highway historians have given the impression that Pope and Roy Stone, head of the National League for Good Roads and first chief of the Office of Road Inquiry, worked largely in concert to pass Good Roads legislation. In fact, Stone essentially forced Pope to resign from the National League for distributing his "great petition to Congress" without the League's approval.

Stone feared the petition would invite criticism because it stopped just short of demanding a new cabinet position. Senator Manderson approved of Pope's removal; he also forwarded Stone a copy of the letter Pope sent to all congressmen, remarking that Pope "is quite persistent in his efforts." Offended by his removal from a movement he pioneered, Pope refused any association with the National League: "I do not ask or expect public recognition of what I have given for so worthy a cause," he wrote to Stone in January of 1893. "My ambition is to have something accomplished in my day and generation which shall be of benefit for all time to this nation."

In February, Stone was furious to learn of the highway line item in the Department of Agriculture's upcoming appropriations bill. He preferred a distinct twelve-person National Highway Commission. He dashed off a letter to Manderson, imploring the senator to amend the item and thereby "accomplish what you set out to do originally."

But right before Stone sent this seething letter he received notice that the House was preparing a bill "providing for a bureau of good roads" in the Agriculture Department. So Stone scribbled a postscript to his fiery note: "This is not at all what we asked for," he wrote Manderson on February 3, 1893—the day before the item was introduced in Congress—"though I believe it is one of Col. Pope's ideas."

Chapter 11

"Rocks, Ruts, and Thank-you-marms"

T HE OLD POST ROAD'S brief stretch as the automotive center of the world began, like many brief stretches of brilliance, with an attractive young lady. And it ended, like so many such stretches, with a lawsuit.

It was spring of 1893 when Hiram Percy Maxim bought a used Columbia tricycle for thirty dollars. "The bicycle was just becoming popular and it represented a very significant advance" in transportation, Maxim later recalled in his memoir of the period. An arms engineer from an inventive family—his father is credited with creating the machine gun, and Maxim himself would later devise a silencer—Maxim knew that one good advance deserves another. The thought had recently occurred to him, as he biked home from an evening courtship session with his "attractive young lady," that surely he could build a motor capable of doing the work his legs were doing. As such, Maxim did not intend to power his new Columbia much longer. He intended to build a Columbia that could power him.

Maxim spent the next two years transforming his used Pope into a "horseless carriage," as primitive automobiles were commonly called. Maxim's efforts required the faithful assistance of a colleague and earned him not a few suspicious glares from the general store clerk who sold him cup after cup of gasoline. Of course, Maxim could not simply declare his efforts to this man, or almost anyone. The notion of replacing horses with a motor engine, at that time, might have gotten him arrested for insanity. Horses had always borne the efforts of personal transportation, and there was no reason to think they ever would not. Editorial cartoons collected later on by Maxim reflected the fears of such a fundamental cultural change: they depicted horses weeping beneath signs reading "Nearly Extinct," and bridles hanging on museum walls.

When Maxim presented his idea to an executive at a top bicycle company in the late spring of 1895, he received a similarly skeptical reaction. Pursuit of the motor engine was a waste of time, Maxim was told. Another man at the company was willing to entertain the young inventor, however, and soon sent an agent to Maxim's work space, ten miles north of Boston. There, on a suspenseful second try, Maxim's tricycle engine roared to life. Two weeks later the terms were complete, and in July of 1895 Maxim moved to Hartford to run the new "Columbia motor-carriage" department of the Pope Manufacturing Company.

The bicycle's influence on the modern automobile goes far beyond a young lover tinkering with a used Columbia tricycle. In a very real sense the car drove into the cultural landscape established by bike riding. Countryside bicycle touring awakened much of urban America to a powerful sense of adventure. Suddenly there was an alternative to crowded, sweaty streetcars. As bikes became more affordable—and, with the invention of the Columbia "chainless" in the mid-1890s, more rideable—this frontier yearning engrossed a wider population.

As Maxim later recalled, the emergence of American automobiles at the peak of bicycle interest was no coincidence:

> The reason why we did not build mechanical road vehicles before this, in my opinion, was because the bicycle had not yet come in numbers and had not directed men's minds to the possibilities of independent, long-distance travel over the ordinary highway. We thought the railroad was good enough. The bicycle created a new demand which it was beyond the ability of the rail-

road to supply. Then it came about that the bicycle could not satisfy the demand which it had created. A mechanically propelled
vehicle was wanted instead of a foot-propelled one, and we now
know that the automobile was the answer.

The automobile owed as much to the technical aspects of bicycle
production as it did to the cultural ones. After all, Henry Ford did not
call his first car the Quadricycle by accident. More often than not Pope
Manufacturing led this side of the industry too. Several years before
Hiram Percy Maxim arrived in Hartford, Charles Duryea had paid
the Pope factory a visit to discuss the problem of automotive engines.
Schooled in bicycle craft, Duryea thought a car would need the type of
differential gear produced by the Pope company. He purchased one during his visit and installed it on the model built by his brother, J. Frank
Duryea, in their work space in Springfield, Massachusetts. The gasoline
car Frank Duryea completed in the fall of 1893 is widely considered the
first modern one in American history.

Pope invested more in technological research than anyone in the
personal transportation business. His campus of innovation and production extended for nearly a mile along the tracks of the New Haven
railroad as they entered Hartford's Union Station. Axles, gears, and early
components of automotive transmissions were developed from Pope
engineering. Car makers adapted aspects of bicycle tubing, bearings,
suspension, and drive shafts. Pope scientists created bevel gears with a
tolerance—the term in mass production for an acceptable range of varia-
tion—of one two-thousandth of an inch. (By 1903 Ford had achieved a
tolerance of only one sixty-fourth.) His techniques of mass production,
inspired by the firearms factories in Springfield and Hartford, stream-
lined the manufacture of specialized parts. He took quality control to
unprecedented lengths; by the mid-1890s two dozen inspectors gave
each bicycle a review of five hundred points.

One critical aspect of automotive development inspired by the
bicycle needs no technical expertise to recognize at all—just a glance at
early photographs of Maxim's cars, which provide a stark example of the
connection: the wheels have spokes.

This is getting a bit ahead. When Maxim first took over the famed Pope company's new venture, the public expected a "remarkable revolution in transportation." (Pointing out the more spectacular components of Maxim's early efforts, the *New York World* wrote of his engine—all 1.5 horsepower—"this motor is one of the most serviceable ever built, as it will not explode.") Over the next several years Maxim did build some of the most serviceable cars in the industry, testing them during midnight spins on his own trial track: the Old Post Road. In the course of these adventuresome lessons over the dark old highway Maxim gained the mechanical wisdom that developed the Columbia motor works into the country's leading auto manufacturer by the close of the nineteenth century.

Maxim drove mostly at night, as bringing out the loud, coughing machine during the day seemed to attract half of Hartford. His first recorded goal, twenty-five miles to Springfield in early 1897, required several tries spanning a couple months. On their first trip Maxim and an assistant managed only a quarter mile before breaking down; the next try ended after two miles, in the same manner. Finally they made the entire trip, in nearly ten hours, terrifying several horses and carriage drivers along the way. At three in the morning they pulled up to the old Massasoit House on Springfield's Main Street, near the railroad embankment, and found the innkeeper "thoroughly rattled." He had taken their car for a derailed Boston & Albany train heading right for his stables. Maxim later drove forty-some miles from Hartford to Saybrook—following roughly the same course John Winthrop Jr. had taken during his overland exploration in 1645—and made a separate journey, in an electric car, all the way to Boston.

Maxim's most impressive trial took him from Hartford to New York over the Old Post Road in the summer of 1898. His recollection of the ride illustrates all the perils of long-distance driving before the time of federally sanctioned highways. He drove one of his gasoline cars, the Mark VIII, in the company of a European agent for Pope who had a meeting in Manhattan. Outside the towns and cities, "rocks, ruts, and thank-you-marms" cluttered the winding old highway. Very few signs marked the way; Maxim's only guide was a bike-tour map printed by the League of American Wheelmen, which he acquired during his many years as a member. Still, the pair frequently got lost.

A great many delays came from encountering carriages along the road. Horses were liable to shake their reins and flee into the countryside at the sight and sound of the oncoming motor engine. These delicate situations usually required Maxim to approach with extreme caution— or even come to a full halt. "It seemed we confronted a road problem every half mile," Maxim wrote in his memoir. "It was a nervous strain."

A bit west of Norwalk, Connecticut, Maxim's passenger had had enough, and hopped a New Haven train from Stamford into Manhattan. Maxim continued on alone, sometimes asking the way toward the Harlem River, other times following the most well-lighted part of the sky—the presumption being that this was New York City. When in doubt he followed the trolley tracks that lined the Old Post Road. Between bits of information and instinct he eventually reached Manhattan. There Maxim experienced a problem millions of New Yorkers would come to know too well: the inability to find parking. "There was not a single garage in all New York in those days," he recalled, "and a livery-stable would not take me in." (He eventually stored the car at a Pope distributing office.)

"I may have been the first man to drive from Hartford to New York in a motor-carriage," Maxim later wrote. The next morning he met the European agent—shocked, and surely a bit impressed, to find that his driver had both arrived and remained in one piece. The pair even braved a return trip by road, but at a "very rough and stony" section of the Old Post Road in Rye the engine fell clean off the Mark VIII, and the first significant road trip along modern U.S. Route 1 puttered to a rest.

Within a few years the Automobile Club of America had marked most of the routes from New York to Boston, and the Old Post Road had become the definitive trial course for automotive development. A weeklong "reliability run" between the cities in October of 1902, following the northern route through Hartford and Springfield, was considered a turning point in American auto engineering. Sixty-seven of the seventy-five cars that began the five-hundred-mile race finished it. "Automobiles have proved by this run that they are capable of covering long distances on schedule time," the head of the American Automobile Association told the *New York Times.*

Considering the poor performance of European cars—six of seven failed to finish—the *Times* went a bit further: "Consequently the contest is considered to have demonstrated that, not only has the American automobile reached a point in its development which makes it a practically reliable vehicle in nine cases out of ten, but also that it is now in point of reliability and endurance the superior of the foreign-made vehicles."

IF AMERICAN CARS indeed led the globe in excellence at the dawn of the twentieth century, then Maxim's jaunts had made the Old Post Road the axis of the automotive world. Of the 4,192 cars made in America during the year 1900, more than two thousand came from Connecticut or Massachusetts. The total value of American cars at the time was $4,899,443; Connecticut alone accounted for about thirty-nine percent of this figure, with the Pope factory powering the way. In the years that followed, Worcester became a leading auto-parts maker; Springfield manufactured welding equipment; Bridgeport produced springs; Boston made superior speedometers. In 1899 the editor of a British technical journal visited the United States after inspecting automakers in England, France, and Germany. "The Town of Hartford, Connecticut," he concluded, "is the greatest center of activity in the automobile industry today."

It didn't take long for Pope to put Maxim's ideas into production. He had spoken of marketability from the moment he tossed his corpulent frame into one of Maxim's new—and, under The Colonel's weight, lopsided—contraptions. At a public unveiling in 1897, attended by a full press corps ranging from *Scientific American* to *Cosmopolitan* magazine, Pope Manufacturing became the first major company to stress the car's commercial value.

As it happened, the Columbia Automobile Company focused on electric cars—producing five hundred within the next year. At the time no one knew gasoline engines would come to dominate the field. Opinion was widely split between the electric and gasoline camps; in fact, more steam-powered cars were built in 1900 than either of the other two.

Early gas cars, in Maxim's words, "shook and trembled and rattled and clattered, spat oil, fire, smoke, and smell"—rather objectionable qualities, particularly to the upper-class clientele who could afford them. The first gasoline-powered ride taken by George Day, Pope's right-hand man, left Day shaken, silent, and in need of a cigarette. Columbia's auto-works did produce gasoline tricycles intended for messengers and deliv-erymen, though these sold so poorly that Pope was forced to open his own package-delivery service in Boston for their deployment. (Maxim had always favored gasoline engines, but stories he collected on the scar-city of petroleum betray his own uncertainty, though any doubt likely disappeared once oil wells gushed from Spindletop, Texas, in 1901.)

In the end the Pope company preferred Maxim's finely groomed Columbia electric, a choice that echoed the high-wheel bicycle trend Pope had started decades earlier. Cars would begin as toys for the rich. Once the technology improved enough to lower prices—as it had with the safety and chainless bicycles—cultural acceptance would drizzle down toward the masses. But although crisp and quiet enough to suit those with high tastes, electric cars could travel only thirty to fifty miles without being recharged. This was fine for urban driving but made lon-ger trips extremely challenging; as high an authority as Thomas Edison questioned the possibility of creating a battery sufficient for this purpose.

Later on Pope's tilt toward electric power played a large role in the company's downfall. But in spring of 1899 it resulted in the most expansive motor vehicle project of the infant era. In early April Pope traveled to New York to meet with William Whitney, the urban transit king of Manhattan, who wanted to start a worldwide network of elec-tric cabs. Pope's army of selling agents already spanned the globe. (One, John Hertz, later went on to start the rental car agency that still bears his name.) The Pope company, it seemed to Whitney, was the only one in the country capable of producing the two hundred cabs he wanted immediately—let alone the 1,600 cars he demanded soon after.

The result of this deal was the Columbia & Electric Vehicle Com-pany, and its undertaking was, in the words of Herman Cuntz, Pope's patent attorney, "the greatest automobile production ever conceived up to that time." Some of Pope's Hartford bicycle factories were reassigned to the new purpose, and a carriage company in New Haven was purchased. Managers, engineers, and workers shuttled between the two locations to meet the unprecedented order. "This influx to the Mecca of a new industry was the most important movement of people that had occurred since the Rev. Thomas Hooker came to found the village of Hartford," Cuntz recalled. Soon Columbia cabs appeared in Boston, New York, and Paris. Some were even sold to the United States Post Office for package delivery.

So for a brief moment in history the center of the Old Post Road and the center of the transportation universe seemed to turn upon the same gear. The symbol of all this success coalesced in an event that took place in August of 1902, when Theodore Roosevelt became the first president to ride in a motorcade. A photograph of the event captured the full range of the Pope hegemony: Roosevelt in a Columbia electric, riding along the fine streets of Hartford, flanked by Secret Service on Columbia chainless bicycles.

As quickly as it captivated the world, however, the Columbia & Electric Vehicle Company slipped from its perch. Overcapitalization, an unsettled industry, and the inferiority of electric cars contributed to its failure. In addition, the public had not yet widely accepted car travel as a form of transportation. When its slide was imminent the company turned to an alternative strategy for success: a little-known, generously broad automobile patent acquired from an unheralded inventor named George Selden.

Pope's bicycle ventures had relied heavily on early patents to secure the industry. The sputtering Electric Vehicle Company would do the same. Immediately following Pope's meeting with Whitney a memo was sent out from the patent department outlining the company's preferred procedure. The directives, according to Maxim's notes, encouraged employees to influence inventions along "legally advantageous lines" and to watch "for infringements and valuable patents." At the advice of Herman Cuntz and eminent legal experts the company bought the rights to Selden's patent.

For a while the Electric Vehicle Company dangled Selden's patent before American automakers, in a bullish attempt to consolidate the industry. In July of 1903 the Selden holders denied use of the patent to an unproven Midwestern manufacturer named Henry Ford, whose company had but $28,000 in capital—less than one percent of the Electric Vehicle Company's $18 million. Come October they filed suit against Ford's diminutive operation.

Within the span of a decade, the very foundations of movement would be uprooted. Ford built his Model T. The Wright brothers entered the sky. Federal regulators took the Morgan railroad monopoly on the proverbial ride. Pope's auto factories struggled, and in August of 1909 he died after a month of illness brought on largely by his company's embarrassment. Two years later Henry Ford won his appeal against the Electric Vehicle Company, ending its remaining hopes of being an industry leader, and rendering the Selden patent irrelevant. By then the Model T had assured Ford a cultural immortality. Before long, Pope's efforts had been forgotten, and Ford's iconic car was hailed as having "started the movement for good roads everywhere"—in the *Hartford Courant,* no less.

WHILE THIS PERIOD of transportation turmoil might have damaged the Pope legacy, it surely boosted his childhood ambition—"started by my early bicycle experience on the suburban roads about Boston"—that the country improve its highways. The year 1907 "marked a change in policy on the part of motorists in the United States," proclaimed the American Automobile Association in its yearbook. Come 1908 the Office of Road Inquiry (by then called the Office of Public Roads) still had no mandate to build roads, but it teamed with the Massachusetts state highway board, which did have such power, to apply an experimental surface material on parts of the Old Post Road.

Between 1910 and 1915 few topics received more news coverage than the effort for good roads. As cars gained general acceptance, and as flight made driving far less futuristic by comparison, motorists were seen less as an elite class trying to support a hobby with taxpayer money and more as the voice of American necessity. During this time

Congress strongly considered expanding the powers of the Office of Public Roads to include road construction. "I deem Federal aid to good roads the greatest, and certainly the most important, economic question now before the American people," said Jonathan Bourne Jr., chair of a joint committee to investigate the question, in April of 1913. Bourne even ventured the iconoclastic statement that the post roads clause of the Constitution surely empowered the national government to lead the highway improvement effort.

The government's first highway contribution program, the Federal Aid Highway Act of 1916, limited federal aid to "rural post roads" running through towns with populations below twenty-five hundred. At the time such a decision made sense. Small towns had little money to build their own roads, yet they still had a right to the mail. Few foresaw, as did one auto association leader who spoke at congressional hearings on good roads, that the "automobile is going to be a factor in commerce greater than the railroads ever were." (Pope himself had envisioned federal aid going to "thoroughfares that facilitate interstate communication," in an article in *Harper's,* published a year and a half before his death.)

After the country's entrance into World War I, in April of 1917, this mind-set began to change. Freight trains struggled to move provisions with speed—particularly in the East. Soon train failures required federal intervention, and by 1918 the government had nationalized the rails. Meanwhile many manufacturers turned to truck delivery; Connecticut factories, finding the railroads completely backed up, made the switch to survive; and one New York company stretched its truck route through to Boston.

After the war the successful trial of truck shipments made them a fixture on the industrial scene. It also left the overworked highways badly worn. Toward the end of the nineteenth century many roads were made from water-bound macadam. Connecticut and Massachusetts made emergency road appropriations in the millions just to keep pace. Road construction, particularly the kind suited to automobiles, was an ongoing science; only a few years had passed since Logan Page, former student of Nathaniel Shaler, realized that dust churned up by cars was actually a sign of macadam being damaged.

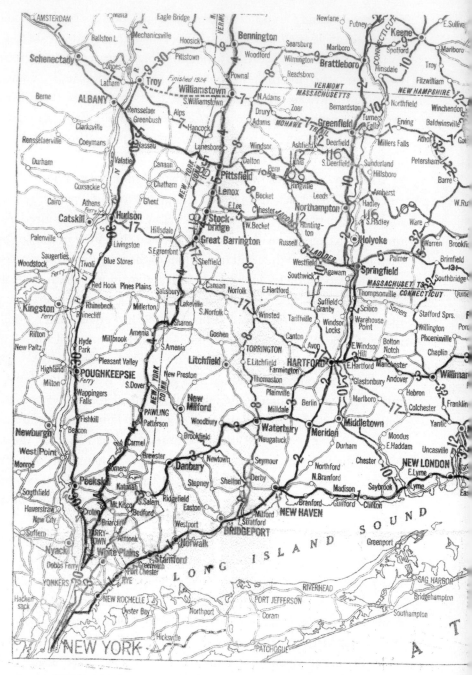

Courtesy of the National Archives

ROAD MARKING SYSTEM
ADOPTED BY
NEW ENGLAND
COMPILED BY
THE AUTOMOBILE CLUB OF AMERICA
BUREAU OF TOURS
For Details, Itineraries, Mileages,
See The Associated Tours Guide

*This 1922 tour map was used to determine the U.S. Highways.
The coastal branch of the Boston Post Road, marked "1" here,
became U.S. Route 1 in 1925.*

Worn-out highways weren't just a problem for truckers. A study by the Department of War found that the very same roads that facilitated commercial flow—interstate roads—would also help military movement. So the dust clouds served as a distress signal of sorts, warning Congress that its misguided rural post road policy might damage the economy and national security alike. In 1921 lawmakers responded by granting a massive $75 million in federal highway aid—equaling five years of aid under the old bill—and directed the Secretary of Agriculture to "expedite the completion of an adequate and connected system of highways, interstate in character."

With that the first truly national interstate era was under way. Roads themselves began to improve. Asphalt and tar were used to dampen wear and tear. Soon new concoctions appeared, like reinforced concrete—slabs of road eight inches deep, supported by half-inch steel bars. By 1925 the problem had shifted from improving roads to organizing them in a manner that made sense to drivers. State highway boards, which oversaw actual road construction, typically created their own individual systems of signage. The driver who crossed state borders without a map did so on a fool's errand. Meanwhile an emergent motor tourism industry began to rewrite atlases across the country. These promoters coined names like the Lincoln Highway—arbitrary designations bereft of geographic significance—confusing drivers and profiting off roads built with taxpayer money.

A push for order came in early 1925, when the association of state highway officials joined the Office of Road Inquiry (renamed, yet again, the Bureau of Public Roads) to select the most important thoroughfares and "give them a conspicuous place among the highways of the country as roads of interstate and national significance." This series of negotiations resulted in 75,800 miles of "United States Highways" emblazoned on a now-familiar white shield, but the process was by no means a simple one.* Eastern states censured Western ones for knighting what they considered local roads with the prestigious "U.S." aegis. Even the word

---

*Among the decisions that slipped through unscathed was the choice of black letters against a "lemon yellow" background for stop signs—a color scheme that remained intact until 1955.

highway itself was debated. New York's road chief went so far as to suggest shields with the letters *T.C.,* for transcontinental. "The word transcontinental won't offend anybody," he said during a meeting in April 1925. "U.S. highway will create criticism."

Finally all the maps were collected and the numbers assigned. Those running north-south would be odd, east-west even, with slight variations based on overlapping routes and levels of importance. The original United States Highways have shifted somewhat since they were first approved—some more than others. But for a converted Indian trail the Old Post Road was admirably represented among the avenues of national importance: The predominant east-west route followed the original northern stretch of the old highway, continuing past Springfield, Massachusetts, all the way to Oregon. Though the route has since changed, maps at the time show definitively that U.S. Route 20 was to pass through the same northern branch of the Old Post Road that George Washington had traveled, by stagecoach, in 1789.*

The principal north-south route described in 1925 has changed far less. It extended from Maine to Florida using the coastal route of the old highway between Boston and New York. It was called U.S. Route 1—though at least one national road map published in 1926 simultaneously lists it as the Boston Post Road, insisting, as J. P. Morgan had with *Hartford* in the name of the New York, New Haven & Hartford railroad years before, that its roots stay represented.

IN 1925, as part of its annual report to the stockholders, the notorious New York, New Haven & Hartford railroad divulged what would appear to be, particularly from the standpoint of a railroad company, a suspicious investment. Circumstances left the New Haven no choice, it told the stockholders; "your Company has been faced for some time

---

*Going west from Boston, the original U.S. Route 20 passed through the Massachusetts towns of Waltham, Watertown, Wayland, Marlborough, Northborough, Shrewsbury, Worcester, Leicester, Spencer, Brookfield, Warren, Palmer, Wilbraham, and Springfield. In 1931 the Southwest Cutoff was built to improve the route to Hartford, and claimed the U.S. Route 20 designation as it veers south after Northborough.

with a serious problem." Passengers were defecting to another form of transportation; it was trolley competition during the Mellen era, revisited. In the absence of a dramatic measure, the company might lose its hold on the region. This, of course, was not an option.

Yes, the New Haven railroad had begun to operate a line of buses on thirty routes of freshly numbered interstates. The New England Transportation Company, as the railroad's bus operation was called, was meant to meet the modern public's travel demands. "A large amount of passenger travel had left the rails and gone to the highways, causing a constantly growing loss of passenger revenue," the New Haven's annual report explained. "It was evident that unless different transportation methods were adopted, considerable rail service would have to be surrendered to the detriment of our revenues, the public convenience and necessity."

At first the New Haven only used its buses to carry travelers along unprofitable secondary rail routes. But very soon the company recognized the need to service the primary corridor too. Beginning October 1, 1927, a bus would depart from the Waldorf-Astoria, in Manhattan, at 9 a.m. and 9 p.m., every day, including Sunday. The coaches had an elevated seating area, with the finest "double-air cushion" seats, capable of carrying seventeen riders. A dozen more passengers could fit in a compartment underneath. "The route will be by the way of Stamford, Bridgeport, New Haven, New London and Providence," reported the *New York Times*. From there the bus would continue north, most likely remaining on U.S. Route 1 all the way to Boston.

Chapter 12

Highway Route 1, Relocated

BETWEEN THE WORLD wars no highway in America carried more traffic than the Boston Post Road. The seventy-mile strip of U.S. Route 1 connecting New York with New Haven, in particular, was red carpet to the automobile's growing celebrity. It was reference point against which other parts of the country compared their own traffic woes. It was laboratory for studies on the nature of highway use. It was, come summer of 1937, put on exhibit among the world's most famous roads—displayed alongside Germany's Bergstrasse, France's Route de Quarante Sous, England's Watling Street, and the Roman Empire's Appian Way. In short, it was a time of road rage, and the Boston Post Road was the nation's road standard.

No surprise, then, that the legacy of the Boston Post Road became a popular platform for the tale of American progress. "The story of this ancient trail," wrote the *Chicago Tribune* in early 1928, "first a post riders' path, now a smooth rigid roadway, is a history of highway building in itself." It was also a history of cultural renovation. During this volatile era, up through the Roaring Twenties and down through the depressed thirties, roads served as a great deal more than mere pieces of infrastructure—they meant great transformations in lifestyle. As the period's highway of record the Boston Post Road acts as a window onto all these behavioral shifts.

The Old Post Road lost more than just its name when it became U.S. Route 1. It lost some essential bits of its purpose. Modern motorists, preferring to be elsewhere and to be there now, had stripped highway travel of its intimacy—the road's milestones, noted one contemporary writer, merely gathered moss. Soon enough their original use, to guide post riders, wasn't needed at all: On July 1, 1926, postal planes flew "for the first time over the country's oldest post route between Boston and New York." As one elderly character in a 1923 short story set on the old highway announced, the "Post Road is not what it used to be."

Indeed it was not. In place of milestones and stagecoach inns, highway scenery was characterized by hot-dog stalls, produce markets, trucker taverns, tearooms, antique stores, roadside motels, and billboards announcing all of the above. Gas stations abounded: even in 1933, smack dab in the Depression, more than a thousand gas pumps dotted the Boston Post Road between Port Chester and New Haven, an average of seven stations per each of that trip's forty-six miles. In New Rochelle for sure, and likely elsewhere along the route, telephone toll lines ran directly beneath the old highway.

A cruising lifestyle emerged, born of a Jazz Age recklessness and bootleg counterculture. The likes of Zelda and F. Scott Fitzgerald took "mad rides along the Post Road" from their home life in Westport to their nightlife in Manhattan. Prohibition agents raided the Boston Post Road Inn near Springfield, and a similar roadside stand in Sudbury, Massachusetts. Booze runners made late-night relays from New York to Boston. Sometimes policemen patrolling the old highway intercepted the jaunts; other times rival gangsters policed the route themselves.

Even after Prohibition was repealed and Depression set in, youths still took to the old highway to satisfy their taste for speed. Franklin Roosevelt Jr. was frequently ticketed for doing eighty or so on the old highway while driving to and from Harvard—once prompting first lady Eleanor to write a judge for a stay so that the young man could attend a class. After September of 1932 drivers had to beware an experimental contraption being tested for the first time on an "unidentified stretch" of the Boston Post Road: an "invisible speed trap" that recorded a motorist's rate without a policeman for miles around.

Trucks also filled the road, making enormous dents in a commercial shipping business once dominated by freight trains. Curious just how deep this gash ran, federal investigators in the mid-1920s found that trucks carried ten times more tonnage than the New Haven railroad for shipments under sixty miles. They concluded that U.S. Route 1 was a trucker's most important route through Connecticut. A similar inquiry in 1932, on a Post Road checkpoint outside of Boston, counted more than a hundred heavy trucks in a single hour. These too ran around the clock: A contemporary post road travel writer found himself unable to sleep in a Norwalk hotel because noisy truck traffic between New York and Boston "persisted all night long."

As sports grew in popularity, stadiums ballooned in capacity, and a newly mobile legion of fans squeezed toward the gates at once. So before Harvard and Yale clashed in Cambridge or New Haven— or in Providence, for the less-anticipated match with Brown—motorists held their own competition along the Boston Post Road. Full maps of U.S. Routes 1, 5, and 20, as well as alternate paths, aided drivers through the cluttered city much as a fullback leads a runner through the defensive line. A writer from *Life* magazine in 1928, anticipating a thing called television, welcomed the chance to view sporting events from one's own living room "without risking life and limb on the Boston Post Road."

Those seeking professional thrills could take Boston Road to the intersection with Third Avenue, in the Bronx, and creep a final mile west toward Yankee Stadium. There, at least after 1927, residents of New Rochelle recognized the left-handed first baseman as a neighbor. To the city's directory he was "ball player"; to baseball fans across America, the Iron Horse; to himself, later, the luckiest man on the face of the earth. But to sociologists Lou Gehrig was just one of many well-off Americans eschewing big-city living for his share of the suburban dream. The white colonial house on a sloping lawn; the screened-in porch facing apple and cherry trees; U.S. Route 1, half a mile away, enticing Gehrig's Packard convertible hither—such was the modern ideal.

So began a heavy departure from the center of the city to its fringes and beyond, for living patterns had relaxed into the flexible frame of automotive transportation. No longer were homes tethered within a mile or two of Union Station; tire tread, not train tracks, dictated residential boundaries, and these were nearly boundless.* Reading the *New York Times* in the middle 1920s, one might have concluded that Westchester County set a new record for real estate every week. In 1927 the county granted the most residential building permits in the country; its aggregate realty value placed it ahead of fourteen entire states. Single-home developments and massive luxury apartment buildings mushroomed east from New York City toward Connecticut. By early 1926 land along the Boston Post Road in Greenwich had increased six times in value within the previous three years.

Once the consumer left the metropolis, the retail stores were not far behind. As family shops shut down near cramped central districts, superstores set up on the capacious outskirts. This shift didn't really take off until after World War II, but already by the early Depression some businesses were choosing suburban locales over downtown shopping districts. In 1930 Best's opened a store on the Boston Post Road in Mamaroneck, its second site in suburbia, so that its customers had "ample parking." In six months between the end of that year and the start of 1931 ten stores were planted in Darien, Connecticut, for the same reason.

By 1930 car registration reached 26.5 million, nearly three times its 1920 figure. The result was a decrease in trolley patronage that soon spelled the end of its era. After 1926 streetcar and commuter railroad patronage decreased at about the same rate that automobile ownership increased. In 1928 the Boston Post Road Coach Company sought to bus New Rochelle commuters into midtown Manhattan. Soon both steam engine and electric railroad companies had substituted their stock for coach buses, until only the essential trunk line trains remained in ser-

---

*The road's most famous home during this period was a "weed-overgrown lot near the Boston Post Road"—residence of Bruno Richard Hauptmann, later executed for kidnapping the Lindbergh baby. In fall of 1934, when Hauptmann was caught, people gathered at the house by the thousands, and tied up traffic on Route 1 for days.

vice. By the start of World War II the New Haven railroad was posting an annual loss in the millions, and the New York, Westchester & Boston railroad had failed entirely.

The United States Highways, like Route 1, scooped up the passenger spillover, but they quickly proved ill-equipped to keep pace with the motoring public. Route 1 was eighteen feet wide for nearly its entire distance—room enough for one lane in each direction, with a brief shoulder. It had no median and often curled around natural terrain in a manner that, while charming to stagecoach travelers, was dangerous to car drivers. Upon this narrow avenue rolled upward of fifty thousand cars a day. On holidays the count jumped to six figures. "It is impossible to see any limit to the growth of highway traffic," John MacDonald, Connecticut's highway commissioner, said in early 1925. "The highway department has no hope now of ever catching up with traffic on the Post road."

As congestion everywhere intensified, so too did the public wail for more roads. The initial response to this plea was to widen the old highways. By July of 1928 U.S. Route 1 had four lanes from the Bronx to Branford, just east of New Haven, as well as from Providence to Boston—the most four-lane mileage of any highway in the United States. Still, before that summer ended, Westchester County had already voted to widen its section yet more. Even this inadequate solution was not easy to achieve. As families flocked to suburbs along the road, land values soared, making it increasingly expensive for states to acquire the extra footage. When historic buildings or even recognizable trees stood in the desired path, protesters roared.

Westchester County responded by building entirely new roads, called parkways. The Hutchinson River Parkway through Westchester, completed by 1928, was built parallel to the Boston Post Road in the hopes of relieving its congestion. As opposed to highways like Route 1, parkways unfurled in harmony with the wilderness and provided places to stop and explore the scenery. Parkway builders nearly eliminated all grade-crossings—intersections with other roads or railroad tracks—replacing them with efficient underpasses or majestic arched bridges. A few traffic lights did remain, but they were fewer and farther between.

Commercial truck traffic was banned, as were billboards. Parkways also had economic advantages, despite being built from scratch: by 1929, one study found, the cost of acquiring land abutting the Post Road—to widen it, perhaps—averaged two dollars per square foot, while land near the Hutchinson River Parkway was going for ten cents.

Engineers near and far flocked to Westchester County to observe the sweetly running Hutchinson and its predecessor, the Bronx River Parkway. Immediately plans were drawn to extend the Hutchinson along the lines of what later became the Merritt Parkway, parts of which opened by 1938. This too was designed to parallel, and therefore relieve, old Route 1. But while these parkways served as models of highway elegance, they proved far less successful in alleviating traffic on the old post road. City commuters, enticed by the beautiful boulevards, considered them an invitation to leave public transit and drive to work. Soon after their completion the new roads paralleling the old post road were packed as well, and Route 1 was again operating at its previous, untenable capacity. To many social critics at the time it seemed automobile traffic could expand indefinitely to fit the space allowed.

Such criticisms didn't stop the urge to build. In the early 1930s the country topped a million miles of improved roadways. When the Great Depression hit, road construction played a major role in many economic recovery plans, promising a stream of jobs that trickled from the roadside to the assembly line.★ Nearly as soon as the federal government released hundreds of millions of dollars for such efforts, in 1933, Robert Moses, the czar of New York City infrastructure, requested $22.8 million to improve, among other highways, the Boston Post Road and the Hutchinson River Parkway.

Ultimately the inefficiency of early twentieth-century highways required an entirely new approach to the problem. Widening the old highways hadn't worked, and parkways had merely relocated, and

★The Post Road figured into another Depression-era initiative. In June of 1935 Hillside Homes was unveiled at the corner of Boston Post Road and East 214th Street, in the Bronx. The $6 million community was considered "the largest housing development in the East" created by the Public Works Administration, part of President Roosevelt's New Deal. The first person to move into the low-income development, which extended west on fourteen acres from the Boston Post Road, was a letter carrier.

slightly prettified, heavy traffic. It wasn't that more roads were needed, it was that the entire concept of a road had to be reexamined. By the time World War II arrived the transportation battle at home still raged. This is no frivolous analogy; by 1940 more than 32,000 people died in motor accidents each year, due greatly to roads ill-suited for the times. A new type of road was needed—the expressway, it was called—to chauffeur life at a speed commensurate with social change.

In 1939, at the World's Fair in New York, a glimpse of this new concept was brought into the public eye by Norman Bel Geddes, in the form of his "Futurama" exhibit. This peek at civilization-to-come depicted an expressway existence filled with free-flowing automobiles. "Today we are still rebuilding old roads that were constructed for another vehicle, instead of starting to build special roads for the special needs of the automobile," Geddes wrote, in 1940, in a book about the exhibit. "The history of the Boston Post Road illustrates this."

And so the road went from exemplifying the "history of highway building," in the *Chicago Tribune*'s words of 1928, to illustrating highway inadequacy, in Geddes's mind—all within a generation.

IT IS NECESSARY to step back in time a moment to follow the first attempt to replace U.S. Route 1 with the so-called "special roads" that would presumably solve the problems of the motor age. Looking back, this effort can fairly be seen as the structural precursor to the national system of interstate expressways that eventually emerged, a quarter century later. As it happened, clearing traffic on the antiquated Boston Post Road was at the heart of the mission.

The story begins on a March day in 1930, sometime around noon, when Franklin Delano Roosevelt, governor of New York, creased his lips into a most disarming smile, and welcomed the wild man into his Albany office. Lester Barlow had prepared for a fight. It was six years in the making, Barlow's plan to revolutionize America's highway system, and though he had come far—as far as the White House, even—he had little to show for his efforts. So he had prepared for a fight, readied his notorious "quick temper," practiced his pitch—only to melt at the famous Roosevelt smile, Barlow later recalled, "which beamed all over his face."

Their guards now down, the two men spoke cordially across the lunch splayed atop Roosevelt's desk. Perhaps they examined the large sheet hanging on one of the walls. Roosevelt had made a special request for it soon after taking office. It showed the status, updated monthly, of every road project in the state. "In other words," Roosevelt had told Frederick Stuart Greene, head of New York's public works department, upon demanding the chart, "I want some visible demonstration of how fast each project is getting on." Now Barlow proposed one addition: a modernized expressway paralleling the Boston Post Road from New York City to New Haven—the first piece to the system that, in Barlow's words, would rank among "the greatest achievements in our Nation's history."

If the term *wild* slightly overstates Lester Barlow's character, then *explosive* fits snugly in its place. In 1914 the American-born Barlow joined Pancho Villa's insurgent forces in Mexico, where he devised an aerial bomb he later sold in secret to the United States government. He spent the next two decades in court fighting for compensation—the War Department had used half a million Barlow bombs in World War I—and when he finally won nearly $600,000 he publicly complained of going bankrupt from income taxes. In 1940 he staged an elaborate publicity event to unveil a new bomb, detonating it in a field filled with eighty-four goats, only to stand bemused alongside congressmen and army officers as it failed to singe even a whisker.

But however volatile his nature, Barlow's technical mind proved sound. He had been a consulting engineer to Gutzon Borglum, the sculptor in charge of Mount Rushmore, even acting at times as Borglum's spokesman. As a resident of Stamford, Connecticut, Barlow also had intimate knowledge about the problems of an antiquated travel artery. Replacing the Boston Post Road with a more efficient highway lay at the very heart of his proposal. He was convinced that the modern automobile required modern road design. "Asphalt, concrete, and gravel have, to some extent, been placed upon the surfaces of these old trails, but most of them are still narrow, rough, and dangerous, and where cities and towns have developed, these old trails have become streets, jammed with street cars, trucks, automobiles, and people," he wrote in late 1928. "There is not one long unobstructed adequate national motorway in all of this great land." In other words, you could drape the old Boston Post Road in signs that read U.S. Route 1, but it remained the old Boston Post Road.

A few leading social critics—though only a few—were thinking along similar lines. "We have tried to adapt the instruments of one age to the demands of another," wrote Lewis Mumford and Benton Mac-Kaye in a 1931 issue of *Harper's* magazine. Mumford and MacKaye had in mind the U.S. Highways in Connecticut, many of which, a federal study had discovered, clung to the route originally cleared for stage-coach travel in the days of Levi Pease. Gutzon Borglum was busy carving the head of George Washington in 1930—but when he did speak out in favor of Barlow's plan, the following year, he too maintained that "we haven't adjusted our roads to the speed we're living at."

Barlow had been calling for his national system of expressways since 1924, back when a single glance at the Boston Post Road served as a powerful illustration of the limitations of the early U.S. Highways. The thinking at the time, one must recall, was that parkways would relieve old highways like Route 1. This was the case with the Pelham–Port Chester Parkway. This road, never built under that name, was first conceived in 1925 for heavier loads. Whereas the Hutchinson River Parkway was designed to relieve Route 1 of private cars, the Pelham Parkway was designed to do the same for truckers. It was planned closer in proximity to the Boston Post Road than the Hutchinson, even—in some places resting literally atop it. The parkway would be eighty feet wide, enough for eight full lanes, and by 1929 its right-of-way had been secured for $6 million.

It is necessary to focus for a moment on a report published that same year: the long-awaited *Regional Plan of New York*. This gigantic discourse on metropolitan New York's transportation problems, and potential solutions, had cost a million dollars and taken a host of planners and engineers nearly a decade to complete. As governor at the time of its completion, Franklin Roosevelt was extremely familiar with its conclusions.* The *Regional Plan* held no official authority over construction; it merely edified a highway-hungry public, merely opined to those truly in charge. By February of 1929 Roosevelt was speaking of the need for a "carefully planned highway system" and he later called the regional plan "the foundation on which all building in the future will be based." Among its conclusions, far too numerous to discuss here in detail, was that a completed Pelham–Port Chester Parkway would replace the Boston Post Road as "the main trunk highway between New York City and New Haven and Boston."

All this lay in the background when Lester Barlow entered Roosevelt's office, with the Pelham–Port Chester route in mind for his new expressway, so the governor had a good idea what the blustering fellow was talking about.

Before meeting with Roosevelt, Barlow had gained the favor of many whose approval would be necessary to run an expressway from New York to New Haven beside the Boston Post Road. He elicited financial pledges from important businessmen. He won over the leading Republican in Westchester County, William Ward, and, by winning Ward, then won the Republican-controlled state legislature. He met with executives from the New Haven railroad and promised them an exclusive bus franchise; the highway ran so close to the tracks, even using the railroad's right-of-way in places, that trains would no doubt lose passengers. All that was left, it seemed, was Roosevelt's blessing.

For Roosevelt, the expressway plan came at just the right time. The full scope of the previous autumn's market crash had started to sink in only recently. In fact, within days of his meeting with Barlow, Roosevelt became the first governor in the country to cite job loss as a mounting social concern, and resolved immediately upon a public works effort that emphasized road maintenance and highway construction.

So come late March 1930 Roosevelt's New York needed a plentiful

---

*FDR might well have known about the findings even without his elected position, as the plan's committee chair, Frederic Delano, was his uncle.

source of jobs, and needed them fast. Here was this man, Barlow, whose $200 million expressway to New Haven meant a mountain of construction contracts. Building could begin within ninety days, and would last more than two years. The employment produced from this type of public works project, Roosevelt felt at the time, represented "the greatest source of hope for the future." Barlow thought the new motorway, by itself, could give work to one-thirtieth of the entire country's unemployed population.

That the proposed expressway would alleviate traffic on the Boston Post Road was an added bonus. On an administrative level, the governor had been pestered twice in recent months to end a two-year delay on a promised widening of Route 1 through Mamaroneck. On a personal level, Roosevelt may then have felt, as he expressed in a letter a decade later, that the Boston Post Road was the most-traveled highway in the country.

Exactly which details of Barlow's plan they discussed are unknown, but it seems reasonable that they overlapped with those Barlow outlined in a memorandum to John Trumbull, governor of Connecticut, around the same time. Barlow's Union Highway, as he originally called it, would eventually stretch from Boston to San Francisco. Cross sections would span the coasts. The four-track expressway would be divided into fast lanes (minimum 35 miles per hour) and slow (maximum 30 mph), with the speeds separated by a twenty-foot gravel median. Access ramps would eliminate crossings with other roads and railroads. A metallic fence would partition the flows of traffic and prevent U-turns. Special sections devoted to gas stations and food stands would contain all commercial encroachment. Barlow might even have mentioned the warm response he had received from several congressmen when he presented the plan to President Herbert Hoover the previous fall, though Hoover himself had not been a fan.

For their time Barlow's plans were sophisticated without being unreasonable (his idea of avoiding Manhattan streets by running the expressway along building tops notwithstanding). In fact, many elements of Barlow's express motorway system presaged the modern interstate system eventually created in 1956. One aspect in particular is a near echo: Barlow called for the federal government to create a road fund dedicated solely to expressway construction, a concept strikingly similar to the Highway Trust formed by the Eisenhower administration to finance the interstates that exist today. Once built, Barlow's roads would collect tolls until they repaid their cost, at which time they would become entirely free. Barlow based both his traffic and financial calculations for the entire system on surveys performed on the Boston Post Road, so it was only natural to propose the "New York-Boston section . . . as a test unit to prove whether the plan is feasible."

By the time Barlow left the governor's office, Roosevelt had agreed to endorse the idea. Take it to the legislature, he told Barlow, and when it gets there tell the newsmen to call me for a comment. So Barlow did just that. On April 2, 1930, the *New York Times* ran a story on the plan with an encouraging quote from Roosevelt. Word spread quickly. "Great public interest has been aroused by your recent suggestion of a super-highway in New York State," the *New York Herald*'s automotive editor wrote to the governor. He requested that Roosevelt prepare an editorial "giving more fully the details of this proposed project and its aims." In turn, Roosevelt asked Barlow to send any other information that might be used to craft the column.

Soon New York Senator Walter Westall and Assemblyman Herbert Shonk, both from Westchester, introduced bills proposing the project. Barlow had acquired building rights to the corridor formerly reserved for the Pelham–Port Chester Parkway. If the bill passed—and "the probabilities point in that direction," the *Times* reported—Governor John Trumbull would consider an emergency session of the Connecticut legislature to approve an identical act there, so the road could continue on to New Haven.

A week later Washington took notice. John Tilson, majority leader of the House of Representatives, telegrammed Westall. He hoped the measure would pass in New York. Soon it would be introduced in Congress as well. "If a New York-Boston express highway is built," wrote Tilson, "I hope it will be a model for the nation."

Shortly after this exchange Senator Lawrence Phipps, chair of the Committee on Post Offices and Post Roads, proposed the creation of a twelve-person committee to study Barlow's plan in detail. "It is time for the Federal Government to recognize more adequately the Nation's transportation needs," the Phipps committee reported. "This is not a matter of pleasure but of business." In early May the Senate passed the bill without a vote. The House seemed poised to do the same.

Then, in a flash, like so much traffic along the Boston Post Road in the days between the world wars, all movement slammed to a halt. In the House, the bill remained trapped in a committee intent upon inaction. The same thing happened in New York, where the state legislature adjourned without advancing the expressway proposal. Attempts to rekindle the plan in subsequent sessions failed to materialize, and after that it faded away.

Later on Tilson revealed to Barlow the reason for this mysterious sea change. The mighty railroad lobby, fearful of losing yet more passengers and freight, had blocked the proposal. The revelation may well have shocked Barlow; he'd had a "very gratifying" audience with the New Haven's vice president just days after meeting with Roosevelt. Yet in the fall of 1930, while at a gathering of New Haven company directors, Barlow received firsthand confirmation. There, during a discussion of highway congestion, J. J. Pelley, then president of the railroad, announced its official position on highway clutter: "If there is anything which we can practically do to increase that congestion," Barlow recalled Pelley saying, "we will do it."

Barlow immediately regressed into his naturally explosive self. In October he telegrammed President Hoover and insisted on meeting with him "at once" about the expressway system. When the acting Secretary of Agriculture declined on Hoover's behalf, Barlow called the president incompetent and told the secretary he was so dumb "you do not know you are alive." In early 1933 Barlow tried again to interest Roosevelt, who by that time had been elected president. Rebuffed, a "hurt" and "pretty much disgusted" Barlow replied that he regretted having ever met with Roosevelt at all. Eventually Barlow abandoned his expressway plan but not his rancor toward public officials. A few years later he publicly demanded that President Roosevelt fire three cabinet members—or else Barlow, somehow, would see to his impeachment.

Ultimately Barlow would live long enough to see the federal inter-state system reach fruition, though one can only guess whether it granted him solace or rather intensified his resentment. No doubt he thought this new system, as one of his obituaries later pointed out, looked a lot like his own. A Highway Trust replenished with gasoline taxes financed the system, whereas Barlow's fund was to be stocked with toll payments. Some pieces, however, were built with toll money, just as Barlow had conceived. These included the New England Thruway—the name for modern Interstate 95 as it runs through the Pelham–Port Chester corridor—and the Connecticut Turnpike, which continued beside Route 1 to New Haven.

Simply put, the expressway between New York and New Haven was built just as Lester Barlow had first described it. But it took a man even more explosive than Lester Barlow to complete the modern expressway beside this stretch of the Boston Post Road—someone whose salvos never failed, like one too many Barlow bombs, to singe the whiskers in their sights.

CLOUDS FILLED THE New York sky on February 5, 1938, but the rain held off and the temperature warmed steadily throughout the day, even into the evening, pleasant enough for Robert Moses and the slew of public officials who accompanied him on a tour of the unrealized Pelham–Port Chester Parkway. A gasoline engine pulled the spectators along the adjacent New York, Westchester & Boston railroad track; the rail's electricity had been shut off with the line's official failure a few months earlier, at the close of 1937. Since then there had been renewed agitation for the Pelham Parkway. At the end of their ride the group lunched at the Pelham Country Club, bounded on the north by U.S. Route 1—a fitting host, since its cluttered lanes had been the very reason for the day's gathering. By then Moses had seen enough. That same day he announced his conclusion to the press: Only a state-of-the-art toll expressway designed for all types of traffic could help clear the Boston Post Road. He considered the matter a "vital necessity."

To refer to Robert Moses by any of his official titles, of which he held many during forty-four years of public service, would be to grossly understate his true influence on roadways—those carved through New York City, for sure, but also those binding cities across the United States. Bertram Tallamy, the man eventually charged with constructing the modern interstate highways, told Robert Caro, Moses's unimpeachable biographer, that the national expressway system owed its creation to lessons Tallamy had learned from Moses dating back to 1926. In that case Tallamy's core curriculum included sizing up vast swaths of vacant land and reconstructing them, upon his neural canvas, until wheels across the country rolled along the strands of Moses's imagination—that skein of the interstates.

On the surface the Pelham Parkway plan seemed perfectly practical. The Post Road, after all, remained packed. Traffic on Route 1 was described in June of 1938 as a "nightmare." Any dreams that the parallel Hutchinson River Parkway would siphon off its surplus had long awakened to a cold, stop-and-go sweat. "Driving over it is a chore," wrote the *New York Times* of Route 1 that July, "and a dangerous one." Westchester County already owned the Pelham route, and the railbed lay unused; together, Moses's veteran vision knew, clearance of these corridors would easily hold a four-lane road, and possibly more.

On closer inspection, however, Moses's decision represented less an inevitable conclusion than a series of discarded alternatives. Building an expressway meant choosing highway transportation instead of railroad rehabilitation. It meant the heavy, ceaseless flow of truck and bus traffic instead of a passenger-only parkway. It meant winding a ribbon of elevated road straight through neighborhoods instead of bypassing cities and towns as New York's official head of public works—whose position would have guided road projects in any state not home to Robert Moses—had recently suggested. It meant, in the words of one resident quoted by the *Times* after Moses's tour, imminent damage to "the fine residential character of the old Boston Post Road."

Within a week of the announcement the protests began. The mayors of Pelham and New Rochelle, among other dissenters, wanted the railroad reopened. Though the Westchester railroad's ridership had steadily declined and had never made a profit for its owner, the New

Haven, the train still carried 8.5 million commuters a year—commuters that would now be nudged off the platform and into the driver's seat. Others sympathized with the need for a highway but preferred it carry only passenger traffic. Trucks and buses made far more noise, and produced a good share of this racket long into the night. (Years later, a study of decibel levels on the Boston Post Road, dubbed "Operation Earmuff," confirmed this fear: Steady truck flow made Route 1 noisier than New York City subways at rush hour.) Not least of all, the expressway would slash through homes and communities while plenty of "virgin territory" remained open for the taking.

America's entrance into World War II, at the close of 1941, temporarily diverted automotive debates across the country. Cities along the old highway made various contributions to the effort: among them, Remington Arms and Sikorsky helicopters from Bridgeport, submarines from Groton, high-tech research from Cambridge. Pratt & Whitney, headquartered in Hartford, produced half of the aviation power used by the American forces. On a national level, car manufacture was suspended to ensure defense production, and railroads felt a brief revitalization. But truck traffic remained prevalent enough on Route 1 that other, lesser routes were designated specifically for civilian use.

Meanwhile the Merritt Parkway, paralleling Route 1 from the Connecticut state line to New Haven, had opened. About five miles north of the Post Road, the Merritt promised thirty-seven fewer intersections, forty fewer minutes of driving time, and a far lower accident rate. But in keeping with the law of automotive averages, it filled up quickly. By 1942, just four years after opening, the parkway was congested while Route 1 remained as jammed as ever. Calls for yet another parallel route gained momentum.

Many of these calls emanated from the mouth of Robert Moses. In early September of 1942 Moses took another tour of the proposed expressway route—this time with William Cox, highway commissioner of Connecticut. Just a few days earlier Moses had secured the cooperation of Westchester County. He had appealed to the federal government that the suggested road held essential military value. This placed the county in something of a patriotic headlock, and it agreed to go along with the expressway plan. Now Moses brought this power of thinly veiled ultimatum to Greenwich, Connecticut. There, he and Cox stood at the spot where New York's new expressway would end, a third of a mile north of the Post Road. Already it had become clear that the Merritt had "failed to relieve an overload on the former main travel artery," reported the *New York Times*. If New York finished its new highway and dumped all this traffic at the Connecticut line at once—from the Hutchinson, Route 1, and soon the expressway—the result, in the day's own terms, would have been something akin to a blitzkrieg, localized entirely on the Boston Post Road.

Cox immediately realized the potential for catastrophe. By the summer of 1943 Connecticut had already started to survey the route for an extended expressway, east of New York toward New Haven. Cox called it the only solution to "an extremely grim and unbearable traffic situation." Simply widening the Post Road, he publicly told the governor, would be more expensive and less efficient. Before anyone realized the full scope of the project, the Connecticut legislature disguised it through to passage. The bill's language cloaked the major expressway as a meager piece of road running through Stratford, a town of roughly 22,000 just east of Bridgeport.

Soon a corridor of critics emerged, from the Bronx to New Haven, spouting with fury. A woman in Mamaroneck filed a grievance in federal court to halt action on the expressway. Greenwich hired an engineer to reroute it. East Port Chester wanted it four miles north. The mayor of Stamford wanted it farther south. Norwalk opposed it altogether on the grounds it would bisect the city.

In 1945 a representative from Westport led a successful "Stop the Road" drive in the Connecticut legislature, and soon the state had curtailed Cox's power to build the project in question. By then the road had a name. In New York it was being called the New England Thruway—part of the state's larger thruway network, hailed as the most important public works since the Erie Canal. In Connecticut, and soon enough in Massachusetts too, it was being referred to as "relocated Route 1." (Today, in all three states, it's Interstate 95.)

Some of the protest, however, was drowned out by the Boston

Post Road's own roar. By 1950 Route 1 from New York to New Haven remained the second-most-congested strip of highway in the country—even as the Merritt and Hutchinson parkways rolled in parallel to ease the load. The towns and small cities on Long Island Sound, a suburban mecca in the early days of sprawl, had been attractive places of residence precisely because they offered escape from the overwhelming bustle of Manhattan to the west and, to a lesser extent, New Haven to the east. Yet traffic on Route 1 in early 1950, a *New York Times* editorial complained, "hinders normal community life."

At the same time, traffic experts insisted that running expressways through towns and cities was the only way to relieve the old highway for good. The Merritt and Hutchinson, after all, had been built away from Route 1 and failed to clear it. Express highways must go through cities "rather than around them," said Robert Moses, who was already calling his new road part of "the so-called Boston-Washington express route." An independent survey, conducted by a Chicago firm hired by protesting towns in Connecticut, concluded that an expressway located fifteen miles north of the Long Island Sound coastline "would not offer a permanent solution to the high-speed traffic problem on the Boston Post Road (U.S. Route 1)." In short, all signs pointed to a major new expressway virtually on top of the old highway.

The situation in suburban Darien, Connecticut, typified the problem's complexity. There, the proposed expressway would slice through thirty homes in just a mile and a half. But as intrusive as an expressway would be, the old highway had become nearly as unappealing. For instance, where Route 1 ran beneath the New Haven railroad tracks in Darien, the twelve-foot underpass, formerly sufficient for all types of traffic, was now too short for many trucks. In one memorable incident several cages of live chickens catapulted from the bed of a tall truck, and "hens cackled in strange places for days." By 1950 only a fifth of Darien residents petitioned against the expressway; many neighboring suburbs had also relented in their opposition.

New York began to build its part of the expressway in 1949. By then it had grown from four to six lanes. It remained, in the eyes of Robert Moses, "one of the most vitally needed arteries" in the state. Connecticut's new highway chief, Albert Hill, stepped up efforts to continue the road beyond New York's border. In a last-ditch attempt to curtail the project, several expressway opponents filed a stop-work suit in Connecticut Superior Court, in late January of 1953.

The trial lasted eight days. A senior state engineer testified that some 8,400 accidents occurred on Route 1 each year, just between Greenwich and New Haven. Federal engineers confirmed that the proposed $120 million expressway could only do its job near the old highway. On the trial's final day Hill disclosed on the stand, for the first time, that he intended to continue the highway east of New Haven toward Rhode Island.

On March 5 Justice John Comley reached a decision: "U.S. Route 1 is outmoded, outdated and far below the present recognized standards for the construction of highways bearing a similar traffic load," Comley ruled. "It is, therefore, concluded that the commissioner has the power to build the proposed expressway." Eleven days later a group of dignitaries, riding in a bus chartered specially for the occasion, toured the route designated, officially now, as "Relocation of U.S. Route 1."

Chapter 13

Changing the Face of America

THE COURSE OF events that led from Robert Moses scouting the Pelham Parkway to an expressway replacing the Boston Post Road reflects the broader development of America's highway system leading up to the passage of the Interstate Highway Act in 1956. In the end it was the sum of smaller decisions made by men like Moses, and not some grand plan etched unto the earth by the signature of Dwight Eisenhower, that formed the foundation of our national infrastructure—the network that would, in Eisenhower's own words, "change the face of America."

First there was the matter of how to keep cars from strangling old highways like the Boston Post Road. In the spirit of Robert Moses refusing to rehabilitate the old Westchester railroad, most experts felt certain that highways, and only highways, could untangle the traffic snarl. But choosing to create modern highways meant, in effect, choosing to destroy railroads. A fatal spiral ensued: as people fled the train cars, railroads had fewer resources to improve their service, which led more people to flee the train cars.

So from 1930 to 1950 automobile and bus commuters entering New York from Westchester and Fairfield, counties traversed by Route 1, rose by roughly 167 percent, while railroad commuters rose less than 4 percent. By the end of 1950 a trolley emblazoned as *The Streetcar Named Expire* made its final run on the Boston Post Road, west from New Rochelle to Pelham, to be replaced thereafter by buses. The situation extended across the country. Between 1947 and 1970 the federal government spent some $58 billion on highways to a paltry $795 million on mass transit. "Why don't they build the thing on top of my railroad and be done with it?" the president of the New Haven told the *New York Times,* in April 1955, of the coming New England Thruway. Soon enough they did.

Yet despite the general consensus that new roads would clear traffic on old ones, agreeing to the precise details of a modern road network proved exceedingly troublesome. In 1938, shades of Lester Barlow perhaps not entirely faded from his mind, President Franklin Roosevelt launched a study "on the feasibility of a system of transcontinental toll roads." The report concluded that although the volume of traffic warranted a national highway network "of a higher standard," only the corridor from Boston to Washington could repay its cost through toll revenue.

Several years later Roosevelt tried again. This time his appointed highway task force proposed a nearly 39,000-mile system that established the plot points of today's interstates. In late 1944 Congress approved the plan but provided no funding for its creation. States and localities were left to address their road problems piecemeal—echoing the old New England style, when one town maintained its portion of the post road only to mire in the next district's unsatisfactory efforts.

After the general expressway scheme had been conceived, there remained the decision of where exactly to place it. A few forward thinkers cautioned against running these roads straight through major cities. "The heaviest route of all," wrote Norman Bel Geddes in 1940, "avoids Boston, Providence, New York . . . as it steers straight toward Washington." The federal Bureau of Public Roads had called for a high-speed Boston–to–New York expressway "away from population centers" as early as 1936.

Far more common, though, was the ideology of Robert Moses, captured in an essay he wrote in 1953: "If the [highway] facility is designed to be of greatest benefit to traffic, it will go through rather than bypass the cities." Moses entered the essay into a contest on planning better highways, sponsored by General Motors; among the forty-four thousand entrants, he came away the winner. Auto industry leaders were not alone in adopting this view. Traffic engineers certainly agreed, and so did local leaders, who used expressway paths to raze and redevelop their slums, often with little regard for existing social tapestries.

Such a mind-set, in its day, could hardly be blamed. Aside from Lewis Mumford, few social critics anticipated the impact of running major highways through cities. To Mumford, whose highway perspicacity stretched far beyond its time, the Moses theory elevated traffic engineers and local officials to the role of cultural architects. "All the current plans for dealing with congestion are based on the assumption that it is a matter of highway engineering, not of comprehensive city and regional planning, and that the private motorcar has priority over every other means of transportation, no matter how expensive it is in comparison with public transportation, or how devastating its by-products," Mumford wrote in his *New Yorker* magazine column "The Sky Line" in April of 1955. After the interstate act passed, Mumford predicted irreparable damage to cities within fifteen years—during which time public opinion on urban road projects indeed pivoted from hopeful to hopeless.

Moses and Mumford feuded on the topic in various media outlets throughout the 1940s and '50s. But whereas Mumford offered only more questions in response to the traffic question, Moses offered answers—politically palatable answers, right around the time Dwight Eisenhower entered the presidency determined to find the expressway solution. In 1919, as part of a coast-to-coast army convoy to promote the good roads movement, Eisenhower had realized America's need for serviceable highways; during World War II he had witnessed, through Germany's impressive Autobahn, just how powerful a true road network could be. In April of 1954, Eisenhower turned to his top aide, Sherman Adams, for a plan. Adams, in turn, looked to Bertram Tallamy and Robert Moses.

That July Eisenhower declared the federal government's intention to build a multibillion-dollar expressway system. For two years politicians hammered out the details, and at the close of June 1956, Eisenhower signed them into law: some 41,000 miles of interstate expressways at a cost of $27 billion—ninety percent of which would come from a federal Highway Trust stocked with gasoline and tire taxes. The money could go to build interstates, and interstates alone.* The routes, as drafted in a 1955 booklet distributed to Congress, would cut straight through cities.

With that the largest public works project in the history of the world was under way. The expressways did, as Eisenhower predicted, change the face of America. But what newspapers first called a "facelift" became seen, over time, as a right cross to the jaw. The blows felt in three Post Road cities, in particular, epitomized the overhaul to urban life that rippled across the country for decades following the interstate act, leaving some people to wonder whether by exchanging the old highway for the expressway they had traded their history for a mess of concrete.

IN LATE JUNE of 1957 Richard Lee, mayor of New Haven, Connecticut, strolled the route of the road that would resuscitate his city. This was Oak Street—or rather, as it lay mostly in rubble, this had been Oak Street—an "infamous" slum being transformed for the good of the downtown district just to its north. Once it was repurposed, the street would lead off the nearly completed Interstate 95, which paralleled Route 1 closely along the coast. The new road would connect I-95 with the streets of downtown New Haven—and so it would be called, appropriately, the Oak Street Connector.

Lee was certainly not the only mayor trying to pump people back into his city at the time. This was the age of urban renewal. Massive redevelopment projects—most subsidized by the federal government, all meant to clot the flow of a suburb-bound populous—cropped up across the country. Local leaders and planners routinely redesigned their

---

*Some of the early expressway segments to parallel the Boston Post Road, including the New England Thruway and the Connecticut Expressway (I-95), were built as toll roads before the 1956 act, and were thus ineligible for federal funding, though subsequent maintenance projects did receive the government benefits.

cities around the routes of expressways to come. They uprooted deteriorated neighborhoods and planted more attractive ones in their place. At the very least they used the paths to nudge well-to-do people, ever so gently, back in the general direction of downtown.

By autumn of 1957 cities large and small all along the old Route 1 were turning with the leaves in a similar process of revitalization. Stanley Church, mayor of New Rochelle, expressed the hope of many in his position when he declared, in anticipation of the interstate's glowing aftermath: "We'll have a renaissance in downtown business when the new road is completed next year."

So Lee was not alone in his efforts, but he was certainly in front of the others. "Lee has put New Haven foremost among New England cities in striking at the illnesses that plague all U.S. municipalities: the exodus to the suburbs, slum growth, downtown decline," wrote *Time* magazine. New Haven was not just foremost among New England cities; it led the march for urban repair even on a national scale. By the end of the 1950s the city ranked fifth in federal redevelopment grants—ahead of Detroit, St. Louis, and San Francisco, among others.

Of course, urban renewal did not come without a social cost. One of the biggest problems at the time was what to do with residents displaced by the new road. Much of the public was "up in arms" regarding the expressway; many refused to vacate their premises marked for destruction. One official in Darien, Connecticut, discussing the lack of alternate housing for residents cleared by the expressway's path, threw up his hands: "Something ought to be done for these people," he said. "But just how are we going to do it?"

New Rochelle literally razed the dead to make way for its part of Interstate 95—demolishing a pair of seventeenth-century graveyards, not to mention stores, churches, and low-income housing structures. Soon afterward, the city cleared space for two multimillion-dollar commercial developments right off the expressway. Whether New Rochelle's "way of life will be 'redeveloped,' along with the city itself," wrote the *New York Times,* "is one of the questions people here are asking."

But in the early interstate era these questions were largely ignored, or poorly answered, or both. After accompanying Mayor Lee's Oak Street tour in June 1957, *Time* magazine mentioned the price of the Connector's redevelopment project ($40 million shared by private investors and public funds); it mentioned that part of the tab was being picked up by the federal government ($6.6 million); it even mentioned the fee for exterminating the neighborhood's fifty thousand rats ($3,000). But the article failed to mention the eight hundred or so low-income families being displaced by the expressway.

Even when social costs were considered, local officials regarded them as an acceptable amount to be paid by the few for the welfare of the many. So the Connecticut woman who camped on her front lawn in a kitchen chair, hoping to deter interstate construction, was labeled a "tardy mover" responsible for the road's delay. Divergence from this mind-set proved a political liability: after failing to secure a major redevelopment program, Bridgeport's Jasper McLevy found himself on the losing end of a mayoral election in 1957, for the first time in twenty-four straight years.

Only a handful of social critics felt an urgency commensurate with the vastness of the expressway program. They were led by Lewis Mumford and largely branded "long-haired planners"—even if, like Mumford, they were clearly going bald. In September 1957, at a conference in Hartford later considered a touchstone of metropolitan planning, Mumford and his cohorts issued an "almost unanimous" call to suspend interstate building until the full breadth of its cultural implications had been properly considered. For Mumford, the exemplary oversight stood right before the audience's eyes: the conference's two keynote speakers, Federal Highway Chief Bertram Tallamy and Federal Housing Chief Albert Cole, were meeting there for the very first time.

At that time no one cared to heed this warning—certainly not state governors receiving ninety cents in return for each dollar spent on interstates. Few denied the deterioration of cities. Across the country, the social movements that began in the twenties and thirties neared an extreme. Well-to-do families sprawled toward the suburbs along improved highways and parkways. Superstores, with super parking structures, followed. Industry and corporate headquarters, seeking cheaper land, were not far behind. Buzzing central districts became ghost lands; slums encircled these blighted cores. The fleeing tax base left cities with a thinning wallet to throw at the problem; with each person or business that left, then, it was harder to keep more people or businesses from leaving.

This master narrative of social movement certainly described New Haven. From 1920 to 1950 the population of its seven closest suburbs increased some 160 percent; residents in the city proper, meanwhile, rose less than 2 percent. Downtown retail stores shrank in number as chains along the Boston Post Road grew in size. The coup de grâce came in July 1956, a month after Eisenhower signed the Interstate Act: plans for what would become New England's largest shopping center, with sixty shops, major department stores, and five thousand parking spots. Its home would be suburban Milford, ten miles west of New Haven, at an exit feeding off the new interstate onto the Post Road.

The general wisdom now held that expressways would halt the movement out of city centers. Dating back to World War II, Maurice Rotival, a professor at Yale's school of architecture, had devised for New Haven a plan to curb urban defection. First he would clear the traffic along Route 1 that strangled downtown streets. Next he would orient this more efficient movement back toward a refurbished central district. Bypassing the city was not an option.

After years of delay Rotival's plan resurfaced in the summer of 1951. Soon transforming Oak Street into the Oak Street Connector became the consensus first step in the city's redevelopment. Shortly after Lee took office, Rotival and several business influences sold the new mayor on the plan, and shortly after this, Lee was selling it to the state highway commissioner, the federal renewal funding agencies, and just about everyone else.

At first it appeared to work. On a chilly afternoon in late October of 1959 some six hundred fifty cars eased along the fifteen-million-dollar, six-lane Connector, behind the vehicle bearing Lee and the governor. Lee pointed out a new sixteen-story apartment building; a thirteen-million-dollar headquarters of the Southern New England Telephone

Company; a major shopping center. Each one glistened along a fresh concrete strip where, not long ago, said Lee, "people once lived in diseased squalor."

Within months Hartford leaped furiously into redevelopment, unwilling "to take a back seat to New Haven." From 1956 to 1963 New Haven's tax base increased; people, it seemed, were returning to the city. Urban officials from all around saw a blueprint for escaping their woes, and pretty soon a sobriquet was coined, and New Haven became known as the Model City.

Underneath the superlatives, however, the long-ignored social problems approached the boiling point. To be sure, many factors aside from interstate placement—racial, military, and economic factors, among them—contributed to urban unrest in the mid-1960s. But the expressways certainly played their role, often exacerbating these factors. The general wisdom had been wrong. Instead of leading people back into cities, expressways had facilitated a broad rush away from downtown. Wealth poured out of New Haven along the interstate. In Orange, eight miles west on Route 1, property values rose more than a thousand percent from 1950 to 1980, while New Haven's fell about ten percent. In Branford, eight miles east on Route 1, half of the town's thirty-one manufacturers in 1966 had emigrated from New Haven.

So began an economic plunge that placed New Haven seventh on a national list of cities with the highest urban poverty in 1983, with nearly a quarter of its residents considered impoverished. Authorities jammed relocated residents into housing projects. Luxurious new buildings on Oak Street memorialized the decision to replace rather than repair a neighborhood, their cool vigil hoisted above a wasteland of intentions. "It would appear that we love the road much more than we do places, certainly more than we love cities, so that our political powers always gather behind the highway network, and we are ready to destroy anything for it," wrote Vincent Scully, a Yale professor and critic of the Oak Street Connector, in 1967.

In August of that year a riot erupted in the Hill neighborhood, an area orbiting Route 1 south of the Oak Street Connector. The violence lasted for several days. Similar revolts occurred elsewhere across the

country that year; New Haven's mayhem was fairly tame, compara-
tively. Then again, no city in the past decade had tried to better itself, at
least ostensibly, with New Haven's fervor.

By November, with some 16,400 miles of interstates remaining to
be built, an alarm began to blare—one that would have sounded, at least
to those in Mumford's circle, strikingly familiar: "So brutal has been the
impact on city life of some of the completed expressways that the Federal Government has cautioned cities against hasty planning that ignores
esthetic, social and economic considerations," reported the *New York
Times*. In several places, expressway hostility grew so great that authorities began to wonder whether some parts of the interstate system would
ever be built at all.

AN ANTI-EXPRESSWAY CONTINGENT four hundred strong gathered
at the Massachusetts statehouse on February 3, 1970, for what the newspapers were calling the "people v. roads issue." The plural, *roads,* was
most appropriate. The group had in its sights Boston's entire expressway establishment. At the hearings that day two dozen witnesses argued
that the proposed expressways would not eliminate traffic but increase
it—that such roads would not slip gently through the city but push it to
the point of revolt. Fifteen cities had halted interstate segments of late,
but the present effort represented a new level of civil unrest. "It cannot
be built," said one protester of Boston's expressway system, "because
the people will stop it."★

By 1960 Bostonians were singing a ballad of road woe familiar to
most of urban America. Thousands of jobs and millions in retail dollars had fled for the fringes. The central shopping district, particularly around Washington Street, had withered in the face of suburban
strip malls. Yet daily traffic downtown continued to rise; by 1964 Bos-

---

★Beneath the great controversy surrounding urban interstates in the 1960s lay a greater
irony: Eisenhower had never intended for expressways to reach cities at all. Until 1959 the
president suffered the illusion that America's road network avoided cities. That year, upon
discovering that Interstate 95 would enter Washington, D.C., he ordered an investigation
into the matter. The resulting White House study recommended removing roughly 1,700
miles of road, but Eisenhower felt things were too far gone to change, and left it at that.

ton ranked second in per capita car use, trailing only the infamous Los Angeles in traffic congestion. "If we don't find an adequate solution," one MIT official told *U.S. News & World Report* that year, "this city is going to choke to death."

Most Boston officials believed that avoiding this asphyxiation meant completing the city's master highway plan from 1948. The plan would imprint a wheel atop the Hub: concentric beltways, an outer and an inner, connected along key corridors by expressways radiating from the core. By the late 1960s several crucial sections, including the Central Artery, which pierced downtown, and Route 128, the outer belt, had been built. Only a few key pieces still remained.

Topping the list of unfinished projects was the so-called Southwest Expressway, meant to carry the twenty thousand or so cars that entered Boston each day from the southwest. Back in 1948 the majority of this traffic traveled U.S. Route 1 from Providence. By the late sixties most used Route 1's replacement, Interstate 95. The interstate stopped at the Route 128 belt, however, forcing traffic into the city along Washington Street, or other local roads. The proposed Southwest Expressway would extend I-95 directly into central Boston.

The expressway's general area of impact had much in common with the old highway. The interstate would relieve Centre Street in Jamaica Plain, the original post road toward Providence. Its right-of-way would straddle the New Haven railroad tracks. The expressway terminal, in Roxbury, would fork into the unfinished inner belt just beyond Roxbury Crossing, where the "parting stone" had once split the old post road's westward and southbound branches.

The path of the eight-lane Southwest Expressway, then, also meant a major rent in the old route's cultural fabric. By 1967 the awareness of such impacts had heightened considerably. A thorough study of families forced by the Southwest Expressway to relocate, the largest of its type at the time, offered a sense of the disruption caused to the corridor's seven hundred or so displaced households. Most of the relocated families earned incomes below the minimum comfort standard, yet because alternate housing was rarely built in advance of expressways, these same people ended up paying more in their new residences. Most of the removed found it harder to get to church from their new location—no small change in a population as likely to define home by parish as by street name. In general the displaced considered their new residences less convenient, and thought the process had upset their household's status quo.

The ultimate unintended impact, perhaps, was that after the move—a move fundamentally designed to ease road congestion—more people drove to work than had before.

Some families refused to move until the bulldozer absolutely insisted. In doing so, they watched their neighborhoods deteriorate before their eyes. Many "lived in fear" of vandals who ransacked homes known to be in the expressway's path. Shops closed. The retail district in Roxbury Crossing, noted one report, was "virtually eliminated." And Boston's relocation program was considered perhaps the "most humane" in the nation by the federal highway department.* The situation elsewhere was certainly far worse.

As bad as the prognosis seemed for the Southwest Expressway corridor, the very existence of a prognosis meant the community was forewarned, and thus forearmed, in a way it would not have been during the early interstate era. So, while the expressway advanced toward completion, residents banded together, under the guidance of local activists, to alter their blueprinted fate.

In June 1968 a group of residents from Jamaica Plain, on the interstate's route, convinced the mayor of Boston, Kevin White, to hear its side of the story. The residents wanted the expressway design changed from a monstrous elevated highway to a depressed one, a less invasive road structure that would run just below ground level. An engineering study agreed with them: "It has been recognized only recently that nonphysical factors play a central role" in road planning, the report admitted. In other words, highway engineers should no longer build massive roads through an established neighborhood without taking the people who make up that neighborhood into account.

---

*The process wore down relocation workers too. Answering questions from tenants was often quite difficult, as many basic facts, like exact dates of road construction, remained unknown. As a result, relocation workers frequently encountered hostility.

Jamaica Plain won its fight. The almighty interstate machine now appeared vulnerable. Anti-expressway groups pressed further, rallying a convincing array of information about the expressway's social disruptions. In the fall of 1969 a rising politician named Michael Dukakis challenged Governor Francis Sargent to halt highway construction. Mayor White amplified the call on December 17, when he wrote a formal letter to Sargent, citing the "anguished objections of neighborhood residents," asking that work on the Southwest Expressway, as well as on the inner belt, be suspended until Boston's entire transportation plan received a full reexamination.

It was a bold request, nothing less than a complete practical and ideological reversal of highway momentum. Before becoming governor, Sargent had been head of the state's Department of Public Works, the office responsible for highway planning and construction. A few years earlier he had successfully lobbied *against* a community's right to veto expressway routes. Sargent was a man of highway roots being asked to stop highway construction.

Because the Southwest Expressway and inner belt were parts of the federal interstate system, halting them would raise federal eyebrows. In particular, such a move would reach the desk of the Secretary of Transportation, John Volpe. Volpe himself was a former governor of Massachusetts, and he had supported Boston's original highway plan during his time in state office.

Initially Sargent refused to commit either way, saying he would await the recommendations of a task force he had commissioned to investigate the matter. As the debate played out in the public sphere during the final days of 1969 and the opening days of 1970, the highway opponents gained ground. The buzz increased leading up to February 3, when the legislature would debate a bill introduced by Dukakis calling for a full moratorium on highway construction. During this time the emerging understanding of expressway impact received a wider audience than ever before. The *Boston Globe* published a complete analysis, with writers and reporters taking each angle, because building urban expressways had "become one of the most basic and sharp social-political issues."

The *Globe*'s pro-expressway side sounded stale, rehashing the same supposed traffic benefits that had been touted since the early interstate era. The anti-highway side, meanwhile, exposed many overlooked complications of expressway construction. Roadwork wouldn't end with the new interstate: to handle the heavy new traffic Boston's local streets would need at least $100 million in upgrades of their own, and the city center would need twice as many parking structures. The public money used to subsidize this construction would, in effect, be a de facto indictment of the poor, since mass transit facilities would experience a relative negligence. In an editorial headlined "Think More," the *Globe* concluded "that the answer to every road problem is not always another new highway."

When he arrived at the statehouse on February 3, 1970, that's all Governor Sargent wanted—a little more time to think. Despite the hundreds of highway protesters in attendance that day, the legislature agreed to withhold action for another week. At that time Sargent would publicly announce the results of his task force, as well as his own decision on the expressway moratorium.

The task force itself represented a new line of thought. It was headed not by highway officials but rather by an independent group that, if anything, was against unabated road construction. Its conclusions strongly opposed many elements of Boston's original highway plan—and, by extension, much of what Sargent had fought for during his time in the public works department. The task force concluded that the interstate system's "applicability to urban areas like Boston is extremely limited."

The governor's "soul-searching" culminated in a rainy tour of the expressway routes on February 10. The following evening he went on television to inform Greater Boston of its transportation future. If Mayor White's call for a highway moratorium had roused the governor on the matter of balanced transportation, then Sargent's thirteen-minute appeal for a "Balanced Transportation Development Program" roused the country. He called for a complete recalibration of Boston's transportation priorities that considered "not *where* an expressway should be built, but *whether* an expressway should be built."

Afterward, on the advice of his task force, Sargent flew immediately to Washington with a rather drastic request: that the government allow cities to tap the sacred Highway Trust for mass transportation. There, a few weeks later, he convinced Secretary Volpe of the need to reexamine Boston's highway plan—the very plan both men had, at one time or another, so ardently endorsed. Volpe's agreement, wrote the *New York Times,* "appeared to mark a new turn in the politics of highway construction and the search for more balanced development of mass transit and urban freeways."

As far as the Southwest Expressway was concerned, Sargent called for all work along it to stop, effective immediately. It "emphatically does not consider the impact on the environment—on housing, on land-use, on people," he said of the proposed Interstate 95 into Boston, along the old highway path. "I have decided that it must."

IN THE IDEAL world of Lewis Mumford, which rotates on the axis of balanced transportation, method of travel is governed by destination. The longest journeys are made by air. More regional movements flow by rail. Long-distance trips can be made in cars, on roadways that sweep through the countryside until they reach the outskirts of the city. From there travelers continue into town on public transit, be it bus or subway. Downtowns are a shrine to the pedestrian. Local streets do exist, but when the system is working as it should they remain relatively unencumbered.

Of course, the constructs of this Mumfordian universe break down if too many people settle in one place. Once this point of saturation nears, Mumford argued, it is simply time to start a new town down the line. He even saw a precedent for this process of populate, rupture, repeat. It had occurred in Puritan New England, along old highways like the post road, when one town's excess became another's new beginning.

Mumford's ideal city can never exist, but toward the end of the twentieth century Providence approached his more realistic goal of becoming a "tolerable" one. The city founded after Massachusetts Bay banished Roger Williams found new life in the years after Boston banished the expressways. It capitalized on key initiatives that followed the challenges made to highway hegemony. It incorporated aspects of its heritage into its transformation, instead of erasing them in a rush to start anew. Eventually it became the model city New Haven had not—became, in the words of a Boston newspaper, no less, "a model for urban revival in the 21st century."

Francis Sargent's opposition to the interstates marked the crescendo of nearly a decade of quieter calls for a more balanced transportation network. Railroad reform had been a mounting cause since the early 1960s. Civil engineers, like those who published the regional survey of Boston in 1962, argued for better harmony between transit and highways. The federal government even joined the chorus that year, when it required cities to submit "comprehensive transportation" plans as a prerequisite to receiving highway aid.

Of course, this well-intentioned policy presupposed a well-running rail system. In the 1960s both commuter and mass-transit railroads were sorely in need of modernization. Decades of focus on highways had left them in disrepair. For the problems were cyclical: equipment desperately needed upgrading, which required capital; private attempts to raise money failed because many investors considered rails a dying industry; instead, fares were raised, which caused more passengers to flee; fleeing passengers demanded upgrades or else.

The poor condition of the New Haven railroad, in part, gave rise to the first federal push to close the vast disparity in public funding between roads and rails. In the course of his work, Claiborne Pell, senator from Rhode Island, frequently rode the New Haven from Providence to Washington. Pell found the ride altogether unsatisfactory; he referred to the sleeper train as a "waker" and described it as "one of the roughest rides since the stagecoach." Yet Pell was even more disturbed by the mighty traffic congestion in the Northeast Corridor, stretching roughly from Washington to Boston, which made up less than two percent of the nation's area yet owned fourteen percent of its cars. He also hated to fly, and had noticed that air travel had likewise been slowed by delays of late.

In the summer of 1962 Pell championed a plan for a high-speed rail network in the Northeast Corridor. In place of failing railroads the plan would establish a fleet of trains that ate up track between D.C. and the Bay at speeds exceeding 100 miles per hour. In fall 1965 Congress passed Pell's High-Speed Ground Transportation Act. One of its primary initiatives was to find out whether more people would ride trains if they were faster and more comfortable. This $18 million investigation targeted two crucial segments of the Northeast Corridor: one ran between Providence and Boston, the other between Washington and New York. In addition to easing transportation in the Northeast, the journal *Science* thought the effort might even ease "those social and economic problems affected by transportation."

The original Metroliner trains, brainchild of this effort, did entice some travelers away from air and auto when they began to run in the late 1960s. They were not enough to save the railroad industry alone, however. By 1968 rail travel between cities had dropped to an alarming 8.7 million passenger-miles—down from 35.3 billion in 1951, just before the interstate era. The New Haven railroad itself failed, for good this time, and began 1969 as part of the Penn Central system. Soon even this last of the great operating companies was chomping at the bit for bankruptcy.

Although the failure would seem a matter of private industry, the government had reasonable grounds for interference. If it simply watched the railroads fold, it would also see millions of travelers—23 million a year on the New Haven route alone—flood the already saturated expressways. Instead, the government did for the railroads what many felt it had been doing for the auto industry for decades: it subsidized them, to the tune of a $3 billion aid package to urban mass transit, signed into law in the fall of 1970. Congress also authorized the national takeover of all railways into the system that would become known as Amtrak. In perhaps the most symbolic victory, Francis Sargent succeeded in cracking open the Highway Trust, making it possible for cities to apply money once restricted to expressways toward mass transportation. Boston, for instance, never built its Southwest Expressway, creating instead the Orange line of the T, the city's name for its transit system.

In the mid-1970s, efforts to recalibrate the country's methods of travel led to a federal program called the Northeast Corridor Improvement Project—and it is this project that served as catalyst of Providence's metamorphosis. For by 1970 Providence commiserated with the distress felt by its post road neighbors. Pockets of blight peppered the historic district east of Main Street and the river. Crossing into the new downtown district meant braving the infamous traffic of Memorial Square—nicknamed "suicide circle." The old New Haven railroad tracks shielded the statehouse, the area's lone pleasant structure, from general view. Interstate 95 swept most shoppers eight miles south to the suburban Warwick Mall, a million-square-foot titan that slowly sucked department stores from downtown Providence until not a single one remained.

Providence did have something going for it that Boston, New Haven, and other cities did not. Instead of pouring money into urban renewal projects that razed entire neighborhoods, Providence largely renovated its existing cultural fabric through a series of city plans. Certainly much demolition took place. But on the whole the process favored restorative nudges over massive overhauls.

The city's first major redevelopment effort, for example, preserved many of the buildings that made up the old College Hill region east of Main Street, parts of which had formed the original post road from Boston. When a new railroad station was built later on, old Union Station was converted into commercial space. Still later, instead of building more roads and bridges between the east and west sides of town, the city cleared several streets to expose the two rivers that run beneath it.

The most dramatic alteration called for relocating the old New Haven tracks that fronted the statehouse. This was the so-called "Chinese Wall"—a gnarled maze of rails, platforms, and overhangs, all perched atop a thirteen-foot embankment. Though first proposed in 1961, only with the passage of the Northeast Corridor Improvement Project did the idea move from concept into reality.

In the words of the federal railroad chief, the project was designed to "get people out of their cars and onto public transportation." Its core mission was to reduce travel time between Boston and Washington; Congress hoped to chop the Boston–New York leg to three hours and forty minutes. An ancillary goal, however, was to improve the general railroad experience, and for this reason some $200 million of the $2 billion package was marked for station upgrades. Most stations along the shoreline route★ received some type of renovation. A concerted effort by local Providence officials to reroute the tracks through an entirely new structure, tapping Senator Pell's influence with the railroad administration, won approval.

From there, several of the city's other plans fell into place. Transportation rearrangement, much of it involving the old post road or its modern derivatives, was at the heart of the Providence renaissance. Though some of the changes continue today, most were finished by the late 1980s. Toward the end of 1986, for instance, the entire Chinese Wall was toppled, freeing the august statehouse from its iron veil.★★ The relocated tracks would run underground through the downtown sector. They would also be pushed back a bit, creating a bubble of land primed for commercial development. The new station itself would be positioned right on Gaspee Street, which in downtown Providence had been designated part of U.S. Route 1.

On the evening of June 19, 1986, at eighteen minutes past six o'clock, an Amtrak train made the inaugural lurch through Providence Station. The engine was named the *Benjamin Franklin*.

More changes stood in the offing. The main downtown interchange of I-95 would be restructured for a smoother transition into the central district. The hazardous traffic circle at Memorial Square would split into two one-way roads between Main Street, on the east side of town, and the west. Many walkways and bridges would be reserved exclusively for pedestrians.

Once these projects were completed, Joseph R. Paolino Jr., the mayor of Providence at the time, predicted that his city would be congestion free. He even launched an advertising campaign, perched on a billboard along the interstate in downtown Boston, aimed at the Bay's

---

★Amtrak's primary corridor runs along the shore. Hartford struggled for years to keep a spur running between New Haven and Springfield, and the inland course through Worcester has been largely ignored, and even occasionally discontinued.

★★In the process of demolishing the tracks construction workers uncovered a few remnants of New York–to–Boston travel past: "We found the old telegraph and electric lines for the railroad company—what was it known as back then?" the site chief reportedly asked, in the *Providence Journal*. "The New York, New Haven & Hartford Railroad Co.?"

weary motorists. The sign, seventy-five feet above, portrayed a traffic jam resembling the one drivers found themselves stuck in so often seventy-five feet below. It declared, in bold letters: "The reasons for moving to Providence seem endless." You might even begin your move on Washington Street, two blocks west of the interstate's Berkeley Street exit, where the billboard taunted the fray from aloft, and creep south along the Old Post Road, toward a new beginning.

Chapter 14

Cruising the BPR

THE LAST MAJOR section of Interstate 95 to open between Manhattan and Boston was a sixteen-mile whip of road connecting the east side of the Thames River, in Groton, Connecticut, with the Rhode Island border. After some gubernatorial words of wisdom several dignitaries hopped into the completed expressway's first ride and took off in a blaze of horsepower. Literally. They rode in a stagecoach, drawn by horses, carrying the influential party as well as the ceremonial ballast of several people dressed in colonial garb.

The idea, in the words of one newspaper, was to recall the interstate's "post Road predecessor of Colonial days, United States Route 1." It seems to me, however, that there's something more to this anachronistic parade than simple homage—something much closer to nostalgia, but not quite that either. Something closer still to a crisis of identity. Something that gets at the very problem of *knowing* a road, particularly this road.

But before proceeding with this examination it's necessary to catch up on some of the more notable events that have transpired along the old route in the past twenty-something years.

In the spring of 1989 a group of rail advocates, led by the Northeast Corridor Initiative, started a campaign to modernize Amtrak's equipment. The electrification of the old New Haven railroad track had never continued east of that city toward Boston. By fall of 1991 the initiative and its supporters had secured the first of many millions of dollars needed to complete the project that had begun in the days of J. P. Morgan.

That year saw Morgan's beloved Hartford continue its long-drawn-out struggle with urban redevelopment. The city became so impoverished that it considered taxing suburban commuters for entering the city during the day then fleeing at night. By 1993 Hartford's iconic department store, G. Fox & Co., had closed its downtown location, on Main Street. A few years later Hartford lost its professional hockey franchise, the Whalers.

The Boston Road in the Bronx was experiencing a similar decay. In early 1990 a livery cab passenger murdered the driver who picked him up in front of a produce store on the Boston Road—the second in a series of killings that prompted an industry scare. In 1994 New York City authorized a $34.7 million upgrade to this section of the road—thirty miles from Morrisania to the Westchester border—the largest improvement since the early days of U.S. Route 1. Boston, with social problems of its own near the terminal of the old highway, began a massive renovation of an area along Washington Street that had earned the undesirable nickname the Combat Zone. In 1996 the Yankees began their domination of the baseball world, to the chagrin of the Red Sox, capturing four World Series in five years.

The 1990s witnessed an explosion of technology along the road. Cell phone towers pierced its surface and fiber-optic wires sizzled beneath it, as information began to flow with an immediacy that rendered the original term "post road" nearly meaningless. By early 2000 the rail electrification project had been completed, and the first high-speed, all-electric Amtrak train—the Acela—pulled out of Boston's South Station en route to New York.

In 2001 Boston Road in the Bronx once again made headlines, for hosting a torrid strip of so-called "hot-sheet" motels, where low hourly room rates encouraged the type of behavior that requires renting a room for a low hourly rate. Vincent "Buddy" Cianci, mayor of Providence, went to jail in 2002 for his own form of objectionable conduct: he was convicted of racketeering conspiracy. Come September of 2003 Joseph Ganim, mayor of Bridgeport, joined Cianci in Fort Dix prison, convicted on charges of corruption.

That year the long-celebrated string of clam shacks sprinkled along the coastal highway earned the highest of gustatory accolades: what Broadway is to theater, declared the *New York Times,* this part of Route 1 was to clam shacks. The New England Patriots—with their new stadium completed along Route 1, in Foxboro—began to overwhelm professional football, winning three championships in four years. The Red Sox turned the tables on the Yankees, with two World Series titles of their own.

The real estate boom was in full swing. National franchises infected mom-and-pop stores and historic buildings, leading to a series of closings—none more lamentable than the destruction of the Tom Thumb house, on the old highway in Bridgeport, knocked out and smoothed into a Walgreens parking lot. In 2005 the Boston Post Road was considered one of the deadliest stretches of highway in Westchester County. Between 2005 and 2007 the Boston Post Road between Stamford and Guilford was, for pedestrians, the deadliest stretch in all Connecticut.

In late January of 2008 an underdog presidential candidate named Barack Obama opened an office in Mamaroneck, New York, at 931 East Boston Post Road. A few days later another underdog, the New York Giants, beat the undefeated Patriots in an upset that ranks high in Super Bowl history. That fall the country's real estate bubble burst, unleashing a wave of foreclosures on the old highway and plunging the region into recession. In early 2009 Obama, by then president, passed a massive economic stimulus package that focused heavily on infrastructure spending. The funding favored "shovel-ready" projects—one of which, a $75 million effort, sought to improve an Amtrak bridge that crossed over Route 1 in Branford, Connecticut.

There was another matter brewing in Branford at the time. Five versions of "Main Street" ran through the town—regular old Main, plus the four directional adjectives appended before it—and the jumble had become a source of frustration for travelers. The town was hoping to clarify the confusion once and for all. They would do this by folding the Main streets that formed part of Route 1 into a single name: the Boston Post Road.

BRANFORD'S DEBATE might be applied to my own description of the road—flitting, as it does, among a loosely assembled system of pseudonyms. The old highway has endured so many transmutations over the years that it becomes nearly impossible to give it a single meaningful name. For most of this book I have tried to call it whatever people called it at the time. Today, on modern maps, it assumes an even more haphazard composite of christenings; if it were the work of a master sculptor, it might be *Schizophrenia in Asphalt.*

There is an old philosophical paradox about the Ship of Theseus, whose planks are replaced with new ones as they wear down with age. Eventually the day arrives when all the planks have been replaced; does the ship then cease being its former self? If someone were to collect the old planks and reassemble them, the problem elevates in complexity. Is the real ship the one made of new planks that still sails the old route, or the one sitting in some basement, assembled from the original boards, incapable of sailing at all?

The Ship of Theseus has much in common with the old Boston Post Road, beginning with the problem of pinpointing the road at its most quintessential state of being. The highway has no internal biology, of course, but in a developmental sense it projects a simulacrum of maturity. It began as the downward fold of those first blades of grass crushed beneath the foot of a wilderness native, and evolved into bituminous macadam seven inches thick, with a four-inch stone bottom, bonded with sand or dust, and sealed with half a gallon of asphalt. Which of these stages, or any of those in between, exhibits a portrait of the road as it truly exists?

Then there are the people. A town might be defined by those who live within its confines. But what population can be considered native to a road? There are those who drive the road most often, and others who live and work directly along it. There are the engineering minds and construction hands who might never step foot on the completed road at all. There are the imprimaturs of litterers, gum chewers, car abandoners, pothole manufacturers, and birds that let loose on the great gray latrine. There are those who technically own the road, which, in the broadest definition of highway aid within the democratic institution, include every single person in the United States. And these are just the people who exist inside the present nook of the space-time continuum; in each of the aforementioned categories there exists a nation of the dead, whose memories howl at the surface of the road from the roots of the earth.

In short, to define the highway in terms of people is, at best, rather difficult, and, at worst, an exercise in distilling the gestalt personality of American society since the landing of the pilgrims.

Next comes the problem of purpose. The name Boston Post Road was never a name at all, so much as a description—a poetic interpretation of where, what, how. My first genuine research inquiry about the old highway elicited the response that its whole story and those of its milestones were one and the same. In some sense this seems true enough. Yet to describe expressways as all about the exit signs doesn't quite convey the magnitude of a system that "changed the face of America," to quote Eisenhower, just as to define George Washington's life through a bulleted list of his battles would fail miserably to convey his importance to the country. And what happens once this purpose shifts, as it so clearly has in the digital age? In the process of writing this book I requested permission to view a manuscript collection on postal records. The archive manager flashed me a look best described as annoyed quizzicality. She couldn't understand the relevance of my request to a book on the Boston Post Road. Despite being familiar with the highway, she had never put the word *post* together with the post office's function.

The completion of the interstate stripped the old road of one last plank of purpose: expressways now bear the bulk of long-distance travel, with the old highway relegated, in most places, to a glorified local street. There's no conceivable sort of transportation reform in the offing that would recalibrate this scale of importance (unless the idea posed in 1909 by Robert Goddard, would-be spaceflight pioneer from Worcester, of a vacuum tube that suctioned people from Boston to New York at 1,200 miles per hour is ever realized, and established along the old highway, for kicks).* Little wonder that in this state of semiretirement the road has assumed an air of senility, a sense of self more scattered than ever.

If we are to know the road at all, then, we must make like the stagecoach at the interstate opening and reach back as we move forward along it. So, armed with four centuries of backstory, I set out one final time on the highway, to gather any latest clues about its identity.

There are, it turns out, some things to know.

I know you attract police sirens in the Bronx for going right on red, and that in western Massachusetts you attract middle fingers for not. I know that when a man drifts down the middle of a major road—literally in the middle; not the sidewalk, not the shoulder, but the middle of the road—he exudes such an aura of derangement that no one honks at all. I know that you can go thirty-seven miles per hour in a fifty zone and enjoy it, and that if you enjoy it too much, very large men in plaid shirts driving monster trucks play a game with you called Tailgating Severely.

I know businesses can display names like Boston Road Collision, Pequot Appliance, Buggy Glo Car Wash, Yankee Discount Muffler, Kings Court Condominiums, Puritan Furniture, Route 20 Redemption, Trailers of New England, Scruples (flanked by silhouettes of fair nudes) Café, and Barnum (a known teetotaler) Wine & Spirits, and that I still prefer these to yet another Super Stop & Shop, or Walgreens, or Walmart. I know that some shopping centers are so large they grow their own shopping centers. I know where there is a seventy-mile boulevard of mad ceaseless neon commerce, and can take you there, if you dare to travel fifteen miles per hour.

I know that if all the maps disappeared tomorrow, a moment after all the street signs spontaneously combusted, one could find the way from town to town across northeast America by following the guiding purple and orange glow of the next Dunkin' Donuts drive-through. I know it's shibboleth to order Dunkin' Donuts coffee with cream and sugar—what you want is your coffee *regular* (in Boston, *reguluh*)—and

---

* It seems worth noting that one of Goddard's boyhood idols was Levi Pease.

that if you insist on further specification, you may identify the precise number and variety of your preferred sugar, so that "Large regular, five Splenda" becomes a reasonable, even civilized transaction.

I know that even though Hartford's Union Station has a sign pointing upstairs to the platform of its tracks, plural, and even though an announcer identifies a train approaching on Track One, implying the existence of other-numbered tracks, there is but one track, singular. I know that if you ask someone whether they enjoy living somewhere, and they say they've lived there for ten years, then say nothing more, that they've given you all the answer they intend to give. I know there are squirrels in Manhattan that literally pose on their hind legs for pictures, but that, overall, there's one less squirrel prancing around the post road than there used to be.

I know that if you think long enough about Ben Franklin's milestones you begin to see them, right there, beneath that street sign, and can make the illegal U-turn to prove it. I know there's a Boston Road in the Bronx, and a Bronx Road in West Roxbury, just outside Boston. I know that the name of the first post rider in this country is not Rider Postington the First, but that it might be Edward Messenger.

I know two local kids in New London—a heavyset Latino boy and a skinny black youth whose partnership seems plucked from the dreams of Cervantes—who have claimed the grounds of John Winthrop Jr.'s old mill as their personal playground. I know that when fire alarms blared when I stayed at Providence's most historic hotel no one bothered to leave, apparently bound by some unspoken consensus that it's perfectly honorable to go down with such an honored house, and I also know, according to the bellhop, that this siren goes off every month.

I know that to Willy Loman the true "death of a salesman" meant being "in his green velvet slippers in the smoker of the New York, New Haven and Hartford, going into Boston"; and that to a character in Don DeLillo's book *White Noise* the question of whether he'd ever crapped in a toilet bowl without a seat elicits the response that he has, once, in a "great and funky men's room in an old Socuny Mobil station on the Boston Post Road"; and that there are still Mobil stations on the old highway, and that I think I'll hold it until I see a BP.

I know where my cousin, whose teenage years in suburban Milford were largely spent "cruising the BPR" with friends, began his high-speed chase one night, near the old cinema at the Connecticut Post Mall. I know a Yale professor who thinks the Howard Johnson motels and fried clam shacks on Route 1 were—in the 1940s at least—"the very best things about our country." I know a great phantasmagoric concourse of memory.

I know it's out there, buried alive beneath asphalt and alias, the backbone of northeast America, smoldering with the stories of a nation. But I also know that sometimes we don't actually want to rediscover the past—that we prefer to keep our history tucked beneath the surface, where it remains inaccessible but stays intact, existing more in mind than in flesh, not so much a place one can visit but the idea of a place, the idea that something special *took* place, here, where I stand, once, and that this idea, even more than the thing itself, leaves open the possibility that something special will rise, here, once more.

MY JOURNEY DOWN the old highway actually began several years ago with what I considered a reasonable question: What the hell is a road called Boston doing in the Bronx? The thought first occurred in Morrisania, where Boston Road veers off Third Avenue across from a McDonald's, and that's where I returned, toward the close of writing this book, to take one final spin. Of course, any good ride on an old colonial highway deserves a good horse, and mine was a delicious strawberry roan—and a British one, at that: a red MINI Cooper with a white top.

I quickly fell upon the task of naming this friend, and my thoughts went back to the first post rider, whose name had escaped my discovery despite a search too extensive to describe here, for fear of retribution from my publisher. So, luckless in pursuit, I had christened the man Rider Postington the First, and now in the absurd hope that the spirit of this pioneer would somehow bless my travels, I passed the name on to my horse, duly pronouncing him Red Rider.

My course had been carefully planned. I would travel to Boston from the spot of my inspiration along the inland route of the old highway, then head back down to New York along the coast of Long Island Sound, finishing at the southern tip of Manhattan, at the erstwhile site of Fort James, where Rider Postington's journey had begun. What I hoped to accomplish with this weeklong ride was far less clear. I wanted to acquire a familiarity with the present road that approached what I had with its historic counterparts, but I didn't want to limit myself to stopping where Ben Franklin stopped, and bunking where George Washington bunked. I wanted to stay at the highway's inns, drink in its taverns, cross atop its railroad tracks, idle below its interstate bridges, but I also wanted to do more than give a running ticker of notable sites. I needed to know if the road lived today in a way that resembled the way it lived inside my head—to know what happened when you took the lone lifeline in an uncivilized world, piled three centuries of civilization on top of it, and said go.

It was a lingering concern of mine, in the days leading up to the trip, that I would have it too easy—that my itinerary, prepared with all the tools technology has to offer, would in some way strip the journey of some essential truth. The first post rider had a vague set of verbal directions and perhaps a few days' horse feed; I had online hotel reservations and a week's worth of Propecia. When I asked the stable to rent a global positioning saddle (which they insisted upon calling a GPS), I did so with a good deal of consternation. Rider Postington had traveled by a narrow slit of poorly groomed earth peeking through the wilderness. Under the circumstances I found it hard to justify pushing a button that measured my distance from a space satellite then explained, nanoseconds later, in a mellow robotic voice, precisely how much time I had to adjust my interior climate until my next turn.

So I established a strict voyager's compromise: When off course I would navigate back to the highway first by wit, then by printed map, and, only failing these, by saddle-ite.

I was just across the Harlem River when the whole damn system collapsed. Lost, I tried to turn right on red, and had my encounter-by-megaphone with the Bronx's Finest. Afterward the GPS was locked and loaded into the cigarette lighter. There it remained until Red Rider and I reached a turnoff where two lanes of traffic merge down to one lane of movement because the entire right lane is filled with parked cars. This is the start of Boston Road in the Bronx.

It was here, just north of where East One Hundred Sixty-third Street meets Third Avenue, that I was introduced to the road several years back. Having finally returned, with a few centuries of relevant knowledge to vouch for the hiatus, I looked around. Beside the McDonald's was a store, gated and padlocked on noon of a Monday. A rusty iron fence slumped outside my passenger window. Behind it stood a drab boxy set of apartment buildings. When a cab passed by it was inevitably an unofficial livery; yellow cabs rarely venture this way. This stretch of the Boston Road had even been issued an alternate name: Edward A. Stevenson Boulevard. In short, there was nothing to imply that I was on a road of any consequence. Anyone else looking at the sign would think this road's greatest significance was that it served as an emergency snow route.

I continued northeast through the Bronx, toward Westchester. For the most part, this section of road traverses a groaning landscape of fast-food restaurants, gas stations, auto shops, bodegas, darting pedestrians, strolling pedestrians, and storefronts that display little in their windows except space to rent. For a brief while an elevated train rumbled directly overhead, dicing the sunlight into white and black squares that turned the old highway into a bit of a chessboard. Traffic lights constantly interrupted the flow of cars. After nearly an hour of driving I had gone eleven miles.

A bit farther along I crossed the bridge over the Hutchinson River, and the entrance to the parkway. Beyond the threshold the run-down vista disappears and, one beat later, leaves in its place the bright frothy verdure of Pelham Manor. The effect is a bit like Dorothy stepping out of monochrome Kansas into Technicolor Oz. Green lawns lead up to stone stairs that run into the neatly nestled homes of residential Westchester County. I was officially on "Boston Post Road" now, though it's also designated U.S. Route 1. At the corner of Split Rock Road I saw, to my right, the general vicinity of Aaron Burr's old country estate, The Shrubberies. The transition from city to suburb was strikingly complete.

In New Rochelle, after passing beneath Interstate 95, the road began to narrow considerably. The storefront pressed up close to the four-lane street, and the unfurled boutique awnings added a vertical element to the general claustrophobia. Red Rider's side mirrors got quite cozy with those on the horses beside him. It continued this way for some time, these close quarters, until I passed through Mamaroneck into Rye.

Here a rather magical transformation took place. Suddenly Red Rider was running with hoof-room to spare. I had come upon the post-prandial effects of the so-called "Boston Post Road diet." Several weeks earlier I had spoken to Christian Miller, Rye's city planner, about the diet. The post road hadn't grown much since the beginning of the twentieth century, but the cars driving on it sure had. Four Red Riders might fit abreast on the road, but four Range Rovers certainly could not. The snug surroundings compromised the safety of motorists and pedestrians alike. To enlarge the old highway in this land of lush green real estate would be extremely expensive; above the cost, such massive overhaul came with a compromise of character. In Rye, Miller told me, the old highway is "very much like it was decades ago," and the residents aimed very much to keep it that way.

So the city chose a simple course of action. Four lanes become two, with padded shoulders and a painted median that vanishes into a left-turn lane at particularly busy crossings. Slimming down to ease over-crowding seems illogical, but there is a psychological element here that steers drivers toward the intended result. Modernity slips away, for a moment, and in its place slides a road that maintains as much colonial simplicity as a twenty-first-century highway can.

For the most part the rest of Route 1 to New Haven sprawled in marked contrast to Rye's controlled asceticism. There was some wilderness, here, but it was a gluttonous commercial wild. That's not meant as a jeremiad against commercial development: downtown Stamford has grown impressively with its status as a regional economic player; pockets of Greenwich maintain a quiet retail elegance; and there are parts of Bridgeport so run-down that any infusion of life, even of the megachain variety, would qualify as an improvement. On the whole, however, I got the sense that something of the old highway had been irretrievably lost, swept over by a thick generic brushstroke the proud region considered anathema. I was marooned on the old highway by a disinterested forest of franchise stores—and I would no sooner reach Boston on this road than Anytown, U.S.A.

A few elms of yesteryear might see a revival on some parts of the road. As of my journey, five areas west of New Haven were mounting a project called the Greening of the Post Road. Through the aid of state and federal grants, Westport, Fairfield, Bridgeport, Milford, and West Haven had arranged to plant trees at strategic points along the old road. The trees will absorb pollutants, and some believe they'll even diminish road rage. Still, I think the attraction to the project is something closer to what Mary Ludwig, whose company, Milford Trees, will plant the saplings in that town, told me before I left: "The pictures I've seen of the old Post Road, and hearing people talk about how things used to be, it makes you feel like you're missing something."

By the time I reached New Haven what I was missing was more than four hours of my life. It had taken me that long to travel some seventy miles: an average of just over fifteen miles per hour. It's hard to convey in prose the precise agony of stuttering through a sea of traffic lights over such a distance. I. Suppose. I. Might. Come. Close. If. I. Wrote. Like. This. It was described to me, traffic on this stretch of Route 1, by people who live along the road, in a gradient of aspersions: from a necessary daily annoyance, to "I hate the Post Road," to feelings of the four-letter variety. Back in Westport I had seen a sign that said "Please Slow Down, We Enforce Our Speed Laws." I couldn't help thinking that if I slowed down from my present pace, I would be driving in reverse.

Eventually I reached my hotel near the Yale campus, and took a stroll past the three churches on the New Haven Green. I stopped inside a tavern beside the original town plots, and with that, the first stage of my trip ended in the same manner that stages ended in the post rider's day. There was even an antique-ish pair of gargoyles perched above my head. (They were resting on high-definition cable boxes, but nevertheless.) Certainly he had experienced hardships that I had missed out on, the first rider. Then again, there were a few aspects of modern highway travel that old Rider Postington had been mercifully spared.

THE STREETS OF New Haven were fairly empty that evening, and even emptier the following morning. Students were still returning from spring break, which, as the cool breeze picked up, must have felt like a bit of false advertising. I walked to the Green and stopped at what was, for the moment, the liveliest spot in the city: the Dunkin' Donuts on Chapel Street. In the process I passed the tavern where I had eaten the previous night. Two puddles of vomit out front indicated that I'd retired before the evening's festivities had truly commenced.

Having filled up on the sweet New England nectar, I began the drive north toward Hartford. Leaving downtown New Haven required that I steer Red Rider down Frontage Street, the local lane of the Oak Street Connector, the symbol of New Haven's recent degradation. Shortly before my trip I spoke with Yale professor Doug Rae, author of *City,* about the destructive impact that highway changes, such as the routing of the connector off Interstate 95, had on New Haven. Sluggish old Route 1 had indeed catalyzed many of the city's redevelopment plans, for better or worse, Rae told me.

"The Post Road figured into this," he said. "Route One ran right through New Haven, as it did through many cities." In *City* I had found the painful statistic that traffic through New Haven on the Post Road averaged five miles per hour circa 1945. "I can't imagine what it must have been like, if you were really trying to drive a long stretch, to pass at five miles per hour through all these towns," Rae said. I almost could after the previous day's travels, and wished I couldn't.

Rae believed the key to New Haven's future prosperity was an improved commuter rail service, particularly the Metro-North line that parallels the Post Road along the coast toward New York. Many transportation experts I spoke to agreed that a resurgence in rail travel was a precondition to progress in the Northeast. That, combined with the redevelopment of small parcels of land near the railroad stations on Route 1, could cause New Haven to "flower again," in Rae's eyes.

From New Haven, Red Rider and I followed the old highway north toward Middletown through the backcountry of Durham. Slow-moving traffic was certainly no problem on this stretch of road. I whizzed by colonial-style homes coated in various shades of pastel—by wide lawns and shuttered windows and thick woodlands and the first (real) horse of my journey—so quickly that I had to drive well below the speed limit to catch it all. Across the Hartford line I passed a car using a piece of cardboard for a rear passenger window and couldn't help but think to myself, what with the wind slipping through the cracks of his makeshift curtain, that he was simulating the experience of stagecoach days better than I.

Once in Hartford I strolled down Main Street, a vestige of the original highway. Soon I neared the intersection where I personally, though unintentionally, had added to the tally of lives ended on the old road during a previous visit. I had been walking along Main when a squirrel suddenly capered toward me. To avoid a sidewalk collision he veered into the street, hopped twice, and then had every ounce of memory and desire crunched out of him by the monstrous right front wheel of a sport-utility vehicle. The all-terrain tread left the furry fellow, now the flatter furry fellow, a last bunch of nerve cells, so that it danced briefly in the street one final time, a morbid little encore.

This captured Hartford for me, in a way: thrusting back toward life beneath an ever-lowering curtain. A news article of a few years ago reported that Hartford had the nation's second-highest poverty rate; at that time, thirty percent of people in the capital of the nation's wealthiest state lived poorly. Things have turned somewhat, but even today there are signs that boast "Hartford: New England's Rising Star" hanging directly above deserted lots.

When I reached the spot where John Winthrop Jr. and Francis Lovelace held their fateful meeting about the "King's best highway" in the summer of 1673, I walked a block east toward the Connecticut River. There was no more meadow, now, no more purling stream. Just the clicking of high heels through a parking garage. It's nearly impossible to see the river, let alone reach it, thanks to the expressway. Still, there is a compact, small-town allure to the city that made me feel it too could flower again with the proper guidance.

That afternoon I drove to the state historical society, just west of downtown Hartford, for a sneak preview of its exhibit on old tavern

signs. Richard Malley, the society's assistant director of museum collections, greeted me. Malley's mellow energy was punctuated on occasion by eyebrows that arched sharply at moments of emphasis. "Tavern
signs," he said, shaking my hand, brows at attention. "Think we have a
couple."

By a couple he meant fifty-seven, hung all about Hoadley Audito-
rium, dating from 1749 onward. Malley and I worked our way slowly
around the room. One sign, marked "Strangers, Resort," pictured two
men drinking some wine at a table on one side, and a carriage scene
on the other. It's thought, said Malley, that the scene was a tribute to
Lafayette, who toured the Post Road on his visit to America in 1824.
Some signs, like the one from a tavern in Saybrook that said only
"Entertainment," came quickly to the point. Others, like one from mid-
nineteenth-century Middletown, offered passing bites of wisdom: "As
we journey through life, let us live by the way."

I asked Malley whether people in Hartford felt any kinship with
the Post Road; after all, it hadn't survived there in name, as it had on
Route 1, and in parts of Massachusetts. As I suspected, Malley thought
most Hartford natives identified the Post Road with the coast of Long
Island Sound. "When people learn there was a post road from New York
that came through Hartford, they're surprised," he said, brows arched.
Similar cultural erasures had been made, mistakenly in many Hartford minds, during urban renewal. The interstates not only cut off the
waterfront from the downtown area, but also sliced the city into distinct
halves. There were a host of social structures rich in potential—from the
Mark Twain and Harriet Beecher Stowe houses to the technical college
occupying the old G. Fox building on Main Street—but on the whole a
great cultural heritage remained relatively concealed.

I unhitched Red Rider and started north onto Palisado Drive,
through Windsor, toward Springfield. We passed the bridge shoot-
ing east where John Bissell's original ferry had once carried passengers
across the Connecticut. Sun spots dressed the river in silver blue lamé,
and a wicked breeze whipped road signs toward me like a matador enticing Red Rider with his cape. In Enfield we found Pease Street, no doubt
named for someone in the family that had been among the region's ear-

liest settlers—perhaps even for stagecoach pioneer Levi Pease himself. Before long we reached the Massachusetts line, and the city of Springfield.

Downtown Springfield has some impressive buildings, to judge by height alone, but the sidewalks themselves give off a subdued, hollow feel. Blight had spread to the stores in the city center. They were all closed up when I passed through except for a Dunkin' Donuts, and even that was surprisingly empty. I walked by a man raining blows with a sledgehammer on the corner of an insurance building; it seemed like an unauthorized bashing, as though he had found a suitable spot to vent a general frustration. I turned off Main Street onto Taylor Street to find the Russell Machine Shop, where Frank Duryea had built his first car. Instead all I found was an empty space where the historical address should have been. I was later told the building had been knocked down during urban renewal.

That afternoon I had my second sneak preview of the day, at the nearly completed Springfield Museum of History. I met the museum's director, Guy McLain, outside a large building hiding behind a construction tarp. McLain had a salt–and–Old Bay beard and a light gravelly voice that accelerated when it hit on a topic he found exciting, which was pretty much everything behind the tarp. In a city that, like New Haven and Hartford, had seen better times, McLain's was a voice of infinite hope.

The plan is for the Springfield Museum to survey general history, but it will also feature a key component of highway transformation at its core: an exact replica of the original gasoline automobile built by Frank Duryea in 1893, widely considered the first modern car made in America. Among the Springfield Museum's primary objectives was redressing a lingering bit of cultural amnesia: that Frank Duryea, and not Henry Ford, built the country's first true car. McLain said that whenever he told this to students during talks at schools, they were always surprised.

"One question I love to ask is, 'Who made the first automobile in America?' They say Ford. And that's here in Springfield!" he said. "I think it's because the Duryea company didn't survive." This was precisely how I felt about the old highway: overshadowed by the interstates, inconsistent in names, it would lose more to history each day, until some crucial cultural root was buried too deep to salvage even for those who lived right by the old way.

"History's written by the winners," McLain said. "This is a real good example of that."

That evening I spoke with Keith Korbut, founder of the Duryea Society, and the person who had arranged my tour with McLain. I told Keith I couldn't find the Russell Machine Shop. He told me the site was clearly marked. I swore I had looked. He swore I should look again. So the next morning I journeyed back to Taylor Street, just off Main, and parked at the bend in the road. There it was after all, etched into the sidewalk, right below my feet—"Duryea Way"—and, tucked some ten yards off the curb, the stainless steel replica of a Duryea car, set on the grounds of the old shop. I would have been glad to see it, if it hadn't made me wonder what else I had missed.

I LEFT SPRINGFIELD and drove east to meet Bob Wilder, Mr. Post Road himself. If the old king's highway still has any right to that name, then Bob Wilder's home in Brookfield, Massachusetts, is the royal court. A silhouette of a stagecoach hangs beside the entrance to his small white cottage. His living room is strewn with warm knitted quilts and an array of colorful, generally Marines-related bric-a-brac. Propped upon the couch was a map of northeast America with a title in the lower right corner: "Post Road, 1763."

For decades now, Bob Wilder has made the Post Road his passionate avocation. He translates this energy in a manner that captivates people who could never find his town of three thousand on a map, let alone visit it, and his tales of the nineteen consecutive milestones still standing between Springfield and Worcester have been told in publications from Palm Beach, Florida, to Billings, Montana. Bob is seventy-five "heading the other way," and keeps his long face hidden behind a full gray beard and truly enormous glasses. Behind the glasses are a set of eyes that see the world a bit more precisely than most. Where I saw windows, trees, and a domed hovel, Bob saw thermal panes, pines, and a military Quonset hut. It might fairly be said of him, I thought as we drove out to the first stone, that Bob Wilder is cut straight from the earth.

We began our tour in Leicester, on Massachusetts Route 9, and worked our way back west. As I steered Red Rider, Bob pointed out milestones like most passengers point out traffic cops or Golden Arches. There's one, under the CVS sign in central Spencer. There's another, in front of Evergreen Cemetery. We had to turn off the road to find one, because, according to Bob, the owner of Spencer Country Inn wanted it on his premises, to attract business. The stones are marked by their distance from Boston—and a few by their distance to Springfield—though many of the engravings have been blasted beyond identification by wind and sand. Many stones have been moved to certain spots simply because Bob has found, through his research, that's where they should be.

When there's a story to the stone, Bob knows this too. We stopped at one wedged along a back road paralleling the state highway. Until a few years ago it had been missing for decades. Then Bob got a call from the chief of police. A man had come down to the station with an old milestone. Turns out he had snatched it up as a teenager, twenty-five years earlier. The man was given immunity in exchange for the stone, and now it rested sixty-four miles from Boston, by mid-eighteenth-century standards. "They put that thing in enough cement to hold down the battleship *Missouri*," said Bob.

We needled through Elm Hill Farms, where Elsie the Cow was discovered by the Borden milk company, and past the site of the old Ayres' tavern that served as a garrison during King Philip's War, in 1675. A spherical wound had dented the Sixty-seven Mile stone above the *t* in "Boston." "Some boy shot it with a .22 years ago," said Bob. On a hilltop in Warren we stopped at a bend in the road at a stone near where George Washington convened with General Israel Putnam, in 1775, on his way to Boston. Bob pointed down a leafy corridor that disappeared into the woodlands. "You're looking at the post road as it existed," he said. "They haven't made it better. They haven't made it worse."

The first several stones were directly on Route 9. In other places the state highway had shifted slightly off the original road in the past few centuries. We weaved onto deeply rutted gravel paths that brought to mind my rental car agreement. The town had wanted to pave them, but Bob wouldn't have it: "The ruts go with it, you know."

I have always treated the road from Boston to New York as a highway, sure, but also as a broader concept—tracking its shifts from Indian trail to railroad to interstate as a reflection of a greater social development. To Bob the highway remained rigidly locked into 1763. Embarrassed at having taken this artistic liberty, I was comforted to find that Bob approved of the communities that had moved stones onto the nearest major road and out of the wilderness, where no one would see them. "Better to move it and preserve it than leave it and lose it," he said. There was some honor, then, in accepting the road as a greater idea—a notion worth preserving in spirit more than a site that must be revered precisely as it lay, or not revered at all.

"Do you ever worry about people forgetting about the post road?" I asked.

"I worry about people forgetting about our history," Bob replied.

As we drove back to the Wilder home, nineteen stones later, Bob slipped a casual note into our conversation that, I thought, went a long way toward explaining his preternatural grasp of the old highway. While discussing his boyhood he revealed that his father had separated him from his mother as a very young child. Later on Bob joined the marines, and right before leaving for war he confronted his father about his past. As he told the story of meeting his mother Bob was directing me through the hilly, winding back roads that clung to the contours of the earth. "I showed up in Maine—we're going to the right, here—I showed up at the door and said, 'Hi, I'm your son.'" She was an Eastern Abenaki Indian, Bob's mother. He was half Native American.

I left the Wilder residence and continued east toward Worcester. There was a milestone just northeast of the city center that Bob swore I couldn't possibly miss, but before I knew it I was entering Shrewsbury, with the Worcester stone somewhere behind me. On Main Street, a short ways before the old highway became U.S. Route 20, I pulled off the road and into Mountain View Cemetery.

The graveyard spread out behind a parking lot at the back of the First Congregational Church. The early evening sky was clear. I passed through two stone pillars balancing marble orbs at the cemetery's entrance. Immediately to my right, peeking through a sizable pile of branches and brush, was a rock honoring the life of Levi Pease. A plaque noted Pease's service in the Revolution, his establishment of the country's first successful stagecoach line, and the contract that made him the first to carry the mail by carriage. He had navigated the Post Road by himself at first, before passengers trusted him to safely make the trip. It was poorly kept, this cemetery, and if I hadn't known exactly where the marker was supposed to be, I never would have found it.

That night I stayed in a colonial inn, alone, in a town none of my friends or family knew even existed. I walked about the grounds briefly before turning in. I could barely see in front of me on the lighted path. Suddenly it didn't matter so much that some of the modern road didn't follow the old road precisely. How did the *old* road manage to follow the old road precisely? There must have been long hours, even for a veteran rider like Pease, when the idea that there was a road from New York to Boston had been enough to guide him through a landscape vast and strange—when the certainty of a destination mattered more than how many road markers were passed along the way.

THE MENU IN the dining room of Longfellow's Wayside Inn, in Sudbury, Massachusetts, says it's been serving "weary travelers" along the Boston Post Road for three hundred years. It began as a tavern run by David Howe in 1716. That explained the Union Jack flying out front. It took Longfellow's name after the poet stopped there in 1862 and authored his famous "Tales of a Wayside Inn," which included a slightly aggrandized description of Paul Revere's ride in April 1775. That explained the men in period dress—three-cornered hats, fifes, and all—practicing a marching formation on the front lawn, in anticipation of the anniversary of the Battle of Lexington, as I pulled Red Rider to a halt.

It was the mere idea of years and years of "weary travelers" that had inspired Longfellow's tales; the inn itself was temporarily closed upon the poet's visit. As I looked around, it occurred to me that while the place was hopping with guests, its purpose as a resting spot for the weary was as defunct in my day as it had been in Longfellow's. In the past three centuries the function of inns—the function, really, of travel—had fundamentally changed. No one had stopped in here because they had spotted a flickering candle of fellowship along a lonely highway. They had planned this excursion for some time—planned it, if they were wise, to take advantage of the "winter getaway" special. Despite the inn's fine efforts, the past and present weren't entirely communicating; they had, a good lawyer might say, irreconcilable differences.

The next morning I rode into Boston on U.S. Route 20. The red hues of a rising sun tickled the hills to the east, and I had time to focus on the sight, because the road was jammed. Bo Bennett, founder of EVcast, a podcast devoted to electric cars, who worked on this stretch of the road, had warned me about the traffic on Route 20. "When you say Boston Post Road you don't get the feeling of nostalgia," he told me before my trip. "You think, you should stay away from there."

One emergency consultation with the global positioning saddle-ite later, I hitched Red Rider to a post in downtown Boston. I spent the rest of the day catching up on some research. The work produced an unexpected gem: there, in a letter written by John Winthrop Jr. in the spring of 1673, was mention of the "returne of Edward Messenger from Boston." He was bearing letters, this Messenger, and not just any letters, but letters from John Leverett, governor of the Massachusetts Bay Colony, the final target of the first post rider's run three months earlier. As evidence of the first post rider's name it was far from conclusive, but it was a step up from Rider Postington the First.

The next morning I ventured to the intersection of State and Washington streets. Here, at the Bay end of the old highway, I started the journey back to New York. The traffic on Washington Street moves one way here, the wrong direction, so I set out on foot along the old highway that once slipped unrivaled along the neck of the Bay.

In former times this intersection was home to the Town House. Merchants from miles around pulled their carts down the road to trade at the region's largest market. Half a block into my walk a Dunkin' Donuts on Washington captured the fervor of the old exchange, supplying the busy downtown population—some so busy they can't actually go inside the store but must order from a walk-through window that opens onto the street—with all the "lahge reguluhs" it needed to subsist.

The brick sidewalk beside Washington Street, still remarkably narrow even today, led me toward the Old South Church, a site once called home by Governor John Winthrop. A group of schoolchildren waited out front to tour the church—a rowdy bunch, similar in spirit to those who had attended the raucous meeting here that preceded the Tea Party. A produce market was preparing for the day under an awning below the Old South spire. Two men called out to someone in the street— "Morning!"—and for a moment modern Boston conjured visions of its small-town roots.

As I walked on I heard one man say to another, "That's the thing about New York—" but, strain as I did, I couldn't catch the finish. The moment sparked a memory. A few years earlier I had met Thomas O'Connor, famed Bay chronicler, at his Boston College office. I had lived in Cambridge a few years before this, a lowly intern at Boston's city magazine, and had felt a palpable—and unrequited—obsession with New York. Midway through our talk I asked O'Connor about this perceived inferiority complex. "Certainly there is a competitive spirit," he allowed before falling silent, and I'll never forget the long seconds of terror that followed, when I was sure I had offended him. Whatever it was the man on Washington Street said during my walk, I'm pretty sure it wasn't: "That's the thing about New York, it's right at the other end of this road."

That competitive spirit has been eased by the recent success of the Red Sox. A vendor at the corner of Summer Street prepared an entire cartful of team paraphernalia. Across Washington people entered the Downtown Crossing station of the Orange T line. This was the line built to service the corridor that escaped the Southwest Expressway, and it rumbled now below the old highway. This intersection has been called the "100 percent corner," as some estimates have placed the foot traffic here at one hundred thousand people a day. Skyscraper window washers swung from their suspended seats above where Washington fanned into three lanes.

Beyond the hospital center the buildings shrank considerably.

Though I was only a mile away from where I had started, in some sense I'd already reached the outskirts of downtown. The window washing here was done by a man with his feet on the ground, dipping his squeegee into a bucket that rested firmly on the sidewalk. Things had changed, of course, as the Prudential Center, high in the distance on filled-in Back Bay, reminded me. But in a symbolic sense this is how things had existed in the early days: a road leading from the busy town center toward the sparsely populated neck, and beyond. The difference between now and then wasn't one of kind but of degree, and of Dunkin' Donuts.

Back atop Red Rider, I pulled to a stop at the corner of Centre and Roxbury streets, in front of a shop called Foreign Car Parts. Flush against the base of the building rested the "parting stone." It had stood there, more or less unmoved, since 1744. In its glory days this stone directed westward travelers toward Cambridge, en route to Springfield, and southbound travelers toward Dedham, en route to Providence. There it was, the side facing Centre: "Dedham X Rhode Island." The Cambridge side faced into the brick facade, hidden from view, but the stone still remained, at least half the stone it used to be.

In Providence the old highway, known there originally as the Pequot Path, rolled down North Main Street, crossed the river at Memorial Bridge, and continued on Weybosset Street until it rejoined Route 1 through southern Rhode Island. Standing on Memorial Bridge, looking north, I saw the stalemate between the city's past and present. To the left, the skyscrapers of downtown puffed their sparkling chests like a young gang of bullies. To the right the short, stocky buildings of College Hill and the Brown University campus maintained a veteran dignity. Only the mellow neutral country of the river ensured a peaceful coexistence.

The theme continued throughout the city. A U.S. courthouse had replaced old Railroad Hall, but a detailed plaque told of Lincoln's speech there, in 1860, and its contributions to his election. The august statehouse, extricated from the old "Chinese Wall" of New Haven railroad tracks, conversed freely with the downtown. A restored granite marker memorialized the burning of the HMS *Gaspee,* and "the first blood in the American Revolution," though when I tried to glance down the river, toward where John Brown and company would have slid that night in 1772, the interstate interfered with my view.

South of Providence, Route 1 took the name Post Road. In Warwick we passed the intermarriage of transportation old and new, as an entrance to Rhode Island's major airport split directly off the old highway. Farther along Route 1 we reached the grounds of Cocumscussoc, Roger Williams's original trading post. The smell of salt from Wickford Harbor filled the air. The bushes chattered in the breeze. Reeds swayed at the bank of the cove as gulls convened upon its rocks. It was an oasis of history along the modern road, tucked just beyond the sounds of the highway, not terribly unlike what John Winthrop Jr. must have found when he stopped there on his tour of the primitive road in 1645.★

Soon I reached Groton and approached the Thames River. The only way across is on the interstate, and so Red Rider and I made our first merge onto the expressway, and into New London. We were so thrown by the experience that I was forced to consult the saddle-ite to find the old home of John Winthrop Jr. The home itself no longer exists, but the mill Winthrop built right near it still does, just off the corner of modern Mill Street and State Pier Road.

Winthrop built the old mill in 1650. It had been torched by the hands of Benedict Arnold, along with the rest of New London, during the Revolution, but it had been finely restored, and was rededicated as recently as the fall of 2008. If hard to find, the re-created scene is peaceful and pleasant—provided one ignores the shadows cast by not one but two expressway bridges, Interstate 95 north and south, which groan incessantly, directly overhead.

At the Connecticut River we merged onto the expressway yet again, to cross the mouth into Old Saybrook, another Post Road town settled by Winthrop. In Clinton I stopped at a traffic light in front of a car carrying a group of teenage girls. They were bopping to the radio and, unmistakably, passing around a joint. It took me a moment to realize,

---

★ One modern disruption on the grounds should be noted: It must be a source of confusion to the ghosts of the *British* settlers who died in the Swamp Fight, which took place nearby during King Philip's War, in 1675, to find the markers honoring their sacrifice surrounded by tiny *American* flags.

as I examined them in my rearview, that there was an element of samsara at work here. They were cruising the BPR, these ladies. Just as my cousin had done a generation before. Just as Zelda and Scott Fitzgerald had done generations before that. Just as teenagers between New York and Boston would continue to do for generations to come.

I stopped for the night at a motel on East Main Street, in Branford, just outside New Haven. This was the same stretch of Route 1 that the town was thinking of renaming "Boston Post Road." Before my trip I spoke about the potential change with Anthony "Unk" DaRos, Branford's first selectman, a position akin to that of mayor. DaRos was very much in favor of the switch, and it didn't bother him that the name Boston Post Road, as a reflection of the highway's function, was becoming obsolete. "You find around here people are very sensitive to the past, and people would cling to that name," he told me. "I think this section of the country is strong that way. We have old ways, but we have new ways too."

I SET OUT back for New York on the final day of my journey in a light but steady rain. It was the same slumping stretch of commerce it had been a week earlier, Route 1 along the Sound, but there were far fewer horses on the old highway this early Sunday morning.

The changes that had taken place on the road upset some of the people I'd had a chance to speak to from the area. The loss of historic sites like the Tom Thumb house, in Bridgeport (just about the only place on the Post Road that lionizes P. T. Barnum above George Washington); the McMansions, or "houses on steroids," constructed in the residential sections of the road that ran through Fairfield; the peremptory division that came from running Interstate 95 through town centers and neighborhoods; the endless refrain of retail chains. Altogether the changes had created a balkanized identity—caused, in the words of one person from Westport, "a loosening of the community feeling."

"There have been discussions about trying to lock in what's left of the small-town character," Robert Yaro, the president of the Regional Plan Association, told me shortly after my trip, regarding Route 1 from Manhattan to New Haven. Oddly, he told me, the recession might help to achieve this aim. "We overbuilt retail everywhere in the country," Yaro said. "We might have the opportunity to reclaim sections of the Post Road that are wall-to-wall retail junk."

What he meant was that in the rush to develop we had lost a vision of the old highway in its prime: of a route leading from home to store, yes, but also of one coursing beneath a canopy of elm trees pierced by some majestic Old World spire—and not just elm trees and spires but *that* elm tree and *my* spire. This is not the hope of returning to a past too quaint to be livable. It's something closer to feeling safe, I think, and not safe in a motor-accident sense, but safe in the sense of having a community, the sort of warm safety Rider Postington must have sought—and likewise dispensed—as he bounded through the darkness toward the next sign of civilization.

For all the advantages of the information age it fails to secure this type of feeling. The early highway rides were missions of intimacy; they required an intimate knowledge of the trails, and left intimate camaraderie at every stop. It was a social network of people who had left an old familiar land for a strange new one, stretching from New York to Boston, bound together by the post riders. Eventually a path appeared, then mile markers added to its prominence, and soon the highway came to symbolize a great continuous chain of conversation. Today conversations are governed by an inscrutable ether living nowhere in particular. It wasn't just the old highway's name that was chipping away. Its essential purpose was fracturing too.

Just west of Pelham I turned onto a road named Kings Highway. This was as close as one could come to the original path leading onto Manhattan through Kingsbridge. The streets here are characterized by hills and twists. In the Bronx I stopped at the corner of Two Hundred Thirty-first Street and Albany Crescent; here, in former times, those traveling on the Albany Post Road, north, split from those heading to Boston. At the corner stood an Irish pub called the Piper's Kilt. A few years earlier I had spoken to one of the bar's owners. He no longer lived in New York, this owner, and I asked him why he'd left. "We never leave New York," he said.

Shortly after reaching Manhattan I left Red Rider and walked the last half dozen miles down the island on foot. It was midafternoon, and the rain politely subsided as I attempted to retrace the course of Washington's victorious parade in 1783. This required a bit of historic license—for about five miles leading south to Madison Square Park the old highway doesn't exist in any meaningful way. The winding young path was wrenched into a perpendicular adulthood by the street commissioners who drew Manhattan's great grid in the early nineteenth century. One New York City street historian has listed the post road here as "obsolete." In a semantic sense I can't help but defend the label. But the lost mileage represents two percent of the highway's entire course to Boston; it would be a bit like calling a person obsolete if he lost a toe.

Whatever their names or shapes, the streets of New York are a great banquet for the senses. The colors swirl in spectroscopic madness; the odors entice and offend; the noise reaches that overwhelming level that can only be described as a strangely silent roar. At the corner of Forty-sixth Street and Third Avenue I neared the former site of the Four Mile stone. Above one corner hung a sign: "Don't Honk: $350 Fine." The law was violated twice before I crossed the street; it seemed about as absurd as Ben Franklin's request that post riders blow their horn every five miles, regardless of whether anyone was around.

The Three Mile stone once stood somewhere near the corner of Madison and Twenty-seventh. Just one block south I reached Madison Square Park, where the old road to Boston once split east off the old road to Bloomingdale, now Broadway, going west. I can't come to this park without thinking of the street commissioners who came here in 1838 and decided to close the road splitting east. The decision had an impact on the road's legacy they might not have intended—the sort of legacy alluded to by the person I passed leaving the park that day. He was explaining to friends that Madison Square Park was the original site of Madison Square Garden. I couldn't help but wonder what this amateur guide would be telling his friends if the park had, at some point, been given another name.

I continued on Broadway past the Flatiron Building and soon encountered the hipster swagger of New York University students buzzing about Union Square. At the southern end of the square a statue of George Washington atop a horse pointed across Fourteenth Street toward a Whole Foods Market. A short way down Fourth Avenue I reached Cooper Union, former site of the Two Mile stone, complete with its requisite plaque describing Lincoln's speech in early 1860. Just south I began to bend through the Bowery on the original line of the old highway. When the final column of the Third Avenue elevated was torn down, in February 1956, exposing the region to sunlight for the first time in nearly a century, one politician suggested changing the name Bowery, "with its connotation of drunken derelicts and broken dreams." Of course the original Dutch word, *bouwerie,* passed down from the settlers of New Amsterdam, meant "farm."

A few blocks later I found that just because the post road seemed gone from New York didn't mean its spirit had completely disappeared. The first and final milestone in Manhattan once stood near the corner of Canal Street and Bowery, at the original Bull's Head tavern. Today this area is right in the heart of Chinatown. There was a steady line of traffic, here, as the Manhattan Bridge carried lines of cars into Brooklyn, but just to the left of the bridge, catty-corner to the site of the old tavern, a different kind of line had begun to form, beneath a large sign with a bright red arrow pointing down to a ticket booth. This was the Fung Wah bus. It runs throughout the day, carrying travelers from New York to Boston.

The skyscrapers lining the last strip of highway, down Broadway, gave it the feel of a dimly lit hallway. The Bowling Green lay in front of the U.S. Custom House at the foot of this hallway, like a grassy welcome mat. It was right about here, in January of 1673, that the first post rider left the fort at the base of Manhattan and headed for John Winthrop Jr.'s home in Hartford, then on to Boston. A mist crept down the skyscrapers in thin wisps, and a foghorn grunted in the harbor, somewhere out of view. I circled the Custom House to its southeast corner, and there I saw another sort of echo, staring back at me from across the street: a retail store for the United States Post Office. It was too fortunate a conclusion to press any further, so I turned around and headed home.

When he returned home to London from one of his youthful

adventures, just before embarking for Boston and the New World, John Winthrop Jr. wrote to his father of feeling like the traveler who has been through so many inns, good and bad, that he "findeth noe difference when he commeth to his Journies end." He had seen war and sickness during his trips, and had no doubt lost the illusion of his immortality, and I'm pretty sure he meant that we're all going to die, and that when we do, and meet that Last Great Difference face-to-face, all the other differences we thought so much of in our lives weren't actually as great as they seemed at the time. But now that I'm done with my tour of the old road, sure that its identity has changed but unsure whether this change has reached an end, I have to allow that Winthrop might have meant something else entirely. He might have been saying that when you're moving, you aren't really in a position to measure anything but where you need to go, and only when you get there can you begin to fairly consider where you've been.

Acknowledgments

A s you cross the road in Manhattan sometimes you must work back against the traffic, something of a lateral movement, so that by the time you reach the other side you are not quite where you thought you'd be, but you're across after all. I've felt this way many times in the process of writing this book, and I feel it again as I compose this page, for a slightly different reason—thinking now that I can no sooner cite everyone involved than I can list the instincts and experiences that shepherd me across a busy street.

To all those who shared their stories with me because they either lived along this old highway or otherwise knew where to locate its secrets, I extend a heartfelt lump of appreciation. (A few individuals who led me to a particularly elusive piece of information are hailed in the Sources and Notes section.) A second lump must go to the staffs of the many libraries and historical societies that became my movable office. Special appreciation goes to David Smith, recently retired gatekeeper of the Wertheim Study at the New York Public Library, in the form of his own sentence.

Many of the aged sources reflected in these pages are available in electronic format—notably, the Colonial Records of Connecticut, the Franklin Papers, and numerous colonial newspapers—and I feel a true debt of gratitude toward anyone in any way responsible for these accomplishments. In that same spirit, those at Google Maps must be added to this debt; if I properly described the thrill I got from cruising the old highway in "Street View" mode—especially when, in doing so, I came upon the "parting stone," first set down in Roxbury, Massachusetts, in 1744—I would never get another date. In honor of these enormous, anonymous efforts, I offer the wimpy admission that I tried to channel every ounce of energy they saved into the creation of this work.

Thanks to Stephen Isaacs, the first to see the potential in this idea, who worked my feeble explanation through his large frame then split into a smile and, odds are, reached for a can of Tab. To Sam Freedman, whose stewardship of the book-writing class at Columbia's journalism school has earned him a second home on the Acknowledgments pages of first-time authors. To my agent, Jim Hornfischer, who guided me so faithfully in the beginning, and my editor, Colin Harrison, who led me so masterfully to the end. And last to Miss Winter, whose early advice—that a book about a road not be "boring as hell"— has served me in better stead than she'll ever know.

Detail. Collection of the New-York Historical Society, negative no. 83134d.

Sources and Notes

A FTER MUCH CONSIDERATION I feel that an annotated bibliography, broken down by chapter, is of greatest use to readers who wish to pursue particular topics within the narrative. Space could accommodate only a selection of individually cited quotes and facts; all quotes come from primary documents mentioned in each chapter, unless otherwise noted. A more complete bibliography is available online, at www.kings besthighway.com.

Some quotations have been adjusted slightly for readability; in these cases, the adjustment is acknowledged in the cited notes. I have also omitted initial and final ellipses in several quotes, again for the sake of the reader, making sure to preserve the original meaning. Dates have been presented as they appeared in the cited sources, with the exception of years, which were adjusted to follow the modern Gregorian calendar. (Until 1752 England and its colonies followed the Julian calendar, which began the year on March 25. Hence a date of March 2, 1683, in the Julian calendar—often written March 2, 1683/84—is March 2, 1684, by today's standards.)

Much of my reason for attempting this book was the lack of a suitable biography of this historic road. The one true general history is Stephen Jenkins, *The Old Boston Post Road* (New York, London: G. P. Putnam's Sons, 1913), a dutiful overview that mixes historical anecdotes with a detailed, almost antiquarian analysis of the road's path. Stewart H. Holbrook, *The Old Post Road* (New York: McGraw-Hill, 1962), is briefer and a bit more approachable than Jenkins, but adds little in the way of substance. Several important popular articles on the old highway have been written over the years. These include Sarah Comstock, "On Boston Post Road" (*New York Times,* Aug. 9, 1914); Donald Barr Chidsey, "The Old Boston Post Roads" (*National Geographic,* Aug. 1962); and Seth Rolbein, "Special Delivery" (*Boston Globe Sunday Magazine,* Jan. 7, 2001). Though providing insight to their times, they generally adhere to the narrative structure established by Jenkins—prizing geography over chronology and character—and, in doing so, limit the larger picture.

I mention these sources here, for they do not appear in the notes to follow. They were read, considered, and set aside to make room for those more directly in contact with the life of the highway.

Chapter 1: The "Ordinary Way"

The exploits and personality of John Oldham were drawn primarily from William Bradford, "History of the Plymouth Plantation" in volume 3, series 4, of *Collections of the Massachusetts Historical Society* (cited as 4 CMHS 3) and the invaluable journal kept by the elder John Winthrop, *The History of New England from 1630 to 1649* (Boston: Little, Brown, 1853), edited by James Savage, cited as Winthrop's Journal. Alexander Young, *Chronicles of the First Planters of the Colony of Massachusetts Bay, 1623-1636* (New York: Da Capo Press, 1970), and Sherman W. Adams, *The History of Ancient Wethersfield, Connecticut* (New York: Grafton Press, 1904), supplemented details on this underappreciated colonist. The indispensable Bernard Bailyn, *The New England Merchants in the Seventeenth Century* (New York: Harper & Row, 1964), supplied context. Several primary sources and maps were used to create a picture of early Boston; the most helpful secondary sources were Darrett B. Rutman, *Winthrop's Boston* (Chapel Hill: University of North Carolina Press, 1965), and Walter Muir Whitehill, *Boston* (Cambridge, Mass.: Belknap Press of Harvard University Press, 1968).

The character of colonial wilderness trails is revealed largely through contemporary travel narratives referenced in the cited notes, as well as the records and laws of the northeast colonies. Prince among these is the *Public Records of the Colony of Connecticut, 1636–1776* (cited as PRCC), which has been digitized and published online at www.colonialct.uconn.edu. Included among these records are those of the New Haven colony. *Records of the Governor and Company of the Massachusetts Bay in New England* (New York: AMS Press, 1968), edited by Nathaniel B. Shurtleff, tracks early Massachusetts Bay life. Isabel S. Mitchell, *Roads and Road-making in Colonial Connecticut* (New Haven: Yale University Press, 1933), supplemented.

Levi Badger Chase and Harral Ayres have devoted a great deal of attention to the precise path of the early highway. See Chase, *The Bay Path and Along the Way* (Norwood, Mass.: Printed for the author, 1919), and Ayres, *The Great Trail of New England* (Boston: Meador Publishing, 1940). Numerous local histories of towns along the route supplemented these accounts, particularly those that composed early town maps based on land records.

The life and character of John Winthrop Jr. was reconstructed largely through his correspondence. The main repository of Winthrop material is the Winthrop Family Papers in the Massachusetts Historical Society (MHS); the collection was being digitized at the time of this writing. These documents have been published in five volumes of the *Winthrop Papers*, and can also be found in various series and volumes of CMHS. Robert C. Winthrop, *Life and Letters of John Winthrop* (Boston: Little, Brown, 1869), supplemented these works. *The Younger John Winthrop* by Robert C. Black III (New York: Columbia University Press, 1966), followed closely by *Puritans and Yankees* by Richard Dunn (Princeton, N.J.: Princeton University Press, 1962), are the best of relatively few biographies on this overlooked colonial figure.

The original travel diary kept by Winthrop in 1645 was viewed at the Beinecke Rare Book and Manuscript Library at Yale University. My primary analysis and all quotes, however, came from William R. Carlton's annotated translation, "Overland to Connecticut in 1645," *The New England Quarterly* 13 (Sept. 1940), as Winthrop kept most of his journal in Latin.

Two superlative secondary sources deserve mention. William B. Weeden's *Economic and Social History of New England, 1620–1789* (Boston: Houghton, Mifflin, 1891) is vital to anyone studying life in colonial New England. Through truly masterful research and storytelling, Sumner Powell, *Puritan Village* (Middletown, Conn.: Wesleyan University Press, 1963), explains colonial social structure and town development; it was my good fortune that he focused on places along the highway.

4   Winthrop's house: Frederick Lewis Gay, "Site of Governor Winthrop's House," in *Publications of the Colonial Society of Massachusetts* 3 (1895), pp. 87–89; Francis J. Bremer, *John Winthrop* (New York: Oxford University Press, 2003), p. 204. Winthrop's first house stood between Kilby and Congress streets. It's often mistakenly placed at modern Washington and Milk streets, also directly on the highway, but that was the location of his second house.

4   Wahginnacut's visit: Winthrop's Journal, 1:62–63.

4   *"thump on ye brich"*: 4 CMHS 3:189–91.

5   *a ferry*: A Record of the Streets, Alleys, Places, Etc., in the City of Boston (Boston: Print Dept., 1910), p. 348.

5   *small clapboard home*: Winthrop's Journal, 1:104.

5   *"bush-burning"*: Adriaen van der Donck, *A Description of New Netherland*, eds. Charles T. Gehring and William A. Starna; trans. Diederik Willem Goedhuys (Lincoln: University of Nebraska Press, 2008), pp. 21–22. Van der Donck originally published his description in 1655.

5   *"making it unpassable"*: William Wood, *New England's Prospect* (London, 1634), p. 15.

5   *"best English houses"*: Daniel Gookin, *Historical Collections of the Indians in New England* (Boston: Belknap and Hall, 1792), p. 10. Gookin wrote in 1674.

6   *"terrifying darkness"*: Sarah Knight, *The Journal of Madam Knight* (New York: P. Smith, 1935). Knight wrote in 1704.

6   *"and returned safe"*: Winthrop's Journal, 1:210.

7 *£2,000:* Ibid., 1:202–3.
7 *"reach of authority":* Winthrop Papers, 3:180.
7 *July 1636:* Francis Jennings, *The Invasion of America* (Chapel Hill: University of North Carolina Press, 1975), pp. 204–10.
8 *"ordinary way":* Winthrop's Journal, 1:281.
9 *fifth moon:* John W. Streeter, "John Winthrop, Junior, and the Fifth Satellite of Jupiter," *Isis* 39 (Aug. 1948), pp. 159–60.
9 Principia Mathematica: Ronald Sterne Wilkinson, "John Winthrop, Jr., and America's First Telescopes," *The New England Quarterly* 35 (Dec. 1962), p. 523.
9 *"loath":* Winthrop, *The Life and Letters of John Winthrop,* 1:252.
9 *size eleven: Winthrop Papers,* 5:242.
9 *"to unnecessarye dangers":* Ibid., 1:352–53.
10 *"his Journies end":* Ibid., 2:150–51. (Edited slightly for readability.)
10 *"for iron works":* Shurtleff, *Records,* 2:71.
11 *Peter Noyes:* Powell, *Puritan Village,* pp. 75–78.
11 *half a mile:* Shurtleff, *Records,* 1:157.
12 *"advantageous for travelers":* Ibid., 4(2):435. (Edited slightly for readability.)
12 *"want of entertainment":* PRCC, 1:103.
12 *"thieves in Holland":* David Peterson de Vries, *Voyages from Holland to America, A.D. 1632 to 1644,* trans. Henry C. Murphy (New York: Kraus Reprint Co., 1971), p. 126.
12 *Richard Fairbanks:* Shurtleff, *Records,* 1:220–21, 281.
12 *"and absolutely necessary":* Great Britain Public Record Office, *Calendar of State Papers, Colonial Series,* 1:275.
13 *"or any merchandise whatsoever":* PRCC, 1:90–91. (Edited slightly for readability.)

Chapter 2: Of Fidelity and Fate

The sources for this chapter include most of those mentioned for chapter 1. The following compilations supplemented the laws and records: Berthold Fernow, ed., *The Records of New Amsterdam from 1653 to 1674* (Baltimore: Genealogical Pub., 1976), and *Laws and Ordinances of New Netherland, 1638–1674* (Albany: Weed, Parsons, 1868), compiled by E. B. O'Callaghan, for the highway in Manhattan; John Russell Bartlett, ed., *Records of the Colony of Rhode Island and Providence Plantations in New England* (New York: AMS Press, 1968), for Providence.

The story of the English capture of Manhattan, and the Dutch recapture that marked the end of the Francis Lovelace era, relied predominantly on: E. B. O'Callaghan, ed., *Documentary History of the State of New-York* (Albany: Weed, Parsons, 1850–51); Peter R. Christoph, ed., *New York Historical Manuscripts, English* (Baltimore: Genealogical Pub. Co., 1980–83); and John Romeyn Brodhead, *Documents Relative to the Colonial History of the State of New-York* (Albany: Weed, Parsons, 1853–87).

In addition to letters found in CMHS, much of the character of Francis

Lovelace was derived from J. H. Pleasants, "Francis Lovelace, Governor of New York, 1668–1673," *New York Genealogical and Biographical Record* 51 (1920).

Any history of New York City would be wise to refer to the great I. N. Phelps Stokes, *The Iconography of Manhattan Island, 1498–1909* (Union, N.J., Lawbook Exchange; Mansfield Centre, Conn.: Martino Fine Books, 1998). John Romeyn Brodhead, *History of the State of New York* (New York: Harper & Brothers, 1853–71), is rich in detail and vast in scope, and J. Franklin Jameson, *Narratives of New Netherland, 1609–1664* (New York: Charles Scribner's Sons, 1909), is also helpful for colonial Manhattan. Russell Shorto, *The Island at the Center of the World* (New York: Vintage Books, 2005), gives a splendid and inspired recent history.

15 Winthrop's children: Lawrence Shaw Mayo, *The Winthrop Family in America* (Boston: Massachusetts Historical Society, 1948), p. 56. From oldest to youngest, they were Elizabeth, Fitz-John, Lucy, Wait-Still, Mary, Margaret, Martha, and Ann. It's possible Winthrop had only seven children at this time, as Ann's date of birth is presumed to be between 1649 and 1653.

15 New London house: Frances Caulkins, *History of New London, Connecticut* (New London: H. D. Utley, 1895), pp. 15–16, 39–47. Thanks to Edward Baker, executive director of the New London County Historical Society, for providing additional information, as well as an image of the house.

15 *"Trustie & swift":* Winthrop, *Life and Letters of John Winthrop,* 2:395.

15 *"along with yow":* 5 CMHS 1:370.

16 *governor of Connecticut:* PRCC, 1:297–298; Isabel M. Calder, *The New Haven Colony* (New Haven: Yale University Press; London: H. Milford, Oxford University Press, 1934), p. 159.

16 Hugh Peter executed: James Savage, *A Genealogical Dictionary of the First Settlers of New England* (Baltimore: Genealogical Pub. Co., 1965), 3:402; Dunn, *Puritans and Yankees,* p. 126.

16 *"an high esteeme":* Glenn W. LaFantasie, ed., *The Correspondence of Roger Williams* (Providence, R.I.: Brown University Press/University Press of New England, Hanover and London, 1988), 2:494. (Edited slightly for readability.)

16 *promise new pants:* Ibid., 1:302.

17 *"this weeks passage":* 5 CMHS 8:55–57.

17 *"spediest oportunity":* 4 CMHS 6:523.

17 *"escape such danger":* Shurtleff, *Records,* 4(2):59–60.

17 *£500:* PRCC, 1:369.

17 *"no small motive":* 5 CMHS 8:73.

18 Fort Amsterdam dimensions: Jameson, *Narratives of New Netherland,* pp. 421–24.

18 *glazed yellow bricks:* James W. Gerard, "The Old Streets of New York under the Dutch" (New York: F. B. Patterson, 1875), p. 17.

18 *Hans Vos:* Stokes, *Manhattan Island,* 2:227.

18 Heere-weg: Stokes (6:595) considers the "Heeren Wegh" modern Bowery Road, and says that Fernow (*The Records of New Amsterdam,* 1:16) called it Broadway by mistake. Willem Sewel, *A Large Dictionary, English and Dutch*

(Amsterdam, 1735, 1:211), a near-contemporary translation, translates *Heere-weg* into Highway.

19 *"was wholly disapointed":* 4 CMHS 7:548–50.

19 *harboring two fugitives:* Lemuel Aiken Welles, *The History of the Regicides in New England* (New York: Grafton Press, 1927), pp. 11, 39–40.

19 *"the son of such a father":* 5 CMHS 1:392. (Edited slightly for readability.)

20 *"effusion of blood":* 4 CMHS 6:527–529.

20 *the Duke's Plan:* Stokes, 1:207 (Plate 10, "A Description of the Towne of Mannados or New-Amsterdam"); Doris C. Quinn, "Theft of the Manhattans," *de Halve Maen* 66 (Summer 1993), pp. 25–30; Jameson, *Narratives of New Netherland,* pp. 419–20; John Beresford, *The Godfather of Downing Street* (Boston: Houghton Mifflin, 1925), pp. 127–28.

20 *"the letter!":* Brodhead, *History of the State of New York,* 1:739.

21 *first regular mail carrier:* Lovelace's mail was the first to provide the sort of service that can be considered systematic in schedule and regional in scope. All quotes from the post rider's oath and official duties are from Christoph, *New York Historical Manuscripts,* 2:520, 524–25. Those from Lovelace's initial letters to Winthrop concerning the post are in 5 CMHS 9:83–86.

21 *"passed daily":* De Vries, *Voyages from Holland to America,* pp. 149–50.

21 *Johannes Verveelen:* Fernow, *The Records of New Amsterdam,* 6:83–84; James Riker, *Revised History of Harlem* (New York: New Harlem Pub., 1904), pp. 678–80; Christoph, *New York Historical Manuscripts,* 2:300–02.

22 *ongoing boundary feud:* Christoph, *New York Historical Manuscripts,* 2:426–65.

22 *"a new road to New England":* Quoted in Robert Bolton Jr., *A History of the County of Westchester* (New York: Printed by Alexander S. Gould, 1848), 1:139.

23 *"handsomer resistance":* 5 CMHS 9:91–92.

23 *"before the causes arrive":* Brodhead, *Documents Relative,* 3:189–90.

24 *"King's best highway":* 5 CMHS 9:83–85.

24 *hardly stirred:* John Winthrop Jr. to Wait Winthrop, Feb. 16, 1673, and Jun. 10, 1673; JWJ to Fitz-John Winthrop, Apr. 15, 1673; in Winthrop Family Papers, microfilm edition, MHS.

24 *"my deare wife":* 5 CMHS 8:163.

25 *"handsomely contrived":* John Josselyn, *An Account of Two Voyages to New-England: Made During the Years 1638, 1663* (Boston: William Veazie, 1865), p. 125.

25 *"affectionate & consolatory letter":* 5 CMHS 8:146.

26 *"all the way by land":* 6 CMHS 3:434–35.

26 *the Connecticut capital:* In addition to PRCC, see William DeLoss Love, *The Colonial History of Hartford* (Chester, Conn.: Centinel Hill Press, 1974), and James Hammond Trumbull, *The Memorial History of Hartford County, Connecticut, 1633–1884* (Boston: E. L. Osgood, 1886).

26 *"and unmannerly carriage":* PRCC, 1:123. (Edited slightly for readability.)

27 *"something ill lately":* 5 CMHS 9:89–91.

27 *"Manning's alarms":* O'Callaghan, *Documentary History,* 3:57. (Edited slightly for readability.)

28 *awoke to the news:* Brodhead, *History of the State of New York,* 2:207, 213; *Calendar of State Papers, Colonial Series,* 7:509–10; Brodhead, *Documents Relative,* 3:198; 5 CMHS 8:150; O'Callaghan, *Documentary History,* 3:57–59.

28 *"is much better":* Brodhead, *Documents Relative,* 3:198.

Chapter 3: Benjamin Franklin, Postman

The primary source for early eighteenth-century travel on the southern route of the post road is Sarah Knight, *The Journal of Madam Knight* (New York: P. Smith, 1935). Two contemporary sources, John Clapp, *An Almanack for the Year 1697* (New York: Printed and sold by William Bradford, 1697), and Thomas Prince, *The Vade Mecum for America* (Boston: Printed by S. Kneeland and T. Green for D. Henchman & T. Hancock, 1732), provided useful context.

Two important maps during this period are Philip Lea, "A New Map of New England . . ." (London, 1690), and Herman Moll, "A new and exact map of the dominions . . ." (London, 1731), viewed at the New York Public Library (NYPL) and the New York Historical Society (NYHS), respectively.

Issues of John Campbell's "Journal of Public Occurrences" appear in series 1, vol. 9, of the *Proceedings of the Massachusetts Historical Society* (cited 1 PMHS 9). Digitized issues of his *Boston News-Letter* are available in most research libraries. Isaiah Thomas, *The History of Printing in America* (Barre, Mass.: Imprint Society, 1970), is a great overview of colonial printing by a colonial printer.

In addition to those already mentioned, several law compilations were needed to follow highway development and postal laws into the eighteenth century. These include *The Colonial Laws of New York from the Year 1661 to the Revolution* (Albany: J. B. Lyon, 1894) and *Journal of the Votes and Proceedings of the General Assembly of the Colony of New-York* (New York, 1764–66), which covers 1691 to 1743. *Report of the Record Commissioners of the City of Boston* (Boston, 1876–98) is a vast collection of early Boston records.

Post office rules and acts imposed on the colonies by Britain appear in *The Public Statutes at Large of the United States of America* (cited U.S. Statutes) and Owen Ruffhead, *The Statutes at Large . . .* (London: Printed by Charles Eyre and Andrew Strahan: and by William Woodfall and Andrew Strahan, 1786). Series 3, vol. 7, of CMHS gathers documents related to the colonial postal system. Wesley E. Rich, *The History of the United States Post Office to the Year 1829* (Cambridge, Mass.: Harvard University Press, 1924), is a thorough analysis.

The career of Benjamin Franklin as postmaster is overwhelmingly traced from *The Papers of Benjamin Franklin,* which have been published online at franklinpapers.org (cited as BF Papers). Unless otherwise indicated, all Franklin quotes come from this source. A helpful supplement was Albert Henry Smyth, ed., *The Writings of Benjamin Franklin* (New York, London: The Macmillan Company, 1905–07). Ruth Butler's *Doctor Franklin, Postmaster General* (Garden City, N.Y.: Doubleday, Doran & Company, 1928) covers this subject for general readers.

29   *"inner and nethermost Dungeon":* 3 CMHS 10:108–09.

29   *"noe power to doe it":* Brodhead, *Documents Relative,* 3:355.

29   *"without baile":* Ibid., 3:721.

30   *King Philip's War:* See William Hubbard, *The History of the Indian Wars in New England* (ed. by Samuel G. Drake; Roxbury, Mass.: Printed by W. E. Woodward, 1865), and Eric B. Schultz, Michael J. Tougias, *King Philip's War* (Woodstock, Vt.: Countryman Press; New York: Distributed by W. W. Norton, 1999).

30   *by double:* Schultz and Tougias, *King Philip's War,* pp. 4, 68–69.

31   *nine pence: The Colonial Laws of New York from the Year 1664 . . . ,* 1:293–96.

31   *"benefit to this country":* 3 CMHS 7:55.

31   *£275:* Ibid., 65–66.

31   *country's first newspaper:* Thomas, *The History of Printing in America,* p. 13.

31   *Elizabeth Spring:* Mayo, *The Winthrop Family in America,* p. 54; Federal Writers' Project, *Rhode Island: A Guide to the Smallest State* (Boston: Houghton Mifflin Company, 1937), p. 329.

35   *late September:* 1 PMHS 9:499. Campbell's letter was dated September 20.

35   *Post Office Act of 1710:* U.S. Statutes, 4:434–45.

36   *Bartholomew Green's shop: Boston News-Letter,* April 17–24, 1704; Thomas, *The History of Printing in America,* p. 85. Green's office was on present-day Washington Street.

36   *modern Washington and Water:* Annie Haven Thwing, *The Crooked & Narrow Streets of the Town of Boston 1630–1822* (Boston: Marshall Jones Company, 1920), pp. 19–20.

36   *applied to start a tavern:* Kym S. Rice, *Early American Taverns* (Chicago: Regnery Gateway, 1983), p. 81.

37   *"little else to do":* Clapp, *An Almanack for the Year 1697,* p. 5.

37   *ninety-four miles:* Prince, *Vade Mecum,* p. 198.

37   *This trend continued:* Charles E. Clark, "The Newspapers of Provincial America," *Proceedings of the American Antiquarian Society* 100 (1991), p. 379; Thomas, *The History of Printing in America,* pp. 231–34, 249.

37   *at a loss:* BF Papers, 14:345–47, 15:58–59.

38   *"now post road":* PRCC, 11:442. See volume 7 for more examples.

38   *"very narrow views":* John Adams, *The Works of John Adams* (Boston: Little, Brown, 1850–56), 9:597–98.

39   *"raised against it":* Alexander Spotswood, *The Official Letters of Alexander Spotswood* (Richmond, Va.: The Society, 1882–85), 2:280–81.

39   *"dropt the Undertaking": New England Courant,* Feb. 4–11, 1723.

40   *free of charge: Colonial Records of Pennsylvania* (New York: AMS Press, 1968), 7:447.

40   *personal inspection:* BF Papers, 4:511; 5:500.

41   *Franklin's office in New Haven:* BF Papers, 2:341–44, 5:187, 13:10–17, 300–11. Also see Alan Dyer, *A Biography of James Parker, Colonial Printer* (Troy, N.Y.: Whitston Pub. Co., 1982).

41   Franklin's postal guidelines: BF Papers, 5:161–68.

41   *"Free B. Franklin":* Butler, *Doctor Franklin,* p. 60.

42   *ten regular newspapers:* See Clarence S. Brigham, *History and Bibliography of American Newspapers, 1690–1820* (Worcester, Mass.: American Antiquarian Society, 1947).

42   *odometer:* Page Talbott, ed., *Benjamin Franklin: In Search of a Better World* (New Haven: Yale University Press, 2005), pp. 178–79.
43   *finally earned money:* Smyth, *The Writings of Benjamin Franklin,* 10:174–75.
43   *"no delays or interruptions":* 3 CMHS 7:87.
43   *"the Publick Revenue":* Ruffhead, *The Statutes at Large,* 7:473–75.
43   *"Death as a Felon":* Ibid., 7:503–8.
43   *"ought to be stampt":* 6 CMHS 9:22–23.
43   *"more than anybody":* BF Papers, 12:65.

Chapter 4: Inflammatory Papers and Tavern Politicians

Most insight into the Stamp Act came from the colonial newspapers published in towns along the post road. Edmund S. Morgan, *Prologue to Revolution* (Chapel Hill: University of North Carolina Press, 1959), contains relevant primary sources. Morgan has also written the definitive scholarly account, *The Stamp Act Crisis* (Chapel Hill: University of North Carolina Press, 1953). The role of newspapers in this era is studied in Arthur M. Schlesinger, *Prelude to Independence* (New York: Knopf, 1958). John Adams, *The Works of John Adams* (details above), was helpful throughout.

Issues of the *Connecticut Gazette* found at the Library of Congress (for 1765) reflect New Haven's enmity toward Jared Ingersoll. An extensive collection of Ingersoll correspondence exists in *Mr Ingersoll's Letters Relating to the Stamp-Act* (New Haven: Printed and sold by Samuel Green, 1766) and in volume 9 of the *Papers of the New Haven Colony Historical Society* (1918; cited, NHCHS Papers). Lawrence Henry Gipson, *Jared Ingersoll* (New York: Russell & Russell, 1969), is the only full-length work.

John Holt's *New York Gazette* of 1765, read in the New York Public Library's Rare Books Division, captures the tone of rebellion in Manhattan. Brodhead (*Documents Relative*) was supplemented by *Calendar of Council Minutes, 1668–1783* (Harrison, N.Y.: Harbor Hill Books, 1987), compiled by Berthold Fernow. Also useful was Henry B. Dawson, "The Sons of Liberty in New York" (Poughkeepsie, N.Y.: Platt & Schram, 1859).

The only full-length work dedicated to the printer William Goddard is Ward L. Miner, *William Goddard, Newspaperman* (Durham, N.C.: Duke University Press, 1962), though the more recent Ralph Frasca, *Benjamin Franklin's Printing Network* (Columbia: University of Missouri Press, 2006), includes a lengthy section on Goddard. Issues of the *Providence Gazette* provided the greatest insight. Context for Goddard's role is examined in Lawrence C. Wroth, "The First Press in Providence," *Proceedings of the American Antiquarian Society* 51 (Oct. 1942). Thomas Williams Bicknell, *The History of the State of Rhode Island and Providence Plantations* (New York: The American Historical Society, 1920), served as an important background source.

Primary documents about the attack on the HMS *Gaspee* are compiled in John Russell Bartlett, *A History of the Destruction of His Britannic Majesty's Schooner Gaspee* (Providence: A. Crawford Greene, 1861), and William R. Staples, *Documentary History of the Destruction of the Gaspee* (Providence: Rhode Island Publications Society, 1990), as well as the papers of some of the figures involved, including Samuel Adams, *Writings of Samuel Adams,* ed. Harry Alonzo Cushing (New York: Octagon Books, 1968).

The basic source for Benjamin Edes is his *Boston Gazette.* Another key primary source was *Letters to the Ministry, from Governor Bernard, General Gage, and Commodore Hood* (Boston: Printed by Edes and Gill; London: Reprinted for J. Wilkie, 1769). Many details were found in various volumes of PMHS. Francis S. Drake, *Tea Leaves* (Detroit: Singing Tree Press, 1970), is a collection of primary matter on the Tea Party. Benjamin Woods Labaree has written the best scholarly look at the event: *The Boston Tea Party* (New York: Oxford University Press, 1964).

William Goddard's crusade for a "constitutional" post was reconstructed using the Boston Committee of Correspondence Records, 1772–84, in the Manuscripts and Archives Division of NYPL (cited as Boston CoC), and the John Lamb Papers, read at NYHS. BF Papers also shed light on this plan. The Lexington alarm was documented in a letter filed as "Battle of Lexington Report, 1775" in the Manuscript Collection of the Historical Society of Pennsylvania. Hugh Finlay, *Journal Kept by Hugh Finlay* (Brooklyn: F. H. Norton, 1867), and Alex L. ter Braake, *The Posted Letter in Colonial and Revolutionary America* (State College, Pa.: American Philatelic Research Library, 1975), provided additional detail.

45   *first issue: Connecticut Gazette,* July 12, 1765. Mecom considered his July 5 issue a "sample" issue, and did not give it a serial number.

45   *New Haven had evolved:* Details from above sources and Rollin Osterweis, *Three Centuries of New Haven 1638–1938* (New Haven, Conn.: Yale University Press, 1953).

46   *about that much money:* Gipson, *Jared Ingersoll* (p. 116), puts the figure at £290,000.

46   *"brethren" and Englishmen "foreigners":* Connecticut Gazette, Aug. 9, 1765.

47   *"the Mother Country":* Ibid., Aug. 30, 1765.

48   New London Gazette: James Hammond Trumbull, "Sons of Liberty in 1755," *New Englander* 35 (1876), p. 299. Many references to Barre's speech are made in colonial newspapers in spring of 1765 (e.g., *Providence Gazette,* April 13, 1765; *Boston Evening Post* and *Boston Gazette,* Apr. 22, 1765). *The Boston Post Boy,* May 27, 1765, has a lengthy reprint of the speech, including the Sons of Liberty line. Trumbull argues the term might have taken root in New Haven as early as 1755. The phrase *Sons of Liberty* appeared in the *Providence Gazette* of Oct. 6, 1764, but Barre's speech popularized it.

48   *"Stamp-Office immediately": Connecticut Gazette,* Sept. 20, 1765.

48   *protection in the state capital: New York Gazette,* Sept. 26, 1765.

49   *a week later:* Ingersoll's account appeared in the Sept. 27, 1765, issue of the *Connecticut Gazette.* Details came from this and NHCHS Papers, 9:341–49.

50   *"in imminent danger": New York Gazette,* Nov. 7, 1765.

50   *"executing their Office":* Brodhead, *Documents Relative,* 7:760.

51   *a special paper called the* Constitutional Courant: Albert Matthews, "The Snake Devices, 1754–1776, and the Constitutional Courant, 1765," *Publications of the Colonial Society of Massachusetts,* 11 (Dec. 1907), pp. 422–32.

51   *mimicked one printed years earlier: Pennsylvania Gazette,* May 9, 1754.

52   *modern Thames and Cedar streets:* W. Harrison Bayles, *Old Taverns of New York* (New York, 1915), pp. 141–42, 202–03.

52   *That night:* The incidents of Nov. 1, 1765 are reconstructed from *New York Gazette,* Nov. 7, 1765; Brodhead, *Documents Relative,* 7:771–72, 775, 791–92; Dawson, "The Sons of Liberty in New York," pp. 92–95; Fernow, *Calendar of Council Minutes,* p. 469.

53   *"the liberty printer":* Adams, *Works,* 2:354.

53   *"and* NO STAMPS": *New York Gazette,* Nov. 7, 1765. (Emphasis from original.)

53   *debauchery as a brothel: Providence Gazette,* Jan, 22, 1763.

53   *"town ever saw":* Bartlett, *Records,* 6:494.

53   *"almost impracticable to pass":* Ibid., 6:269.

54   *Goddard traveled the Post Road:* Clarence S. Brigham, *Journals and Journeymen* (Philadelphia: University of Pennsylvania Press, 1950), p. 105.

54   *listed each tavern:* Benjamin West, *The New England Almanack, for the Year of our Lord Christ, 1764* (Providence: William Goddard, 1763).

54   *multipart history of Rhode Island:* Wroth, "The First Press in Providence," p. 367; *Providence Gazette,* Oct. 20, 1762. The series didn't continue until January 12, 1765, but then appeared in nearly every issue until March 30th.

55   *"Dog bays the Moon":* Henry Ward, *Peter Mumford, post-rider, doth, upon oath, declare . . .* (Newport, R.I., 1764), broadside.

55   *special issue: Providence Gazette,* Aug. 24, 1765.

55   *a pamphlet, written by Hopkins:* Stephen Hopkins, *The Rights of Colonies Examined* (Providence: Printed by William Goddard, 1764), p. 23.

56   *"first blow for freedom":* Staples, *Documentary History of the Destruction of the Gaspee,* p. xxxvii; Samuel Greene Arnold, *The Spirit of Rhode Island History* (Providence: G. H. Whitney, 1853), p. 28; Bartlett, *Gaspee,* pp. 22–24.

57   *within an inch of killing:* Bartlett, *Gaspee,* pp. 22–24. Mawney at first thought the bullet struck Dudingston's femoral artery, a potentially fatal wound.

57   *Samuel Adams advised:* Adams, *Writings,* 2:389–91, 395–401, 427–28.

57   *excuses poured forth:* Bartlett, *Records,* 7:154–58.

57   *"against the King": Massachusetts Spy,* Dec. 31, 1772.

58   *a few steps from the Town House:* Thomas, *The History of Printing in America,* p. 258. Edes and Gill later moved to Queen Street, modern Court Street.

58   *"working the political engine":* Adams, *Works,* 2:219; Thomas, *The History of Printing in America,* p. 258. (Edited slightly for readability.)

58   *Paul Revere supplied:* Rollo G. Silver, "Benjamin Edes, Trumpeter of Sedition," *Papers of the Bibliographical Society of America* 47 (1953), pp. 258–59.

58   *the many pseudonyms of Samuel Adams:* William V. Wells, *Life and Public Services*

of Samuel Adams (Freeport, N.Y.: Books for Libraries Press, 1969), 1:444–45. The appearance of these names was confirmed in issues of the *Boston Gazette,* respectively: Jan. 8, 1770; Sept. 16, 1771; Apr. 24, 1769; Apr. 20, 1770; Sept. 25, 1769; Mar. 27, 1769; and Oct. 2, 1769.

58   *"never divul'g authors":* John E. Alden, "John Mein," *Publications of the Colonial Society of Massachusetts* 34 (Feb. 1942), pp. 583–84.

58   *"chicanery and cowardice":* Adams, *Works,* 3:447, 457–58.

58   *agreed to resign:* 2 PMHS 44:688–689; *Boston Gazette,* Dec. 23, 1765; NHCHS Papers, 9:328; Anne Rowe Cunningham, ed., *Letters and Diary of John Rowe* (New York: New York Times, 1969), pp. 88–89.

59   *"trumpeters of sedition":* Boston Evening Post, Sept. 19, 1774.

59   *"Measure of Administration":* Boston Gazette, Nov. 29, 1773. (Capitalizations from original.)

60   *roster of names:* 1 PMHS 12:174–75. Peter Edes later wrote that he thought this list the only complete roster of Tea Party participants.

61   *"A mob!":* 1 PMHS 13:172–73,

61   *supposed Tea Partiers:* All names from Drake, *Tea Leaves,* pp. 95–172.

61   *"interesting event":* Samuel Adams letter, Dec. 17, 1773, Boston CoC.

61   *nothing less than the country's freedom:* Thomas Young to Lamb, Mar. 18, 1774; Goddard to Lamb, Mar. 23, 1773; Revere to Lamb, Mar. 28, 1774; Goddard to Lamb, May 1774, Lamb Papers; Miner, *William Goddard,* pp. 128, 133–35.

62   *"Plan I am forming":* Goddard to Lamb, Dec. 16, 1773, Lamb Papers. Goddard writes this letter the same day the Tea Party takes place.

62   *"as they can":* Finlay, *Journal,* p. 45.

62   *just beginning to do the same:* BF Papers, 13:124–58; Ingersoll, *Letters,* pp. 25–27; New York CoC to Boston CoC, Feb. 28, 1774, Boston CoC; Thomas Young to Lamb, Mar. 18, 1774, Lamb Papers; Adams, *Writings,* 3:80–82.

63   *"banish Tyranny from our Land":* Marlborough CoC to Boston CoC, Jan. 1773, Boston CoC. (Edited slightly for readability.)

63   *broken seals:* Major Durkee to Isaac Sears, Feb. 10, 1766, Lamb Papers.

63   *"Our secrets are in the hand":* New York CoC to Boston CoC, Feb. 28, 1774, Boston CoC.

63   *"constitutional":* Goddard to Lamb, Mar. 23, 1774, Lamb Papers.

64   *Providence and Newport committees:* Boston CoC to Providence and Newport CoCs, Mar. 29, 1774, Boston CoC.

64   *"success to the Design":* Adams, *Writings,* 3:80–82.

64   *"foundation of and precedent for":* Massachusetts Spy, Mar. 17, Mar. 24, 1774.

64   *subscription cards:* Miner, *William Goddard,* p. 126.

64   *"late affairs of the Tea":* Revere to Lamb, Mar. 28, 1774, Lamb Papers.

64   *the central office:* Goddard to Lamb, Mar. 23, 1774, Lamb Papers; *New York Journal,* May 11, 1775; Boston CoC to NY CoC, Mar. 24, 1774, Boston CoC.

65   *"America had enough":* Peter Force, *American Archives,* series 4, vol. 1, p. 504.

65   *third-in-command: Letters of Delegates to Congress, 1774–1789* (Washington, D.C., 1976–2000), 1:170.

65   *"sinister plan":* Goddard to Isaiah Thomas, Apr. 15, 1811, box 6, folder 2, Isaiah Thomas Papers, 1748–1874, American Antiquarian Society.

65   *another set of constitutional messengers:* "Battle of Lexington Report, 1775," at the Historical Society of Pennsylvania. Signatures appear from representatives

of Worcester, Brookfield, Norwich, New London, Saybrook, Killingworth, Guilford, Branford, New Haven, and Fairfield. Many thanks to Bob Berthelson, a collateral descendant of one of the messengers—Israel Bissell—and to David Haugaard of the Historical Society of Pennsylvania, for helping me locate this account.

66 *"a long time":* Thomas Jones, *History of New York during the Revolutionary War,* ed. Edward Floyd De Lancey (New York: *New York Times,* 1968), 1:39.

Chapter 5: The General and the Blacksmith

The fighting on Manhattan was reconstructed primarily from dozens of letters and reports reprinted in Henry P. Johnston, *The Battle of Harlem Heights* (New York: AMS Press, 1970), and others collected in series 5, vol. 2, of Peter Force, *American Archives* (cited as 5 American Archives 2). Stokes (*Iconography* vol. 5) supplemented the picture, as did Douglas Southall Freeman, *George Washington* (New York: Scribner, 1948–57). Bruce Bliven, *Battle for Manhattan* (New York: Holt, 1956), is the most elegant secondary account of this fight. For a slightly alternative take read Victor Paltsits, "The Jeopardy of Washington, September 15, 1776," in *NYHS Quarterly* 32 (Oct. 1948).

The most helpful of many contemporary accounts were Joseph Plumb Martin, *Memoir of a Revolutionary Soldier* (Mineola, N.Y.: Dover Publications, 2006); Frederick Mackenzie, *Diary of Frederick Mackenzie* (New York: New York Times, 1968); and James Thatcher, *A Military Journal during the American Revolutionary War* (Boston: Cottons & Barnard, 1827).

The description of Evacuation Day, in 1783, came mainly from James Riker, *"Evacuation Day," 1783* (New York: Printed for the author, 1883). Also helpful were the *Public Papers of George Clinton* (Albany, N.Y.: The Universities of the State of New York, 1899–1914), and Henry P. Johnston, "Evacuation of New York by the British, 1783," in *Harper's* (Nov. 1883).

Two excellent maps provide geography of Manhattan during this period: "B. F. Steven's facsimile of the unpublished British headquarters . . ." (London, 1900) and Otto Sackersdorff, "Maps of farms commonly called the Blue book, 1815" (New York, 1868), both viewed in the NYPL map collection. Edward Hagaman Hall, *McGown's Pass and Vicinity* (New York, 1905) includes a useful map as well. Richard J. Koke documents the road during this time in "Milestones Along the Old Highways of New York City," in *NYHS Quarterly* 34 (July 1950).

Details about the first stagecoach trip were based on newspaper ads from the *American Mercury* (Hartford); *New York Packet*; *Massachusetts Spy* (Worcester); *Connecticut Journal* (New Haven). Contemporary sources have filled in the portrait of such a journey, chiefly George Washington, *Diary of George*

Washington, from 1789 to 1791, ed. Benson John Lossing (New York: C. B. Richardson & Co., 1860); Timothy Dwight, *Travels in New England and New York* (Cambridge, Mass.: Belknap Press of Harvard University Press, 1969); John Quincy Adams, *Diary of John Quincy Adams* (Cambridge, Mass.: Belknap Press of Harvard University Press, 1981); J. P. Brissot de Warville, *New Travels in the United States of America* (London: Printed for J. S. Jordan, 1792).

The only place to begin a study of Levi Pease is with the writings of Oliver W. Holmes (1902–1981). See "Levi Pease, Father of New England Stage-Coaching" in *Journal of Economic and Business History* 3 (1930–31); "Stagecoach and Mail from Colonial Days to 1820" (PhD diss., Columbia University, 1956); and *Shall Stagecoaches Carry the Mail?* (Washington, D.C., 1972). The closest contemporary account comes from Andrew H. Ward, *History of the Town of Shrewsbury, Massachusetts* (Boston: S. G. Drake, 1847), read at Columbia University's Rare Book & Manuscript Library. Ward reports having conversed with Pease for his biography. Contemporary newspapers added detail.

Pease's work with the U.S. Post Office is documented in *Journals of the Continental Congress* (cited JCC) and *Papers of the Continental Congress, 1774–1789* (cited PCC) and the *American State Papers* (cited ASP). Additional correspondence of Ebenezer Hazard has been published in volumes 2 and 3 of CMHS, series 5.

67   *Clinton had just shaken: Public Papers of George Clinton,* 8:257, 282. Clinton complained of illness as recently as November 12.

67   *sense of vindication:* Numerous accounts were used to assess the Battle of Harlem Heights as one of Washington's lowest hours. The most telling was from Nathaniel Greene to Nicholas Cooke, Sept. 17, 1776, describing Washington as having "sought death rather than life" after watching his men flee.

68   *Nathan Hale had been executed: NYHS Quarterly Bulletin* (Apr. 1918), pp. 12–13.

68   *owned by Roger Morris:* William H. Shelton, *The Jumel Mansion* (Boston & New York: Houghton Mifflin, 1916), pp. 4–6, 8–9.

69   *"a lady's man":* W. W. Abbot, ed., *The Papers of George Washington* (Charlottesville: University Press of Virginia, 1984), 4:302. (Edited slightly for readability.)

69   *"Main Road":* Johnston, *Battle,* p. 161.

70   *the only avenue to span the entire island:* Johnston (p. 46) puts the end of Bloomingdale Road near One Hundred Fifteenth and Riverside Drive. The British Headquarters Map suggests it ends a bit farther north, as does Sackersdorff, Plate 21. Also see Stokes, 6:589.

70   *wind whipped toward them from the southwest:* Ambrose Serle, *The American Journal of Ambrose Serle* (New York: New York Times, 1969), p. 105.

71   *Hessians hymned:* Barnet Schecter, *The Battle for New York* (New York: Walker & Co., 2002), p. 182.

71   *"from New York to Kingsbridge":* Mackenzie, *Diary,* 1:48.

72   *making no move to withdraw:* Johnston, *Battle,* p. 163; 5 American Archives,

2:369–70; Bliven, *Battle for Manhattan,* p. 51; Freeman, *George Washington,* 4:194.

72   *"rather to be wished for than expected":* 5 American Archives, 2:351.

73   *Casualties and prisoners:* Ibid., 2:369, 379. In a letter two days after the battle, Washington counts three or four prisoners, one or two dead. On September 21 Howe reports 300 killed and wounded, and an equal number of prisoners.

73   *long-term morale:* Johnston, *Battle,* pp. 129–32, 134–36, 139–42, 231–34.

74   *John Loudon McAdam:* Robert Spiro, "John Loudon McAdam in Revolutionary New York," *NYHS Quarterly* 40 (1956), pp. 46, 51–52; *Rivington's Royal Gazette* (N.Y.), Apr. 4, 1778.

74   *At Cape's tavern:* Bayles, *Old Taverns of New York,* pp. 202–03, 311; Stokes, 6:611.

74   *"gratitude and joy":* Riker, *Evacuation Day,* p. 14.

74   *When Washington was told:* Freeman, *George Washington,* 5:463. Riker (p. 18) reports that Washington was present as Van Arsdale tried to climb the pole.

75   *first successful New York–to–Boston:* Pease's enterprise was the first to succeed for any substantial length of time. The Nov. 25 trip was one of the company's first complete runs.

75   *Presuming they kept schedule:* See Pease's advertisements in *American Mercury,* Oct. 25, 1784; *New York Packet,* Sept. 30, 1784; *Massachusetts Spy,* Nov. 4, 1784.

76   *"is really the Paradise":* Warville, *New Travels,* p. 132.

76   *read the newspapers:* The latest issues would have been *Connecticut Journal* (New Haven), Nov. 24, 1784; *American Mercury* (Hartford), Nov. 22, 1784; and *Massachusetts Spy,* Nov. 24, 1784.

77   *"Zealous Americans":* L. H. Butterfield, ed., *John Adams Diary and Autobiography* (Cambridge, Mass.: Belknap Press of Harvard University Press, 1961), 2:160.

78   *"New England Roads":* *Massachusetts Spy,* Jan. 17, 1810. (Emphasis removed from original.)

78   *The Pease family:* Details come from vol. 1 of Francis Olcott Allen, *The History of Enfield, Connecticut* (Lancaster, Pa.: The Wickersham Printing Co., 1900).

78   *New England hosted:* See James Truslow Adams, *New England in the Republic* (Gloucester, Mass.: P. Smith, 1960), for the region from 1775 to 1850 and Jacqueline Carr, *After the Siege* (Boston: Northeastern University Press, 2005), for the Bay to 1800.

78   *Washington traveled the southern branch:* John C. Fitzpatrick, ed., *The Writings of George Washington* (Washington, D.C.: U.S. Govt. Print. Off., 1931–44), 4:473–79.

78   *Pease was made an adjutant:* *Massachusetts Soldiers and Sailors of the Revolutionary War* (Boston, 1896–1908), 12:38.

79   *General John Thomas:* See Charles Coffin, *The Lives and Services of Major General John Thomas* (New York: Egbert, Hovey & King, 1845), and 2 PMHS 18.

79   *Jeremiah Wadsworth:* See John D.R. Platt, "Jeremiah Wadsworth, Federalist Entrepreneur" (PhD diss., Columbia University, 1955), and Robert Abraham East, *Business Enterprise in the American Revolutionary Era* (New York: AMS Press, 1969).

79   *"better clad and more healthy":* Jared Sparks, ed., *Writings of George Washington* (Boston: Little, Brown, 1855), 6:192.

80   *"upper Post road":* *Connecticut Courant,* Feb. 25, 1772.

80   *July* and *twice a month: New York Journal,* July 23, 1772; *Connecticut Courant,* Apr. 28, 1772.

80   *highly variable:* H. E. Scudder, ed., *Recollections of Samuel Breck* (London: S. Low, Marston, Searle, & Rivington, 1877), p. 90.

80   *"occasion of pleasure":* Edmund Quincy, *Life of Josiah Quincy* (Boston: Fields, Osgood & Co., 1869), pp. 55–56.

81   *the man running it, John Ballard: Proceedings of the Bostonian Society at the Annual Meeting, January 9, 1894* (Boston: Old State House, 1894), p. 33.

81   *"common walk": Independent Chronicle* (Boston), June 27, 1793.

82   *"your day or mine":* Ward, *Shrewsbury,* p. 408.

82   *same page: Connecticut Journal,* Oct. 15, 1783. The ad appeared in the third column of page 3; the legislative notice ran in the first column.

83   *"as soon as possible": Boston Gazette,* May 3, 1784.

83   *"ten minutes' notice": Loudon's New York Packet,* May 26, 1785. (Punctuation edited for grammatical correctness.)

84   *"exorbitant" contract proposal:* JCC, 29:526. The office paid riders £275 to go from New York to Boston by Hartford once a week. The new system would go twice a week, for £550. Talmage Hall requested £750.

85   *Portland, Maine, to Philadelphia combined:* PCC, 61:421. For the year 1786 Pease was paid $2,490.72 for the Boston–to–New York section; the others combined to cost the post office $1,841.47.

85   *about $2,500 a year:* ASP, Post Office Dept., pp. 9, 14.

86   *now asked roughly $4,000:* PCC, 61:421. According to Hazard it had cost the post office $813 to send the mail between New York and Boston by lone rider.

86   *demanding an extra $226:* JCC, 31:922.

86   *his Boston tavern up for sale: Massachusetts Centinel,* Apr. 4, 1787.

87   *Enraged printers:* Holmes, *Shall Stagecoaches Carry the Mail?,* pp. 18–20; *Massachusetts Centinel,* May 7, 1788.

87   *"new arrangement in the post-office":* Sparks, *Washington,* 9:393–95.

87   *a right eye that smarted:* 5 CMHS, 3:48–49.

87   *Calling himself "the first":* JCC, 34:207–08; PCC, 41:250, 254–55.

87   *comparing himself to Adam:* 5 CMHS, 3:194.

Chapter 6: Setting the Business in Motion

Several excellent works have been authored on transportation in the early nineteenth century. Philip Elbert Taylor, "The Turnpike Era in New England" (PhD diss., Yale University, 1934), and Frederic J. Wood, *The Turnpikes of New England* (Boston: Marshall Jones Company, 1919), focus on the Northeast. Edward Chase Kirkland, *Men, Cities and Transportation* (Cambridge, Mass.: Harvard University Press, 1948), is essential for a study of New England. George Rogers Taylor, *The Transportation Revolution, 1815–1860* (New York: Rinehart, 1951), and Adna Ferrin Weber, *The Growth of Cities in the Nineteenth Century* (Ithaca, N.Y.: Cornell University Press, 1963), are more general.

Sources listed in the previous chapter, particularly contemporary newspapers and diaries, remain relevant. To these must be added Isaiah Thomas, *The Diary of Isaiah Thomas, 1805–1828* (Worcester, Mass.: The Society, 1909), which focuses on the turnpike into Boston, and The Westchester Turnpike Road Company Records, viewed at NYHS, for the Manhattan end. The story of Aaron Burr developed from a reading of Stephen Wray, "The Boston Road and Aaron Burr," in *Valentine's Manual of Old New York* (New York: Valentine's Manual Inc., 1920); additional sources appear in the cited notes. Also helpful was "Letters Sent by the Postmaster General" in the Records of the Post Office Department at the National Archives in Washington, D.C. (cited as PMG Letters).

Important post road maps published during this period include Abraham Bradley, "Map of the United States" (Philadelphia, 1796), and "Map of the United States Exhibiting the Post-roads . . ." (1804). Christopher Colles, "A Survey of the Roads of the United States of America" (New York, 1789) follows the highway from Manhattan to New Haven. Richard J. Koke, "Map Showing Milestones along the Post Road in 1769 and Along the Middle and Harlem Bridge Roads in 1801" (1950), focuses on Manhattan. Bradley (1804) and Koke were viewed at NYHS. Bradley (1796) and Colles were seen at NYPL.

Anyone venturing into the cotton era would be wise to begin with Caroline F. Ware, *The Early New England Cotton Manufacture* (New York: Russell & Russell, 1966). William Bagnall, *The Textile Industries of the United States* (New York: A. M. Kelley, 1971), supplemented. Slater's character is gleaned from George S. White, *Memoir of Samuel Slater* (Philadelphia, 1836); his technical prowess, from Bagnall, *Samuel Slater and the Early Development of the Cotton Manufacture in the United States* (Middletown, Conn.: J. S. Stewart, 1890), read at Columbia University's Rare Book & Manuscript Library. Quotes related to Slater come from White or Bagnall unless noted.

Robert F. Dalzell Jr., *Enterprising Elite* (Cambridge, Mass.: Harvard University Press, 1987), offers an outstanding study of the Boston Manufacturing Company. The main archival source on Francis Cabot Lowell are his papers, at MHS. Additional primary information came from Kenneth Wiggins Porter, *The Jacksons and the Lees* (Cambridge, Mass.: Harvard University Press, 1937), and Nathan Appleton, *Introduction of the Power Loom* (Lowell, Mass.: P. H. Penhallow, 1858). Kenneth Frank Mailloux, "The Boston Manufacturing Company of Waltham, Massachusetts" (PhD diss., Boston University, 1957), is valuable as well.

89   *He "is the only person"*: PMG Letters, vol. A, pp. 19–21.
90   *"Post-Office and Post-Roads"*: Fitzpatrick, *The Writings of George Washington,* 30: 493.
90   *"complete consolidation": American Traveller,* June 30, 1826.
90   *"set the Business in motion"*: PMG Letters, vol. DD, p. 192.

90   *every detail of the line: Philadelphia Gazette,* May 6, 1799; PMG Letters, vol. DD, pp. 302, 391.

90   *faster, safer, and more efficient:* PMG Letters, vol. EE, p. 514.

90   *lifestyle:* Jack Larkin, *The Reshaping of Everyday Life, 1790–1840* (New York: Harper & Row, 1988). See also Curtis P. Nettels, *The Emergence of a National Economy, 1775–1815* (New York: Holt, Rinehart and Winston, 1962); and Henry Adams, *The United States in 1800* (Ithaca, N.Y.: Great Seal Books, 1955).

91   *"Boston and New York packet[s]": Boston Gazette,* Oct. 25, 1813. The item comes under the heading "Horse Marine News."

91   *New towns sought inclusion:* PMG Letters, vol. A, pp. 331, 527; vol. DD, p. 193; U.S. Statutes, 1:354–55, 2:579–89; Bradley map (1804).

91   *now took only thirty-six hours:* Oliver W. Holmes and Peter T. Rohrbach, *Stagecoach East* (Washington, D.C.: Smithsonian Institution Press, 1983), p. 131.

92   *"road-destroying":* Patrick Shirreff, *A Tour Through North America* (Edinburgh: Oliver & Boyd, 1835), p. 37.

93   *Major Graves's tavern:* J. H. Temple, *History of the Town of Palmer, Massachusetts* (Springfield: 1889), pp. 15, 146–47.

93   *"on the great road": Massachusetts Spy,* Oct. 21, 1795.

94   *nearly enough miles of road:* Kirkland, *Men, Cities and Transportation,* 1:38. Turnpike mileage reached 2,500 by 1806.

94   *thirteen times:* Roger Parks, *Roads and Travel in New England, 1790–1840* (Sturbridge, Mass.: Old Sturbridge Village, 1967), p. 19.

94   *one humble opinion:* My own.

95   *a toll bridge across the Harlem River: Laws of the State of New-York* (New York: Francis Childs and John Swaine, 1790), p. 30; *The Colonial Laws of New York from the Year 1664 to the Revolution,* 5:708–09.

95   *new attorney general, Aaron Burr:* Solid evidence of the relationship among Burr, Browne, and Bartow is clear from the Aaron Burr Papers, 1777–1836, in the Manuscript Collection at NYHS. Further documentary support came from Harry B. Yoshpe, *Disposition of Loyalist Estates in the Southern District of the State of New York* (New York: Columbia University Press, 1939), pp. 104–06; Westchester County Records of Land Conveyances; *Daily Advertiser* (New York), Mar. 19, 1789, Jan. 30, 1795; *New York Evening Post,* Apr. 1, 1817. Many thanks to Pelham historian Mark Gaffney for helping me secure these documents, and for clarifying this historic transaction.

96   *bridge to John Coles: Minutes of the Common Council of the City of New York,* 2:202, 223, 248.

96   *"old Boston Post Road": New York Courier,* June 13, 1816; *New York Columbian,* May 30, 1818.

97   *John Brown's brother Moses:* The discussion of Brown relied heavily on James Hedges, *The Browns of Providence Plantations* (Providence, R.I.: Brown University Press, 1968), and Mack Thompson, *Moses Brown* (Chapel Hill: University of North Carolina Press, 1962), as well as Paul E. Rivard, "Textile Experiments in Rhode Island, 1788–1789," *Rhode Island History* 33 (May 1974). Much context for this period came from Peter J. Coleman, *The Transformation of Rhode Island, 1790–1860* (Providence, R.I.: Brown University Press, 1963).

98   *2.5 million water-whizzing spindles:* David J. Jeremy, *Transatlantic Industrial Revolution* (Cambridge, Mass.: MIT Press, 1981), p. 19.

98   *"to break up the Business":* Alexander Hamilton, *The Papers of Alexander Hamilton*, ed. Harold C. Syrett (New York: Columbia University Press, 1961–87), 9:436–37.

99   *"than I expected":* Ibid., 9:434–35.

101 *"celebrated cotton mill":* Ibid., 10:330.

101 *"is ordinarily promoted":* Ibid., 10:311.

102 *Lowell had reached the same conclusion:* Lowell to P. T. Jackson, Nov. 20, 1811, Box 6, Folder 17, Francis Cabot Lowell Papers, MHS.

102 *made £1.5 million a year:* Mary Strickland, *A Memoir of the Life, Writings and Mechanical Inventions of Edmund Cartwright* (London: Saunders and Otley, 1843), pp. 182–83.

102 *British frigate captured their ship:* Robert Sobel, *The Entrepreneurs* (New York: Weybright and Talley, 1974), p. 21.

102 *just about everything to memory:* Most accounts of Lowell's time overseas claim he memorized everything. Jeremy (*Transatlantic Industrial Revolution*, p. 95) says that Lowell secured drawings of a frame at some point.

102 *acquire, within months:* Lowell to P. T. Jackson, Nov. 2, 1810, Box 6, Folder 9; Lowell to Jackson, Apr. 8, 1811, Box 6, Folder 12, Francis Lowell Papers, MHS.

103 *storeroom-turned-laboratory:* Frances W. Gregory, *Nathan Appleton* (Charlottesville: University Press of Virginia, 1975), p. 148.

103 *through the center of town:* Mailloux, "The Boston Manufacturing Company," p. 154. Other details of Waltham came from Edmund Sanderson, *Waltham as a Precinct of Watertown and as a Town, 1630–1884* (Waltham, Mass.: Waltham Historical Society, Inc., 1936), and "A Topographical and Historical Description of Waltham, in the County of Middlesex, Jan. 1, 1815," in 2 CMHS 3:262.

104 *held classes above an apothecary:* Thomas H. O'Connor, *The Athens of America* (Amherst, Mass.: University of Massachusetts Press, 2006), p. 67.

104 *"parting stone":* See "Old Mile-stones Leading from Boston," in PMHS 42 (1909).

104 *Mrs. Bowers found room: Massachussets Mercury,* Sept. 8, 1795; Feb. 22, 1799.

105 *stock dividend of seventeen percent:* Joseph Martin, *Martin's Boston Stock Market* (Boston, 1886), p. 90. Beginning in 1820 the company began to issue its dividends semiannually. In 1822, with three mills in operation, it issued a first dividend of 15 percent, and a second of 12.5 percent.

105 *"most prosperous in the United States": Niles Register,* June 23, 1821.

105 *enough cotton cloth each year: Boston Commercial Gazette,* Sept. 26, 1822. The company made 1,820,000 yards of cotton for the year. Assuming a 500-mile round-trip between New York and Boston, this leaves 34 miles left over; Shrewsbury is 38 miles from Boston on the old highway.

Chapter 7: The Great Boston–New York Rivalry

No book-length biography exists of Nathan Hale. My understanding of his personality came primarily from his articles in the *Boston Daily Advertiser* from 1825 to 1835, found in the Newspaper Room of the Library of Congress, and the Hale Family Papers in the library's Manuscript Reading Room. Samuel K. Lothrop, "Memoir of Hon. Nathan Hale, LL.D.," in vol. 18 of PMHS (Dec. 1880), was helpful, as were works by or about his son, Edward Everett Hale, particularly *A New England Boyhood* (Boston, 1927).

Boston's railroad-canal debate was tracked in official reports: Loammi Baldwin II, *Report of the Commissioners of the State of Massachusetts: on the Routes of Canals from Boston Harbour to Connecticut and Hudson Rivers* (Boston, 1826); *Remarks on the Practicability and Expediency of Establishing a Railroad on One or More Routes from Boston to the Connecticut River* (Boston, 1827) and *Remarks on the Practicability and Expediency of Rail Roads from Boston to the Hudson River, and from Boston to Providence* (Boston, 1829), compilations of Hale's articles; and *Report of the Board of Directors of Internal Improvements of the State of Massachusetts on the Practicability and Expediency of a Rail-road from Boston to the Hudson River, and from Boston to Providence* (Boston, 1829), printed by Hale.

George Bliss, *Historical Memoir of the Western Railroad* (Springfield, Mass.: S. Bowles and Company, 1863), gives an insider's view on this era. Alvin F. Harlow, *Steelways of New England* (New York: Creative Age Press, 1946), offers a reliable popular account. Vol. 4 of Winsor's *The Memorial History of Boston* supplemented the period. George Pierce Baker's *The Formation of the New England Railroad Systems* (Cambridge, Mass.: Harvard University Press, 1937) is an excellent overview.

Scholars debate whether jealousy toward New York or industrial needs determined Boston's decision. See Stephen Salsbury, *The State, the Investor, and the Railroad* (Cambridge, Mass.: Harvard University Press, 1967), for the latter position; Kirkland, the former. Julius Rubin, "Canal or Railroad?" in *Transactions of the American Philosophical Society,* 51 (1961), examined the responses of three major cities (Boston, Philadelphia, Baltimore) to the Erie Canal.

111   *New York papers with contempt: Boston Daily Advertiser,* Oct. 28, 1825. This emotion is gleaned from the nasty editorial regarding the Erie Canal that appears in this issue signed "Daily Adv."; Nathan Hale wrote all such articles.

112   *more stagecoach lines traveled through:* Peter R. Knights, *The Plain People of Boston, 1830–1860* (New York: Oxford University Press, 1971), p. 11.

112   *"convenient and unalterable": Resolves of the General Court of Massachusetts: Passed at the Session Began and Held at Boston, on the Twenty-fifth Day of January* (Boston, 1809), p. 230.

112   *"metropolis of her own State":* Nathan Hale, "Poussin on American Railroads," *North American Review* 44 (1837), p. 428.

114   *"Who ever heard of such a thing?":* Charles Beebe Stuart, *Lives and Works of Civil and Military Engineers of America* (New York: D. Van Nostrand, 1871), p. 122.

114   *"provincial towns":* Hale, "Poussin," p. 438.

114 *quickly became "the most important":* Communication from the Secretary of the Treasury . . . (32d Cong., 1st sess. Senate; Washington, D.C., 1853), p. 297.

115 *"wholly without Reason":* Nathan Hale to Enoch Hale, June 3, 1776, Box 28, Hale Family Papers.

116 *thesis:* Williams College thesis, Box 1, Hale Family Papers.

116 *"importance and responsibility":* Boston Daily Advertiser, Apr. 6, 1814.

116 *In his middle years:* Hale's physical description is taken from two portraits printed in Hale, *Tarry at Home Travels* (p. 22), and Winsor (4:124).

116 *"capacity of usefulness":* Lothrop, PMHS 18:278.

117 *twelve miles to Stockton's port:* L. T. C. Rolt, *The Railway Revolution* (New York: St. Martin's Press, 1962), p. 65.

117 *averaging nearly ten miles per hour:* Rolt (p. 86) puts the speed at 8.5 mph; the Boston Daily Advertiser (Nov. 11, 1825) puts it as high as 12 mph.

118 *"require its execution":* Bliss, *Historical Memoir,* p. 5.

118 *"no hesitation":* Canal Report (1826), p. 133. When the Hoosac tunnel was built, fifty years later, the project cost over ten times Baldwin's estimate.

118 *"Highways, of intercommunication":* Canal Report (1826), p. 160. (Emphasis from original.)

120 *"great benefit from your labors":* Levi Lincoln to Nathan Hale, Feb. 16, 1827, Box 1, Hale Family Papers. The word *corrected,* nearly illegible in the original, is presumed from the context of the letter.

121 *"from Boston to the Moon":* Joseph Tinker Buckingham, *Personal Memoirs and Recollections of Editorial Life* (Boston, 1852), 2:15.

121 *"the horse rides himself":* letter to Hale, May ?, 1829, Box 1, Hale Papers.

123 *"If the rail-road don't go to my house":* Boston Daily Advertiser, Jan. 26, 1830. (Emphasis removed from original.)

123 *gilded pinecone perched atop:* Ellen Mudge Burrill, *The State House, Boston, Massachusetts* (Boston: Wright and Potter, 1921), p. 21.

124 *the* Rocket, *the* Comet, *and the* Meteor: Harlow, *Steelways,* pp. 97, 100; Hale, *Boyhood,* p. 153.

124 *"like a dream":* Christopher Columbus Baldwin, *Diary of Christopher Columbus Baldwin* (Worcester, Mass.: The Society, 1901), p. 355.

125 *important railroad figures had convened:* Boston Daily Advertiser, July 9, 1835.

125 *"effectuating the most safe, cheap, and expeditious":* Third Annual Report of the Directors of the Boston & Providence (Boston, 1834), pp. 7, 17.

125 *to New York's twelve:* American Railroad Journal 7 (July 1843), pp. 205–06.

125 *"our enterprising neighbors":* New York Journal of Commerce, Apr. 29, 1940.

125 *"such men as these":* New York Journal of Commerce, Apr. 25, 1940.

Chapter 8: Toward Union

My discussion of Manhattan streets is based on many early New York City maps. A thorough catalog appears in vol. 1 of Stokes; some of the most important were Plate 26 (A Plan of the City of New York, c. 1730), Plate 27 (The Bradford Map, c. 1730), Plate 32-a (A Plan of the City and Environs of New York, c. 1742),

Plate 34 (A Plan of the City of New York from an actual Survey, c. 1754), Plate 40 (The Montresor Plan, c. 1766), Plate 41 (The Ratzer Map), Plate 42 (The Ratzen Plan), and Plate 64 (The Taylor-Roberts Plan, c. 1797). Several listed here were viewed in full at the NYHS and NYPL map collections.

Maps directly related to the commissioners who laid out Manhattan were viewed at NYHS: William Bridges, "This Map of the City of New York and Island of Manhattan as Laid out by the Commissioners" (New York, 1811), with accompanying text in William Bridges, *Map of the City of New York and Island of Manhattan: With Explanatory Remarks and References* (New York: Printed for the author by T. & J. Swords, 1811); and John Randel Jr., "The City of New York as Laid out by the Commissioners with the Surrounding Country" (New York, 1821). The NYHS manuscript department also holds John Randel's Field Books, 1812–22. Randel wrote about his work years later: "City of New York, North of Canal Street, in 1808 to 1821," in *Manual of the Corporation of the City of New York* (New York, 1864). A history of Broadway in the *Manual* of 1865 helped as well (cited as *Valentine's Manual,* 1865).

My reconstruction of the Norwalk crash was drawn primarily through reports in the *New York Daily Tribune*. Context and detail of the road came through William Guild, *A Chart and Description of the Rail-road from Boston to New York* (Boston: Bradbury & Guild, 1850); *A Compilation of the Ferry Leases and Railroad Grants Made by the Corporation of the City of New York* (New York: The Council, 1860); and the original survey of the New Haven, prepared by Alexander Twining, *Engineer's Report on the Survey and Primary Location of the New York and New Haven Railroad* (New Haven: Hitchcock and Stafford, 1845).

The stock fraud of Robert Schuyler is explored in the legal document *The New York and New Haven Railroad Company, against Robert Schuyler and Others* (New York, 1860); the magazine articles, Robert B. Shaw, "The Great Schuyler Stock Fraud" in *Railroad History,* 141 (1979), and Clarence Deming, "The Upbuilding of a Railroad System" in *The Railroad Gazette* (April 29, 1904); and contemporary newspapers, in particular the *New York Times*. Some quotations came from the undated Sidney Withington, *The Strange Case of Robert Schuyler*.

An immense debt of gratitude is owed to Harold Holzer's superlative *Lincoln at Cooper Union* (New York: Simon & Schuster, 2004), which inspired my section on Lincoln in New England. The journey itself is reconstructed through contemporary newspapers, specifically *Providence Daily Journal, Providence Daily Post, Hartford Courant,* and *New York Daily Tribune*. *Lincoln* (New York: Simon & Schuster, 1995), by David Herbert Donald, provided background. Details about the New Haven cars of 1860 came from John H. White Jr., *The American Railroad Passenger Car* (Baltimore: Johns Hopkins University Press, 1978).

A special collection of the Railway Mail Service, as well as other resources made accessible by the library of the National Postal Museum, gave a good overview of the era. Population figures come from the U.S. Census.

126   *they filed their official Street Committee report:* The legislative decisions regarding the closing of the original Boston Post Road in Manhattan are found in *Journal & Documents of the Board of Assistants, of the City of New York*; *Proceedings of the Board of Aldermen*; and *Minutes of the Common Council of the City of New York*.

127   *Stokes marks that year:* Stokes, *Manhattan Island*, 6:589. The first consideration of extending Bloomingdale Road to meet the Post Road at Harlem Heights came in 1792, but it was not officially completed until at least July 1795.

127   *"in reality an accident":* John Flavel Mines, *A Tour Around New York, and My Summer Acre* (New York: Harper & Brothers, 1892), pp. 155–56.

130   *219 Broadway:* New York City Directory (1807), p. 408.

130   *"destined to be trodden by more people":* Mines, *A Tour Around New York*, p. 155. Mines attributes this saying to Horatio Seymour, who served twice as governor of New York.

132   *"on the Third Avenue": Minutes of Common Council*, 18:653.

132   *"the finest drive":* "At the Old Bull's Head," *Scribner's Monthly* (Jan. 1879), p. 424.

132   *"no longer necessary": Board of Assistants*, vol. 13, Doc. No. 3.

133   *"name of Broadway": Board of Assistants*, 13:174. Despite this petition the name Broadway doesn't completely overtake the Bloomingdale Road until 1867

133   *burned to the ground:* Philip Hone, *The Diary of Philip Hone* (New York: Dodd, Mead, 1927), 1:398.

133   *"mode finally adopted was the* railway": Henry V. Poor, *Manual of the Railroads of the United States for 1868–69* (New York, 1868–1924), p. 10. (Emphasis from original.)

134   *"old Post Road":* Boston & Providence Railroad Corp., *Report of the Board of Directors . . .* (Boston: 1832), p. 14.

134   *Boston postmaster O. B. Brown: History of the Railway Mail Service* (Washington, D.C., 1885), p. 21.

134   *"goods all received in good order":* David M. Henkin, *The Postal Age* (Chicago: University of Chicago Press, 2006), pp. 47–48.

134   *three-cent coins: U.S. Statutes at Large*, 9:587–88, 591.

135   *seven of the top nine populations:* Knights, *The Plain People of Boston*, p. 22; Percy Bidwell, "Population Growth in Southern New England 1810–1860," *American Statistical Association Publications* 15 (Dec. 1917), p. 815. In descending order of population these were Boston, Providence, New Haven, Hartford, Cambridge, Worcester, and Roxbury.

136   *"the suburbs of New-York": Morning Courier and New-York Enquirer*, Nov. 15, 1832.

136   *Boston's 85 percent:* George Rogers Taylor, "The Beginning of Mass Transportation in Urban America: Part 1," *Smithsonian Journal of History* 1 (summer 1966), p. 36. Also see Part 2 in fall 1966.

136   *village was building around Thirtieth Street:* Edward K. Spann, *The New Metropolis* (New York: Columbia University Press, 1981), p. 296.

136   *"improvement in travelling": Recollections of Samuel Breck*, p. 275.

137   *sixth annual meeting: New York Daily Tribune,* May 7, 1853; *New-York Medical Gazette and Journal of Health,* May 1853.

139   *"Probably no road in this country": Scientific American,* July 5, 1851, quoting the *New York Daily Sun* of June 25, 1851.

141   *"negligent or reckless": New York Journal of Commerce,* Aug. 1, 1854.

142   *"bankrupt in character and confidence": Scientific American,* Oct. 7, 1854.

142   *"grief and mortification": New York Times,* Dec. 20, 1855.

142   *took his own life: New York Times,* Sept. 11, 1858.

143   *eight o'clock express train to Boston:* Frank Williams, "A Candidate Speaks in Rhode Island," *Rhode Island History* 51 (Nov. 1993), p. 111.

143   *"beaten about":* John Forster, *The Life of Charles Dickens* (Boston: Estes and Lauriat, 1872–73), 3:363.

143   *quarter past four: Providence Daily Journal,* Feb. 29, 1860; *Providence Daily Post,* Mar. 1, 1860. The railroad schedules indicate that the 8 a.m. train from New York reached Providence at 4:15.

143   *"chances were about equal to the best":* James A. Briggs, "A Reminiscence of Abraham Lincoln," *New York Evening Post,* Aug. 16, 1867.

144   *Cooper had buried beneath his institute:* Edward C. Mack, *Peter Cooper, Citizen of New York* (New York: Duell, Sloan and Pearce, 1949), p. 243.

144   *osmotic approach to speechwriting:* Ward Hill Lamon, *The Life of Abraham Lincoln* (Boston: J. R. Osgood and Company, 1872), p. 417.

145   *Lincoln chiseled away at Douglas's statement: New York Daily Tribune,* Feb. 28, 1860. The reprint of the speech in this issue was prepared under Lincoln's guidance, according to Holzer.

146   *typical Boston Road train of 1860:* Details for this section come from John H. White Jr., *The American Railroad Passenger Car.* Thanks go to New Haven railroad expert Jack Swanberg for his input.

147   *"Mr. Lincoln's doctrine": Providence Daily Post,* Feb. 28, 1860. (Capitalization from original.)

148   *"the finest constitutional argument":* James B. Angell, *The Reminiscences of James Burrill Angell* (New York: Longmans, Green, and Co., 1912), p. 117.

148   *a seat beside Cassius Clay: Hartford Courant,* Mar. 6, 1860. Lincoln mentions having met Clay "in the cars at New Haven one day last week." As he went up to Boston after speaking in Providence, this could only have been during his trip east from New York after Cooper Union.

148   *immediately preceded Lincoln:* David L. Smiley, *Lion of Whitehall* (Madison: University of Wisconsin Press, 1962), p. 164.

149   *Not ten days earlier:* J. Doyle DeWitt, *Lincoln in Hartford* (undated), p. 13.

149   *invited to parade beside Lincoln:* Julius G. Rathburn, "The Wide Awakes," *The Connecticut Magazine* 1 (1895), p. 334. Despite the invitation, there's no indication that the group accompanied Lincoln to Washington.

150   *"hearts of thousands": Hartford Courant,* Mar. 9, 1860. (Emphasis from original.)

150   *"as in his own State": Providence Daily Journal,* Mar. 8, 1860.

150   *"post-office in this city?":* Briggs, *New York Evening Post,* Aug. 16, 1867.

150   *zero public talks until he was elected:* Holzer, *Lincoln at Cooper Union,* p. 236.

Chapter 9: Barnum, Morgan, and New England's "Invisible Government"

The basic source for the Massachusetts Sixth is John W. Hanson, *Historical Sketch of the Old Sixth Regiment of Massachusetts Volunteers* (Boston: Lee and Shepard, 1866). The Baltimore riot was reconstructed in the *Baltimore Sun;* a book by George William Brown, then mayor, *Baltimore and the Nineteenth of April 1861* (Baltimore: N. Murray, 1887); and *The Massachusetts Register* (Boston: George Adams, 1852–1872) for 1862. John Niven, *Connecticut for the Union* (New Haven, Conn.: Yale University Press, 1965), gives superior context to the state during the era.

The *Hartford Courant* of 1865 published complete daily reports of the Connecticut legislative sessions. Of P. T. Barnum's many autobiographies, I focused on *Struggles and Triumphs* (Buffalo, N.Y.: Courier Co., 1889), the 1889 edition being the most comprehensive. The Leonidas Westervelt Circus Collection at NYHS, often referred to as the "Barnum scrapbook," contains a great deal of relevant and unique material. A. H. Saxon, *P. T. Barnum* (New York: Columbia University Press, 1989), is the best single biography.

The Interstate Commerce Commission's investigation, officially titled *Evidence taken before the Interstate Commerce Commission relative to the financial transactions of the New York, New Haven & Hartford Railroad Company . . .* (Washington, D.C., 1914; cited as ICC Report), is the primary document related to the New Haven's monopoly. George B. Baehr Jr., "The Attempt at a Transportation Empire in New England" (PhD diss., University of Notre Dame, 1969), gives an exhaustive analysis, as does Robert Levine, "History of New York, New Haven and Hartford Railroad Company 1842–1913" (M.A. thesis, Clark University, 1931). Many thanks to Laura Katz Smith, curator of the New York, New Haven & Hartford archive at the University of Connecticut, for bringing these studies to my attention. John L. Weller, *The New Haven Railroad* (New York: Hastings House, 1969), gives the best popular account. Henry Lee Staples and Alpheus Thomas Mason, *The Fall of a Railroad Empire* (Syracuse, N.Y.: Syracuse University Press, 1947), also helped.

Details on Morgan's life came primarily from his authorized biography, Herbert L. Satterlee, *The Life of J. Pierpont Morgan* (New York: Priv. Print, 1937), as well as Satterlee's *J. Pierpont Morgan* (New York: The Macmillan Co., 1939). Frederick Lewis Allen, *The Great Pierpont Morgan* (New York: Harper, 1949), is the leading popular text, and Vincent P. Carosso, *The Morgans* (Cambridge, Mass.: Harvard University Press, 1987), the leading scholarly analysis. These were supplemented with contemporary newspaper and magazine pieces, chiefly Garet Garrett, "Things that were Mellen's and things that were Caesar's," *Everybody's Magazine* 31 (July 1914).

Two contemporary trolley guides furnish the description of the route across the Northeast: *Trolley Trips through Southern New England* (Hartford, Conn.: Trolley Press, 1907) and *Trolley Trips through New England and Hudson River Valley* (Hartford: Trolley Press, 1914). The role of streetcars in suburbia is meticulously covered in Sam Bass Warner, *Streetcar Suburbs* (Cambridge, Mass.: Harvard University Press, 1978).

151   *havens for escaped slaves:* Sources included Wilbur Henry Siebert, *The Underground Railroad in Massachusetts* (Worcester, Mass.: American Antiquarian Society, 1936); Horatio T. Strother, *The Underground Railroad in Connecticut* (Middletown, Conn.: Wesleyan University Press, 1962); William Grimes, *Life of William Grimes* (Chapel Hill: University of North Carolina Press, 2001); Thomas Wentworth Higginson, "Cheerful Yesterdays," *Atlantic Monthly* 79 (Mar. 1897).

151   *"peace flag" ceremony:* Newton Brainard, "The Saybrook Peace Flag," *Connecticut Historical Society Bulletin* 27 (Jan. 1962), p. 8.

151   *Word of success at Gettysburg:* Gideon Welles, *Diary of Gideon Welles* (Boston, New York: Houghton Mifflin, 1911), 1:357.

152   *direct ancestor, Matthew Grant:* Henry Reed Stiles, *History of Ancient Windsor, Connecticut* (Albany, N.Y.: J. Munsell, 1863), 1:157, maps; W. A. Croffut and John M. Morris, *The Military and Civil History of Connecticut during the War of 1861–65* (New York: L. Bill, 1868), p. 756; Edward C. Marshall, *The Ancestry of General Grant* (New York: Sheldon, 1869), pp. 3, 12–13.

152   *display Davis's "petticoats":* A. H. Saxon, ed., *Selected Letters of P. T. Barnum* (New York: Columbia University Press, 1983), p. 132.

153   *could not reach the desperate president:* Michael Burlingame and John R. Turner Ettlinger, eds., *Inside Lincoln's White House* (Carbondale: Southern Illinois University Press, 1997), p. 11.

154   *"Do they know our condition?":* Croffut and Morris, *Connecticut,* p. 839.

154   *Charles A. Taylor:* Details of Taylor came from documents supplied by the Massachusetts State House, where Taylor's musket was on display for many years. Thanks to Susan Greendyke, art collections manager of the State House, for her help.

154   *private tracks Colt had constructed:* William Hosley, *Colt* (Amherst: University of Massachusetts Press, 1996), p. 109.

154   *three firearms every five minutes:* Michael H. Frisch, *Town into City* (Cambridge, Mass.: Harvard University Press, 1972), pp. 73–77.

154   *record profits:* Thomas Weber, *The Northern Railroads in the Civil War, 1861–1865* (New York: King's Crown Press, 1952), p. 49.

155   *"amicable arrangements":* Hartford Courant, June 21, 1865.

156   *"invisible government":* ICC Report, 1:37–38.

157   *museum drew praise from scientists:* Joel J. Orosz, *Curators and Culture* (Tuscaloosa: University of Alabama Press, 1990), pp. 184, 228–29.

161   *news of the fire "very coolly":* Hartford Courant, July 14, 1865.

161   *"The state had better have been called":* Harvey W. Root, *The Unknown Barnum* (New York, London: Harper & Brothers, 1927), p. 199.

161 *"through the legislature": Hartford Courant,* June 28, 1871.

161 *"put on another":* Clarence Deming, "The Retirement of President Clark," *Railroad Gazette* (Nov. 24, 1899), pp. 803–4.

162 *many years as a highway surveyor:* Henry M. Burt, *The First Century of the History of Springfield* (Springfield, Mass.: H. M. Burt, 1898–99), 1:193, 227, 235.

163 *have its own entrance into Boston:* Edward Hungerford, "Mellen: Transportation Overlord of New England," *Success Magazine* (Sept. 1911), p. 11.

163 *remove the name* Hartford: Garrett, *Everybody's Magazine,* p. 111. Mellen added: "We might call it New York & Hartford, the New York, Hartford & Boston, or simply the Hartford Railroad, if we liked, but we had to keep Hartford."

163 *"Morgan has more":* Clarence W. Barron, *More They Told Barron* (New York: Harper, 1931), p. 121.

164 *"I have leaned on you much":* Elting E. Morison, ed., *The Letters of Theodore Roosevelt* (Cambridge, Mass.: Harvard University Press, 1951–54), 3:605.

164 *divided New England: Commercial and Financial Chronicle,* May 20, 1893.

165 *typically rode only twenty-five miles:* Baehr, "Transportation Empire," p. 218; *Statement of the Affairs of the New York, New Haven and Hartford Railroad Company* (1925), p. 45

166 *"work and back again": New York Daily Tribune,* Feb. 2, 1866.

166 *created Rochelle Park:* Samuel Swift, "Community Life at Rochelle Park," *House & Garden* 5 (Jan.-June 1904), p. 236; Roger Panetta, ed., *Westchester: The American Suburb* (New York: Fordham University Press; Yonkers: Hudson River Museum, 2006), p. 184.

168 *conversion to alternating current.* J. W. Swanberg, *New Haven Power, 1838–1968* (Medina, Ohio: A. F. Staufer, 1988), pp. 308–10.

168 *already more heavily traveled:* White Jr., *American Railroad Passenger Car,* p. 636.

168 *"pet road": Wall Street Journal,* Apr. 1, 1913.

168 *"invested in New Haven stock": New York Times,* Dec. 11, 1913.

168 *"glaring instances of maladministration":* ICC Report, 1:2.

168 *widely debated:* See Carosso, *The Morgans,* p. 607; Staples and Mason, *The Fall of a Railroad Empire,* pp. 11–12; Barron, *More They Told Barron,* p. 170; Allen, *The Great Pierpont Morgan,* p. 236; and Satterlee, *J. Pierpont Morgan,* p. 399.

169 *"messenger boy": Boston American,* Dec. 30, 1912.

169 *"last resting place in Connecticut": Wall Street Journal,* Apr. 1, 1913.

169 *"Its great days have returned": Trolley Trips* (1914), p. 10.

Chapter 10: Colonel Pope and the Good Roads Movement

The life and work of Albert Pope emerged from his lectures and articles. Individual mention must go to Pope's chapter "The Bicycle Industry," in *One Hundred Years of American Commerce,* ed. Chauncey M. Depew (New York: D. O. Haynes & Co., 1895). Also see Willa Cather, *The Autobiography of S. S. McClure* (Lincoln: University of Nebraska Press, 1997); Edwin M. Bacon, *Men of Progress* (Boston: New England Magazine, 1896); and Charles W. Burpee, *History of Hartford County, Connecticut, 1633–1928* (Chicago: S. J.

Clarke, 1928). Pope's family history is traced in Charles Pope, *A History of the Dorchester Pope Family* (Boston, 1888). Stephen B. Goddard, *Colonel Albert Pope and His American Dream Machines* (Jefferson, N.C.: McFarland, 2000), is the only full-length biography. The Connecticut State Library houses two important Pope archives: the Correspondence of the Pope Manufacturing Company and the Hartford Cycle Company Correspondence (cited PMC Corr and HCC Corr, respectively). Contemporary newspapers, primarily the *New York Times,* added details and some quotes.

Context for the early American bicycle era comes from Robert A. Smith, *Merry Wheels and Spokes of Steel* (San Bernardino, Calif.: Borgo Press, 1995); Gary Allan Tobin, "The Bicycle Boom of the 1890s," *Journal of Popular Culture* 7 (1974); and Phillip Mason, "The League of American Wheelmen and the Good Roads Movement 1890–1905," (PhD diss., University of Michigan, 1957). Regional cycling guides, cited in the source notes, show the relevance of popularity of biking along the post road.

Pope's involvement with highway reform emerged from correspondence found at the National Archives in College Park, Md., in the Bureau of Public Roads Records; see the "Records of National League for Good Roads, Letters Sent, 1892–1897," and the "Office of Public Roads, General Correspondence 1893–1916" (cited RNL and OPR, respectively).

173   *"aid of the* Federal *Government":* ASP, Misc., 1:725. (Emphasis from original.)

173   *New England method of road maintenance:* Charles L. Dearing, *American Highway Policy* (Washington, D.C., 1941), p. 40; Nathaniel Shaler, "The Common Roads," *Scribner's Magazine* (Oct. 1889), p. 477.

174   *"regard work as* unconstitutional": *Report of the Commissioner of Agriculture for the Year 1868* (Washington, D.C., 1869), p. 348. (Emphasis from original.)

175   *"growth of the railway system":* J. W. Jenks, "Road Legislation for the American State," *Publications of the American Economic Association* 4 (May 1889), p. 154.

175   *"a lot of 'cranks' ":* Congressional Record, 24(3):1883. (Edited slightly for readability.)

175   *Ford Motor Company: Hartford Courant,* June 21, 1927; *New York Times,* Dec. 22, 1927.

176   *moved to Harvard Street:* deed, Marshall Stearns to Charles Pope, Mar. 7, 1846, Liber 162, Folio 253, Norfolk County Registry of Deeds, in Dedham, Mass. The house was on the west side of Harvard Street, near the intersection of Vernon Place. Many thanks to Albert Pope of Hartford, direct descendant of Col. Pope, for responding to an inquiry on the matter.

176   *many more lots:* Charles Pope was engaged in far too many real estate transactions to list. Many of the deeds and mortgages he dealt involved property on Harvard Street and Washington Street, parts of the old highway. These records were viewed at the Norfolk County Registry of Deeds, in Dedham, Mass.

177 *Popes lived on Washington Street:* Boston City Directory (1874). The directory states only that the Popes lived on Washington Street, "near Newton line, Brighton."

177 *Pope sold his products:* Charles E. Pratt, *The American Bicycler* (Boston: Houghton, Osgood and Company, 1879), p. 71; *Price list of separate parts of bicycles . . .* (Boston, 1881), found at Connecticut Historical Society.

178 *"rapid collective circulation":* Edward Howland, "A Bicycle Era," *Harper's* (July 1881), p. 281.

179 *"sway over the affairs of the L.A.W.":* undated note to George Pope, HCC Corr: "You and the Colonel will have to 'hump things' in order to retain your single (or double-) handed sway over the affairs of the L.A.W."

179 *publication of travel-sized bicycling guides:* Arthur Atkins, *Cyclist's Road Book of Boston and Vicinity* (Boston: For the author, 1885); Charles G. Huntington, *Cyclist's Road Book of Connecticut* (Hartford: Brown & Gross, 1890); League of American Wheelmen, *Road Book of Massachusetts* (Boston, 1894).

179 *About forty percent of this membership:* Mason, "The League of American Wheelmen" (p. 50) reports 1898 membership at 103,000; his statistics show that Conn., Mass., N.Y., and R.I. combined for about 43,000 members.

179 *"Boston and New York in six days":* Isaac B. Potter, "The Bicycle Outlook," *Century* 52 (Sept. 1896), p. 789.

179 *"changed completely":* *Scientific American* (June 20, 1896).

180 *"how admirably these things are constructed":* Mark Twain, "Taming the Bicycle," in *What Is Man? and Other Essays* (New York, London: Harper & Brothers, 1917), p. 286.

180 *"bicycle squad":* Theodore Roosevelt, *An Autobiography* (New York: Da Capo Press, 1985), p. 187.

180 *futuristic bicycle-railroad:* Boston Daily Globe, Mar. 31, 1892.

181 *"irresistible demand for them":* Joseph B. Bishop, "Social and Economic Influence of the Bicycle," *Forum* 21 (Aug. 1896), p. 689.

181 *the kind of heavy government oversight:* Albert A. Pope, "Highway Improvement" (Syracuse, N.Y., 1889), p. 10; Albert A. Pope, *The Movement for Better Roads* (Boston: Pope Manufacturing Co., 1892), in the Rare Book and Special Collections Division, Library of Congress, p. 4.

182 *"in general the line of":* Pope, *Better Roads,* p. 14.

182 *"if wheelmen secure":* *New York Times,* Sept. 11, 1892.

183 *League began a furious race for support:* New York Times, Nov. 12, 1892; Albert Pope to Roy Stone, Jan. 12, 1893, Box 31, OPR; Roy Stone to Charles Manderson, Nov. 19, 1892; form letters, Roy Stone; Roy Stone to Smith Ely, Dec. 6, 1892, Box 1, RNL.

183 *Pope called for a Department of Roads:* Albert Pope, *A Memorial to Congress on the Subject of a Road Department at Washington, D.C.* (Boston: Sam A. Green, 1893), pp. 1–3.

183 *"wheeled to the Committee on Inter-State Commerce":* New York Times, Dec. 21, 1893. Pope signed the petition on February 27, 1893, which suggests it was sent to Washington on this date. However, the complete petition was not officially exhibited until Dec. 20 of that year, likely because the congressional session ended in early March.

184   *about three total miles:* Nathaniel Shaler, "The Move for Better Highways," *Harper's* (Jan. 6, 1894).

184   *essentially forced Pope to resign:* Roy Stone to Albert Pope, Nov. 18, 1892, Box 1, RNL.

184   *"quite persistent in his efforts":* Charles Manderson to Roy Stone, Dec. 22, 1892, Box 31, OPR.

184   *"My ambition is":* Albert Pope to Roy Stone, Jan. 12, 1893, Box 31, OPR.

185   *"Col. Pope's ideas":* Roy Stone to Charles Manderson, Feb. 3, 1893, Box 1, RNL.

Chapter 11: "Rocks, Ruts, and Thank-you-marms"

Sources listed in chapter 10, particularly PMC Corr and HCC Corr, remain relevant. Anyone interested in the early New England car industry should leap directly to Hiram Percy Maxim's energetic memoir, *Horseless Carriage Days* (New York: Dover Publications, 1962). All quotes by Maxim come from here unless otherwise indicated. This work is supplemented by the Maxim Collection (cited MC) at the Connecticut State Library.

Herman F. Cuntz, "Hartford: The Birthplace of Automobile Industry," in the *Hartford Times* of Sept. 16–18, 1947, gives another Pope employee's perspective. General background came from James J. Flink, *America Adopts the Automobile, 1895–1910* (Cambridge, Mass.: MIT Press, 1970), and Allan Nevins, *Ford* (New York: Scribner, 1954). William Greenleaf, *Monopoly on Wheels* (Detroit: Wayne State University Press, 1961), examines the Selden dispute. Glen Norcliffe, "Popeism and Fordism," in *Regional Studies* 31 (1997), and Bruce Epperson, "Failed Colossus," in *Technology and Culture* 41 (Apr. 2000), offer scholarly analyses of the transition from bicycle to car manufacture.

Congressional battles over highway improvement are captured in the *Congressional Record* of the 52nd Cong., 2nd Sess., and in two sets of hearings: *Federal Aid to Good Roads, April 25, 1913* (Washington, D.C., 1913), and *Good Roads* (Washington, D.C., 1913). The debate on highway numbering came from material in the Classified Central Files, 1912–50, of the Bureau of Public Roads Records at the National Archives in College Park, Md. (cited, CCF). *Grant's Auto Route Guide* (New York: Evans-Brown, 1926), vol. 1, viewed at NYPL, helped as well.

187   *Editorial cartoons:* Box 1, Scrapbook 1893–95, vol. 1, MC.

187   *invention of the Columbia "chainless":* Russell Stone, "The Columbia Chainless," *McClure's* 10 (Nov. 1897), pp. vi–viii.

188   *"the automobile was the answer":* Maxim, *Horseless Carriage Days,* pp. 4–5.

188   *Quadricycle:* Norcliffe, "Popeism and Fordism," p. 273.

188   *Charles Duryea had paid:* J. Frank Duryea, *America's First Automobile* (Spring-

field, Mass.: D. M. Macaulay, 1942), pp. 5, 9; Donald Berkebile, "The 1893 Duryea Automobile," *Bulletin of the United States National Museum* 240 (1964), pp. 5–6.

188   *Pope invested more in technological research:* George Pope to David J. Post, Jan. 24, 1893, HCC Corr.

189   *"remarkable revolution in transportation":* Boston Herald, Sept. 30, 1895, in Box 1, Scrapbook 1893–95, vol. 1, MC.

189   *"will not explode":* New York World, Sept. 15, 1895, in Box 1, Scrapbook 1893–95, vol. 1, MC.

190   *"reliability run":* New York Times, Oct. 10–12, 15–16, 1902. *Automobile and Motor Review* (Oct. 18, 1902) gives a comprehensive account of the race.

191   *Of the 4,192 cars:* J. T. Sullivan, "New England a 1900 Leader," *Motor World* 19 (Mar. 2, 1911), p. 1.

191   *"automobile industry today":* Hartford Courant, Aug. 24, 1958.

192   *stories he collected on the scarcity of petroleum:* undated article, "Our Petroleum Supply Failing," Box 1, Scrapbook vol. 2, 1895–1901, MC.

192   *could travel only thirty to fifty miles:* Scientific American (Oct. 31, 1903); chart, Jan. 1, 1900, Box 1, Scrapbook 1893–95, vol. 1, MC; *Hartford Courant,* May 14, 1897.

192   *as high an authority as Thomas Edison:* New York World, Nov. 17, 1895. The impetus for this interview, coincidentally, was the effort of the senior Hiram Maxim to build an airplane.

192   *agents already spanned the globe:* Pope Mfg Co to Htf Cycle Co., July 16, 1894, PMC Corr.

192   *only one in the country capable:* Mark D. Hirsch, *William C. Whitney, Modern Warwick* (New York: Dodd, Mead, 1948), p. 557.

193   *first president to ride in a motorcade: Automobile and Motor Review* (Sept. 20, 1902), p. 14; *Hartford Courant,* Aug. 24, 1958; *New York Times,* Aug. 18, 2002. In 1899 William McKinley became the first president to ride in a car, though the steam-driven engine that carried him was soon obsolete.

193   *"infringements and valuable patents":* "Patent Dep't memo," May 8, 1899, Box 1, Maxim Workbook from 1896–1900, vol. 1, MC.

194   *"good roads everywhere":* Hartford Courant, June 21, 1927.

194   *"roads about Boston":* Depew, One Hundred Years, 2:552.

194   *1907 "marked a change in policy":* American Automobile Association, *Yearbook* (New York, 1907), pp. 61–64.

195   *"facilitate interstate communication":* Albert Pope, "Good Roads and the Nation's Prosperity," *Harper's* (Mar. 16, 1907).

195   *World War I:* Walker Hines, *War History of American Railroads* (New Haven, Conn.: Yale University Press, 1928), p. 9; Bruce E. Seely, *Building the American Highway System* (Philadelphia: Temple University Press, 1987), p. 50.

195   *turned to truck delivery: Engineering News-Record,* 79 (July 19, 1917), p. 98.

195   *Logan Page:* Seely, *Building the American Highway System,* p. 28.

198   *Department of War found: Engineering News-Record,* 84 (Mar. 25, 1920), p. 636.

198   *"interstate and national significance":* Report of Joint Board on Interstate Highways, p. 1, File 481, Box 1695, CCF.

198   *by no means a simple one:* Richard Weingroff, "From Names to Numbers," read at www.fhwa.dot.gov/infrastructure/numbers.cfm. The author thanks Mr.

Weingroff for directing him toward the primary documents regarding the naming and numbering of the U.S. Highways.

199 *Old Post Road was admirably represented:* Maps and documents used to verify these routes include Report of Joint Board on Interstate Highways, pp. 49–51, Box 1695; "The Federal Aid Highway System of the United States with Interstate Highways Selected and Numbered by the Joint Board on Interstate Highways on October 31, 1925," Box 1701; William F. Williams to Edwin Warley James, Aug. 27, 1925, Box 1700; maps, Report of Joint Board on Interstate Highways, Box 1693, all in File 481, CCF. Also see *Grant's Auto Route Guide,* vol. 1.

199 *lists it as the Boston Post Road: Grant's Auto Route Guide,* 1:124–25.

200 *"a serious problem":* This and other quotes in this section come from *Statement of the Affairs of the New York, New Haven and Hartford Railroad Company* (1925).

200 *"The route will be": New York Times,* Sept. 29, 1927.

Chapter 12: Highway Route 1, Relocated

A majority of the details of life along the Boston Post Road between 1925 and 1940 comes from contemporary newspapers and magazines. Quotes are from issues of the *New York Times* during these years unless otherwise indicated. Frederick Lewis Allen, *The Big Change* (New York: Harper, 1952), is an excellent popular overview of the period.

The primary material for the meeting between Franklin D. Roosevelt and Lester Barlow was found in the Office of the Governor of New York, Official Papers of Gov. Roosevelt, General Correspondence files, viewed at the Franklin D. Roosevelt Library in Hyde Park, New York (cited as Gov NY, GC). Also there, the Papers of the President, Official File, and the Governor Papers offered additional insight. Barlow's book, *What Would Lincoln Do?* (Stamford, Conn.: The Non-partisan League Pub. Co., 1931), was an important supplement, as were his journal articles, cited in the notes. Coverage of his expressway plan appeared in newspapers and magazines. Kenneth S. Davis, *F.D.R.: The New York Years, 1928–1933* (New York: Random House, 1985), gave context. Local legislation came from *Journal of the Senate of the State of New York,* as well as the Assembly's journal, for the 153d Session. Federal legislation came from the *Congressional Record* of the 71st Cong., 2nd Session. Also see Senate Report No. 513, *Commission to Study Proposals for National System of Express Motorways.*

The role of Robert Moses in building an expressway to parallel the Boston Post Road came primarily from contemporary news articles. Unless otherwise noted, quotes in this section came from the *New York Times* published between 1938 and 1953. Moses's book *Public Works* (New York: McGraw-Hill, 1970) showed his philosophy. Robert Caro's triumphant effort *The Power Broker* (New

York: Knopf, 1974), is of course the best place to begin a Moses examination. The essays in *Robert Moses and the Modern City,* eds. Hilary Ballon and Kenneth T. Jackson (New York: W. W. Norton, 2007), provide a more sympathetic view of Moses's work, as does Cleveland Rodgers, *Robert Moses* (New York: Holt, 1952).

Reports of official road investigations include *Report of a Survey of Transportation on the State Highway System of Connecticut* (Washington, D.C.: Govt. Print. Off., 1926); *Report of the Westchester County Park Commission for the Acquisition of Parks, Parkways or Boulevards* (1923); and *Regional Plan of New York and Its Environs* (New York, 1929–31), prepared by the Regional Plan Association. *Public Transportation for New England* (Boston, 1957), a compilation of reports presented at a conference of New England Governors, addresses the traffic problem on a regional level.

America's Highways, 1776–1976 (Washington, D.C.: U.S. Govt. Print. Off., 1977), compiled by the Federal Highway Administration, is a comprehensive overview of highway reform. Mark H. Rose, *Interstate* (Knoxville: University of Tennessee Press, 1990), examines this subject's political aspects. Contemporary transportation expert Wilfred Owen offers leading insight; see *The Metropolitan Transportation Problem* (Washington, D.C.: Brookings Institution, 1956) and, with Charles L. Dearing, *Toll Roads and the Problem of Highway Modernization* (Washington, D.C.: Brookings Institution, 1951). John Rae, *The Road and the Car in American Life* (Cambridge, Mass.: MIT Press, 1971), is a first-rate analysis of the car's social impact. Richard O. Davies, *The Age of Asphalt* (Philadelphia: Lippincott, 1975), reprints many important primary documents. Michael R. Fein, *Paving the Way* (Lawrence: University Press of Kansas, 2008), is an excellent recent account of New York's roads in the first half of the twentieth century.

201   *no highway in America carried more:* Though debatable, traffic on the Boston Post Road was considered the country's worst by a range of contemporaries, including major newspapers (e.g., *New York Times,* Aug. 23, 1925, and Feb. 19, 1929; *Chicago Daily Tribune,* July 16, 1928, and July 21, 1929; *Washington Post,* Feb. 5, 1928, Jan. 25, 1931), prominent citizens (Elliott Roosevelt, ed., *F.D.R.: His Personal Letters*; New York: Duell, Sloan and Pearce, 1947–50), and travel writers (Thomas Murphy, *New England Highways and Byways from a Motorcar*; Boston: L. C. Page & Company, 1924). The best case is made from a federal survey conducted in the late 1930s (*Toll Roads and Free Roads*; Washington, D.C.: U.S. Govt. Print. Off., 1939), which estimated that the country's heaviest traffic corridor stretched from New Haven to Jersey City, New Jersey; approximately seventy of this route's ninety-two miles ran on the Boston Post Road.

201   *world's most famous roads: New York Times,* July 22, 1937. The "Roads of the World" exhibit was presented by Ford in Dearborn, Michigan. Several other American highways were represented, including the Lincoln Highway.

201   *"history of highway building in itself":* Chicago Daily Tribune, Mar. 25, 1928.

202   *"for the first time":* Washington Post, July 1, 1926.

202   *"what it used to be":* Mason, *Saturday Evening Post,* July 14, 1923.

202   *Zelda and F. Scott Fitzgerald:* Matthew J. Bruccoli and Margaret M. Duggan, eds., *Correspondence of F. Scott Fitzgerald* (New York: Random House, 1980), p. 245.

202   *Franklin Roosevelt Jr.: Los Angeles Times,* Jan. 4, 1935.

203   *"unidentified stretch": Washington Post,* Sept. 29, 1932.

203   *"persisted all night long":* Murphy, *New England Highways and Byways,* p. 307.

203   *"without risking life and limb":* Agnes Smith, "The Radio," *Life* (Aug. 23, 1928).

203   *"ball player":* New Rochelle City Directory (1933).

203   *The white colonial house:* Jonathan Eig, *Luckiest Man* (New York: Simon & Schuster, 2005), p. 121.

204   *record for real estate:* A representative headline appears Sept. 27, 1925: "Westchester Lot Market Boom Is Making a County Record." See Dec. 4, 1927, and Mar. 22, 1931, for articles linking these suburbs to the automobile.

205   *"highway department has no hope now":* Chicago Daily Tribune, Feb. 17, 1925.

207   *"Post Road illustrates this":* Norman Bel Geddes, *Magic Motorways* (New York: Random House, 1940), pp. 13, 21.

207   *six years in the making:* Barlow to Guernsey T. Cross, Apr. 11, 1930, Gov NY, GC.

207   *"quick temper": New York Times,* Sept. 6, 1967.

208   *"how fast each project is getting on":* memo, FDR to Frederick S. Greene, Nov. 4, 1929, Gov NY, GC. Roosevelt made this request two weeks after taking a meeting with Robert Moses, though there is no evidence that the two events are connected.

208   *"greatest achievements in our Nation's history":* Lester Barlow, "Financing the 'Barlow Plan' for Public-Owned Toll Roads," *Highway Engineer & Contractor* 34 (June 1929), p. 42.

208   *won nearly $600,000: Time,* Sept. 23, 1940; *New York Times,* Sept. 8, 1940, Aug. 28, 1940.

208   *eighty-four goats: New York Times,* May 26, 1940.

209   *"not one long unobstructed":* Lester Barlow, "Government-Owned Toll Motorways," *Highway Engineer & Contractor* 19 (Nov. 1928), p. 35.

209   *"speed we're living at": New York Times,* Feb. 8, 1931.

210   *"carefully planned highway system": The Public Papers and Addresses of Franklin D. Roosevelt* (New York: Russell & Russell, 1969), 1:131.

210   *"future will be based":* Ibid., 1:498.

210   *"main trunk highway": Regional Plan of New York,* 1:244.

210   *Pelham–Port Chester route in mind: New York Times,* Apr. 2, 1930; Barlow to John H. Trumbull, Mar. 19, 1930, in "New York & New England Motorways Corporation," Gov NY, GC.

210   *using the railroad's right-of-way:* "Motorways," *Time* (Apr. 14, 1930); Barlow to John H. Trumbull, Mar. 19, 1930, in "New York & New England Motorways Corporation," Gov NY, GC.

210   *within days of his meeting with Barlow:* Barlow fails to provide the exact date, saying only that the expressway bill was introduced "a few days later." The bill was introduced in both houses on April 1; if "a few" means three, the meeting

occurred on March 29. However, Roosevelt's diary of appointments shows he was at his home in Hyde Park, from March 27 to March 30. Most likely they met a bit before these dates.

211 *"source of hope for the future"*: The Public Papers and Addresses of Franklin D. Roosevelt, 1:447.

211 *through Mamaroneck:* A. W. Brandt to FDR, Feb. 7, 1930; F. E. O'Callaghan Jr. to FDR, Jan. 30, 1930, Gov NY, GC.

211 *in a letter a decade later: F.D.R., His Personal Letters,* 4:789.

211 *Barlow's Union Highway: New York Times,* Oct. 11, 1925.

212 *"plan is feasible"*: Barlow, "Government-Owned," p. 39.

212 *"proposed project and its aims"*: Bert Pierce to FDR, Mar. 31, 1930; FDR office to Bert Pierce, Apr. 5, 1930; FDR office to Barlow, Apr. 5, 1930, Gov NY, GC.

212 *consider an emergency session:* Barlow to John H. Trumbull, Apr. 4, 1930, in "New York & New England Motorways Corporation," Gov NY, GC.

212 *"a model for the nation"*: telegram, John Q. Tilson to W. W. Westall, Apr. 8, 1930, in "New York & New England Motorways Corporation," Gov NY, GC. (Edited slightly for readability.)

213 *mighty railroad lobby:* Barlow, *What Would Lincoln Do?,* p. 99; C. M. Sheafe Jr. to FDR, Gov NY, GC.

213 *"you are alive"*: Barlow, *What Would Lincoln Do?,* p. 76.

213 *"pretty much disgusted"*: Barlow to Louis McHenry Howe, Mar. 11, 1933, Papers of the President, Official File 4110, FDR Library.

213 *see to his impeachment: New York Times,* Aug. 8, 1937.

214 *"vital necessity": New York Times,* Feb. 6, 1938.

215 *lessons Tallamy had learned from Moses:* Caro, *Power Broker,* p. 706.

216 *various contributions:* Ann Markusen, et al., *The Rise of the Gunbelt* (New York: Oxford University Press, 1991), pp. 127–36.

217 *"unbearable traffic situation"*: Hartford Courant, Sept. 13, 1943.

217 *piece of road running through Stratford:* Connecticut General Assembly, *List of Bills, Etc. . . . January Session, 1943* (Hartford, 1943), p. 297.

218 *second-most-congested strip: New York Times,* Feb. 21, 1950.

218 *"so-called Boston-Washington express route"*: Robert Moses, "New Highways for a Better New York," *New York Times,* Nov. 11, 1945.

219 *intended to continue the highway east: Hartford Courant,* Feb. 6, 1953. Today this extension of the expressway continues to New London as modern I-95, then splits northeast as I-395. I-95 east of New London was a separate project.

219 *"Relocation of U.S. Route 1": New York Times,* Mar. 17, 1953.

Chapter 13: Changing the Face of America

Several federal reports must be examined as background to the Interstate Highway Act of 1956. The four primary documents are *Toll Roads and Free Roads* (Washington, D.C.: U.S. Govt. Print. Off., 1939); *Interregional Highways* (Washington, D.C.: U.S. Govt. Print. Off., 1944); *A Ten-Year National Highway Program* (Washington, D.C.: U.S. Govt. Print. Off., 1955); and *General Location of National System of Interstate Highways* (Washington: U.S. Govt. Print. Off., 1955), also known as the Yellow Book, prepared by the Bureau of Public Roads for members of Congress. Rose, *Interstate* (Knoxville: University of Tennessee Press, 1990), and Gary T. Schwartz, "Urban Freeways and the Interstate System," in *Southern California Law Review* 49 (Mar. 1976), provide accessible analysis of these technical manuscripts.

My sources on the development and impact of the Oak Street Connector included G. William Domhoff, *Who Really Rules?* (New Brunswick, N.J.: Transaction Books, 1978); Jeanne R. Lowe, *Cities in a Race with Time* (New York: Vintage Books, 1968); and Mandi Isaacs Jackson, *Model City Blues* (Philadelphia: Temple University Press, 2008). The best single volume on modern New Haven is *City* (New Haven, Conn.: Yale University Press, 2003) by Douglas W. Rae, professor at the Yale School of Management; additional insight was drawn from an interview of Rae. Supplementary detail was provided by "Life in the Model City," published online by the New Haven Oral History Project; an interview with the project's director, Andy Horowitz; and contemporary issues of the *New Haven Journal-Courier*. Unless otherwise indicated, quotes came from issues of the *New York Times* printed between 1954 and 1957.

My study of the aborted plan to build the Southwest Expressway into Boston came primarily from material available in the Government Documents collection of the Boston Public Library. In chronological order by publishing date, these are: *The Boston Regional Survey Transportation Inventory: Chapter Four: Highways* (Cambridge, Mass., 1962); *Basic Design Report Southwest Expressway* (1966); *Inner Belt / Southwest Expressway Summary Relocation Report* (1967); *Impact of the Proposed Southwest Expressway on Jamaica Plain* (1968); *Southwest Corridor Study* (1970); *Report to Governor Sargent on Immediate Action Opportunities* (1970), by the task force on transportation chaired by Alan Altschuler; and John Mogey, Mary Donahue, and Else Wiersma, *Social Effects of Eminent Domain* (Boston: Boston University, 1971). *The Master Highway Plan for the Boston Metropolitan Area* (Boston, 1948), gave technical background leading up to this era. Thomas H. O'Connor, *Building a New Boston* (Boston: Northeastern University Press, 1993), offers a broader context. The *Boston Globe* gave a good deal of space to the battle; quotes came from issues between 1969 and 1970 unless otherwise noted. Special recognition goes to Alan Lupo, *Rites of Way* (Boston: Little, Brown, 1971), an exceptional journalistic treatment of the affair.

Research on the transformation of Providence centered on a pair of scholarly efforts: Francis J. Leazes Jr. and Mark T. Motte, *Providence, the Renaissance City* (Boston: Northeastern University Press, 2004), and Gene Bunnell, *Making Places Special* (Chicago: Planners Press, American Planning Association, 2002). Brent D. Ryan, "Incomplete and Incremental Plan Implementation in Downtown Providence, Rhode Island, 1960–2000," in *Journal of Planning History* 5 (2006), was an essential supplement. *College Hill* (Providence: City Plan Commission, 1967) was a highly informative contemporary plan. Articles in the *Providence Journal* provided context and detail.

In countless articles Lewis Mumford championed a move toward balanced transportation. Some of the most useful were the essay "Highway and the City" in *Highway and the City* (New York: Harcourt, Brace & World, 1963); "The Intolerable City," in *Harper's* (Feb. 1926); and "Townless Highways for the Motorist," written with Benton MacKaye, in *Harper's* (Aug. 1931). "The Roaring Traffic's Boom," a four-part series that appeared in Mumford's *New Yorker* column, "The Sky Line," in 1955, is also notable. Senator Claiborne Pell of Rhode Island made an excellent contribution to the subject with *Megalopolis Unbound* (New York: Praeger, 1966). Articles published in academic journals and newspapers, as well as an interview with James R. Repass, president of the National Corridor Initiative, formerly the Northeast Corridor Initiative, rounded out the context.

220   *"change the face of America":* Dwight D. Eisenhower, *Mandate for Change* (Garden City, N.Y.: Doubleday, 1963), p. 549.

220   *roughly 167 percent:* Regional Plan Association, *Bulletin* no. 77 (July 1951), pp. 3–6.

221   *a nearly 39,000-mile system: Interregional Highways,* pp. iii, 4, 52. This included a core system of roughly 34,000 miles and an estimated 5,000 miles of interstates running through major cities.

221   *"steers straight toward Washington":* Geddes, *Magic Motorways,* p. 279.

221   *"away from population centers": New York Times,* May 17, 1936.

221   *"go through rather than bypass":* Moses, *Public Works,* p. 288.

222   *Moses and Mumford feuded:* Their notable face-offs included Mumford's four-part series, "The Roaring Traffic's Boom," *New Yorker* (Mar.–June, 1955); Mumford, "The Skyway's the Limit," in *The Highway and the City* (1963); and "Mr. Moses Dissects the 'Long-Haired Planners,'" *New York Times Sunday Magazine,* June 25, 1944.

222   *In 1919:* Dwight D. Eisenhower, *At Ease* (Garden City, N.Y.: Doubleday, 1967), p. 157.

223   *"facelift":* "New Haven Mayor Sees Turnpike As Big Face-Lifter," *Hartford Courant,* Feb. 9, 1956.

223   *"infamous":* "Forward Look in Connecticut," *Time,* June 24, 1957.

224   *New Rochelle literally razed the dead: New York Times,* May 31, 1956; Oct. 6, 1957; Nov. 28, 1957; "Still 45 Minutes From Broadway," *New York Times Sunday Magazine,* July 31, 1955. Many thanks to Barbara Davis, of the New Rochelle Public Library, for her help on this part of New Rochelle's history—and several others throughout this book.

225   *failed to mention the eight hundred or so: Redevelopment Plan for the Oak Street Redevelopment Area* (New Haven, 1959), p. 19.

225 *branded "long-haired planners"*: "Mr. Moses Dissects the 'Long-Haired Planners,'" *New York Times Sunday Magazine,* June 25, 1944. On the cover of *Time* (Apr. 18, 1938) a balding Mumford is slouching in the nook of a tree.

225 *at a conference in Hartford:* See Wilfred Owen, *Cities in the Motor Age* (New York: Viking Press, 1959).

225 *"almost unanimous": Hartford Courant,* Sept. 15, 1957.

225 *meeting there for the very first time:* See Richard Weingroff, "The Genie in the Bottle," read at www.tfhrc.gov/pubrds/septoct00/urban.htm.

226 *Maurice Rotival:* In addition to the sources noted above, *New Haven Journal-Courier,* Oct. 17 and Oct. 26, 1953, were particularly helpful.

227 *"in diseased squalor": Hartford Courant,* Oct. 27, 1959.

227 *"back seat to New Haven": Hartford Courant,* Feb. 14, 1960.

227 *"we are ready to destroy anything for it":* Vincent Scully, "America's Architectural Nightmare," *Zodiac* 17 (1967), p. 165. In that same issue, see Scully, "The Threat and Promise of Urban Redevelopment in New Haven."

228 *"ignores esthetic, social and economic considerations": New York Times,* Nov. 13, 1967.

228 *Fifteen cities had halted: New York Times,* Feb. 15, 1970; Juan Cameron, "How the Interstate Changed the Face of the Nation," *Fortune* (July 1971), p. 81.

228 *Eisenhower had never intended:* "Urban Freeways and the Interstate System," pp. 444–46; Helen Leavitt, *Superhighway—Superhoax* (Garden City, N.Y.: Doubleday, 1970), pp. 298–99.

229 *ranked second in per capita car use:* "Boston Makes a Comeback," *U.S. News & World Report* (Sept. 21, 1964), pp. 57–58.

229 *meant to carry the twenty thousand: The Master Highway Plan for the Boston Metropolitan Area,* p. 36.

229 *seven hundred or so displaced households: Basic Design Report Southwest Expressway,* p. 2; *Impact of the Proposed Southwest Expressway,* p. 9. Some reports list the number closer to 1,000 families.

230 *"virtually eliminated": Southwest Corridor Study,* p. 11.

230 *"a central role":* Ibid., p. 4.

232 *"is extremely limited": Report to Governor Sargent,* p. 5.

232 *"whether an expressway should be built":* Jack Flannery, ed., *The Sargent Years* (Boston, 1976), p. 56. (Emphasis from the original.)

233 *"appeared to mark a new turn": New York Times,* Feb. 27, 1960.

233 *"that it must": The Sargent Years,* p. 56.

234 *"model for urban revival": Boston Globe,* Jan. 12, 1997.

234 *"comprehensive transportation" plans:* See *U.S. Statutes at Large,* 76:1145–48.

234 *"roughest rides":* Claiborne Pell, "The Proposed High-Speed Railroad System," *New England Law Review* 1 (1965), p. 8; Pell, *Megalopolis Unbound,* p. 10.

235 *"problems affected by transportation":* Luther J. Carter, "Northeast Corridor: Transport Project Gains Headway," *Science* (Mar. 4, 1966), p. 1066.

236 *"onto public transportation": Washington Post,* June 20, 1978.

237 *tracks through an entirely new structure:* Leazes and Motte, *Providence,* pp. 82–90. Stamford was the only other city on the Boston–New York leg to get funding for a new station.

237 Benjamin Franklin: *Providence Journal,* June 17, 1986.

238 *launched an advertising campaign: Providence Journal,* July 29, 1986, Jan. 13, 1987, Jan. 19, 1987; *Boston Globe,* Jan. 13, 1987.

Chapter 14: Cruising the BPR

The bulk of this chapter was written based on my experiences traveling the old highway. In addition, I conducted dozens of interviews with people who lived or worked along the route either now or then. While I can't begin to list them all, I must note that my meeting with Thomas O'Connor and my discussion with the owner of the Piper's Kilt occurred several years before my trip. And I must give special thanks to Keith Korbut of Springfield, founder of the Duryea Society, who suffered severe burns in an auto repair accident the day before we were to meet, yet arranged my museum tour nonetheless, for which I will always be as impressed as I am grateful.

239   *"United States Route 1": New York Times,* Dec. 13, 1964.
240   *authorized a $34.7 million upgrade: New York Times,* Mar. 6, 1994. Thanks also to the New York City Department of Transportation for supplying additional information in response to a Freedom of Information request.
241   *one of the deadliest stretches: New York Times,* Mar. 6, Mar. 20, 2005; *Connecticut Post,* Oct. 28, 2008.
243   *idea posed in 1909 by Robert Goddard: Scientific American* (Nov. 20, 1909), p. 366.
259   *"returne of Edward Messenger":* John Winthrop Jr. to Fitz-John Winthrop, Apr. 15, 1673, Winthrop Family Papers, microfilm edition, MHS.
260   *"100 percent corner": Boston Herald,* Dec. 6, 1997.
265   *"obsolete":* John J. Post, *Old Streets, Roads, Lanes, Piers, and Wharves of New York* (New York: R. D. Cooke, 1882).
266   *"with its connotation": New York Times,* Feb. 17, 1956.

Index

About the Author

ERIC JAFFE, a former online editor at *Smithsonian* magazine, is a writer in New York City. He's a graduate of the Columbia University Graduate School of Journalism, where he began to write this book, his first. Visit www.kingsbesthighway.com.